THE WAY OF THE SHARK

THE WAY OF
THE SHARK

Lessons on Golf, Business, and Life

GREG NORMAN
with DONALD T. PHILLIPS

ATRIA BOOKS

New York   London   Toronto   Sydney

ATRIA BOOKS
1230 Avenue of the Americas
New York, NY 10020

Library of Congress Cataloging-in-Publication Data is available.

ISBN-13: 978-0-7432-8774-6
ISBN-10:   0-7432-8774-6

First Atria Books hardcover edition October 2006

10 9 8 7 6 5 4 3 2 1

ATRIA BOOKS is a trademark of Simon & Schuster, Inc.

Photo Credits: Unless otherwise credited, all photos are from the author's collection or courtesy of Great White Shark Enterprises. Insert I: p. 3 bottom,
courtesy The Grange Golf Club; p. 4 bottom, Phil Sheldon; p. 5 top, Getty
Images; p. 7 top, Getty Images; p. 8 bottom, Robert Beck. Insert II: p. 1 top,
Lawrence Levy; p. 1 middle, AP photos © 1995; p. 1 bottom, Getty Images;
p. 2 top, Corbis; p. 2 bottom, Golf Australia; p. 3 bottom, Brian Smith for *Golf
Digest*; p. 4 second from top, Robert Nelson; p. 6 top, courtesy World Golf Hall
of Fame; p. 6 bottom, courtesy Reebok; p. 7 top, Michael O'Bryon; p. 7 bottom,
Rossa Williams Cole; p. 8 second from top, Matthew Harris; p. 8 third from
top, courtesy Nakheel; p. 8 bottom, Michael O'Bryon.

Greg Norman gratefully acknowledges the contributions of *Travel + Leisure
Golf* magazine in the development of this book.

Manufactured in the United States of America

For information about special discounts for bulk purchases,
please contact Simon & Schuster Special Sales at
1-800-456-6798 or business@simonandschuster.com.

"There are no ordinary moments."

—DAN MILLMAN

CONTENTS

ACKNOWLEDGMENTS

Like so many things I have done on and off the golf course, I began the process of writing this book with the end in mind. It has proven to be a cathartic experience, and I have enjoyed both the opportunity and the challenge.

One of the great benefits is that it has given me reason to reflect on those individuals who have had a profound impact on my life. Throughout the process I have dusted off memories of people, events, and locations that I hadn't thought about in years.

As I look back, it occurs to me that at each stage of my life the person I came into contact with—be it positive or negative—touched me at just the right time in just the right circumstance. Most all these people and anecdotes are chronicled in the pages that follow, but there are a distinct few who warrant specific acknowledgment.

My mother not only steered me toward the game of golf but gave me the support and encouragement to achieve my dreams and aspirations. Every effort, every sacrifice she made is appreciated more than she will ever know.

My father is my foundation, the very fabric of my being. He instilled in me many of the core values that I live by to this day. There were times, early on, that I did not appreciate his methodology, but today I realize his teachings are the very essence of who I am.

Janis, my sister, older and wiser, was perhaps the first to truly understand my insatiable appetite to succeed, to go to the next level. She helped me shine and helped build my self-esteem, for which I am eternally grateful.

For all those years I maintained an arduous schedule, Laura was a stabilizing force at home and a tremendous support during my playing career. Her direction and guidance to Morgan and Gregory helped prepare them for the world they are about to enter as young adults.

I have tried to instill in my children values and lessons that will last them a lifetime, and I cherish my relationship with them more than anything else. In recent years, Morgan has taught me to open my heart, to have a greater appreciation for those I come in contact with. From a very early age Gregory demonstrated great clarity and perspective on important issues, which just recently I have adopted into my own approach.

As my mentor Charlie Earp once said, "You are judged by the company you keep." To that end, I have been extremely fortunate to interact with so many wise, gracious, and caring individuals from all walks of life. All of whom helped influence the person I have become.

PART ONE

LESSONS THAT LAST A LIFETIME

CHAPTER ONE

IN OUR JOURNEY through life, we learn many small lessons that mold us, shape us, and influence how we deal with others. But once in a while something happens that seriously alters the path on which we're headed. Such lessons stick with us like glue. We *never* forget them. We relive them over and over again, in our private moments, in our conversations, in our dreams. I was only eighteen years old when I experienced my first life-changing lesson. I was by myself, and it really was a pivotal moment. It turned me toward the great sport of golf.

A few years after my family moved to Brisbane (Australia's third-largest city, located on the southeastern coast of Queensland), a major cyclone swept along the shoreline a few hundred miles to the northeast and caused the ocean to produce a heavy swell. Not wanting to miss a terrific opportunity to get in some bodysurfing, I grabbed my gear and drove to Noosa Heads. Arriving by midmorning, I hiked about half a mile along the headlands to where I was sure to catch the biggest wave possible. Then I perched myself on some high rocks and studied the waves before I dove in. I knew I'd be committed once in the water because the only way out then was to make it all the way to the beach.

Instead of catching a breaker I could easily ride into the beach, I found myself in an uncontrollable dumper that quickly sucked me down, bounced me hard on the sandy bottom, and rolled me around like a rag doll. The sheer force of the water tore the flippers off my feet and ripped away my hand board. It was like being inside a washing machine. Looking back on it now, I think of it as a terrifying and humbling experience. Until then, I thought I was bulletproof. But when it was actually taking place, I had this inner calm come over me. Everything seemed to be happening in slow motion. Rather than panic, I started thinking of a way to survive the situation. I know it sounds crazy, but the more pressure I'm under, the calmer I become. For me it has always been that way: I take stock of the situation and analyze the best way to deal with it.

Finally the wave released me from its powerful grip and, slowly, I struggled back to the surface. I must have been under for quite a while because that first gasp of fresh air felt like nothing less than the gift of life. But it didn't take me long to realize that I was facing another major problem. I was now nearly half a mile away from the beach, and the surf was pushing me rapidly toward the rocks. The only thing I could do was swim against the tide, which violates all the rules of safety in the ocean. But it was my only option. I'm not sure how long it took me to reach the beach, but when I finally got there, I fell, utterly exhausted, facedown into the sand and just stayed in that position until I could garner strength and count my blessings.

The next day I sat down and thought about what had happened. "Oh, man, what an ordeal," I said to myself. "I'm really lucky to be alive. Surely, there must be something I can do that isn't quite as dangerous."

And what was the lesson I learned? Well, there was a movie out that year called *Magnum Force.* I had seen it just before the cyclone hit, and as I sat there thinking about my near-death experience, I swear that the image popped into my head of Clint Eastwood saying: "A man has got to know his limitations."

And right then and there, I decided to dedicate myself to golf. Up to that point, golf was just another activity for me. I liked it. I was good at it. But I'd taken it up less than three years before, and to tell you the truth, I'd spent a lot more time in and around the water. I was born in Mount Isa, a small outback mining town populated largely by Finnish immigrants who had migrated to Australia after World War II. Because of their experience and work ethic, the

Finns gravitated to the mines of Mount Isa. My mother, Toini, was the daughter of a Finnish carpenter, and my father, Merv, was an electrical engineer for the company. When I was still an infant, we moved to Townsville, on the Queensland coast. It was there, on the edge of the Coral Sea and the Great Barrier Reef, that I spent the first fifteen years of my life. I took it for granted back then, but now I realize that I grew up in paradise: a pristine rain forest area just north of the Tropic of Capricorn, with white sandy beaches, clear coastal waters, and year-round warm weather. The Great Barrier Reef extends more than 1,200 miles and consists of more than 600 islands and 3,000 living reefs.

Back then, life for me was all about having fun. At the age of ten or twelve, I ran with a kid named Peter Rawkins. If we weren't spearfishing together, then we were on horseback, galloping along the beaches with my black Labs, Pancho or Sambo, running alongside. We always rode bareback with a cut lunch (air-dried sliced meat) in bags slung across our backs. Peter and I would ride all day, sometimes covering twenty miles from sunup to sundown. At frequent intervals, we would walk the horses into the shallows and tumble off their backs for a quick swim. And when our parents gave us permission, Peter and I would camp out and fall asleep under the stars, eagerly looking forward to the next day's adventure.

Our horses were kept in a paddock just behind our homes that was surrounded by a barbed wire fence. Each morning we had to ride our bicycles more than three miles around to the main gate to get the horses. Well, one day I decided there was an easier way. I took a pair of wire cutters and cut a hole in the fence big enough for me to squeeze through. Then I caught my horse, put the bridle on him, and rode out through the main gate. But my indiscretion in trying to make life a little easier for myself ended when I was caught and my parents were informed. The consequences of my actions involved some pretty tough punishment. Of course I had to repair the hole in the fence, which was no easy feat because I had cut the tension wire. The entire episode taught me not to take shortcuts.

That was one of my early lessons, but it didn't really slow me down. When the conditions were right, I was on the beach and in the water straightaway. And all too often, I pushed the envelope a bit too far. While spearfishing one day I shot a large coral trout only to have the spear go through the fish and embed itself deep into a coral head. As I was tugging on the spear, I glanced to my left and saw a seven-foot shark moving rapidly in my direction. Instinctively, I let go of the spear and simply floated back to the surface. Glancing back, I could see the shark devouring my catch. After a while, I swam back down, retrieved my spear, and continued fishing. There were a lot of times when sharks chased me off and ate my fish. I didn't like sharks back then.

There were other sea creatures that were quite dangerous as well. One was a kind of jellyfish, but probably unlike any you've ever seen before. We called it a sea wasp or a bluebottle because of its color. But this is no Portuguese man-of-war; it has tentacles that are ten to twenty feet long, and its sting is very toxic. One day I was spearfishing with my older sister, Janis, out in Nelley Bay off Magnetic Island, where my parents owned a little holiday shack. Janis became entangled in the tentacles of a sea wasp. I had just pulled myself up in our small boat when she breached the surface with a terrifying scream. I dove back in the water and dragged her to the boat. Seeing the welts on her legs and torso, and realizing that it was a bluebottle, I rowed to the beach as fast as I could. Janis was screaming and writhing in agony the entire way. My parents then rushed her to the local clinic, where she received the appropriate medical attention. Janis recovered fully, and rather than being life-threatening, the entire episode was more of a mental trauma than anything else for both of us.

Diving in to help my sister was a natural reaction and part of life in and around the Great Barrier Reef. Nothing scared me back then. I didn't think twice about riding a horse bareback at full speed along the beach, or strapping a tank on my back and scuba diving without lessons, or surfing in high waves with or without a surfboard. Actually, I taught myself to do all those things. Never had a lesson. I saw other people doing it. I spent some time thinking about it. And then I gave it a shot. I was always challenging myself to learn and understand new skills.

I did have a good teacher when it came to boating, however. One day my father came home from work and announced to Janis and me that he was going to help us build a small boat. Our house was built on stilts for cooling. And for the next several months, the dirt floor underneath looked like a small construction site as we studied our plans, laid out the materials, and assembled our small sabot, *Peter Pan*. I really enjoyed working with my father on that project. We immersed ourselves in the engineering of that little boat: crafting the ribs, overlaying the planks, making it watertight, and varnishing it. Janis and I joined the Townsville Sailing Club, where we learned how to sail and read the wind, how to get the maximum performance of our boat, and how to race it. In short, we learned all about boats on the water. Navigating, rules of the road—you name it, we learned it. We won several competitions with me as the skipper and Janis as the crew. Little did I know, many years later I would build a boat that would be heralded as the highest technical achievement in a motor yacht by *Showboats* magazine. My father taught me well.

Even though I was a curious kid and absorbed things that were happening around me, I really didn't like school very much. I participated in cricket, Aussie Rules football, rugby, track and field, swimming, and squash. The classroom, however, was too confining for me, and my mind was always wandering to the outer world. As a matter of fact, I was frequently getting the cane rapped across my knuckles (literally) for daydreaming, or for being brutally honest and telling people exactly what was on my mind. The subjects in which I did not do well were the ones that simply didn't interest me. I did like geography, however. I think it had something to do with being attached to the land and the outdoors. I loved the aspects of geography that went beyond memorizing cities, continents, and oceans. Learning to read topographic maps was enjoyable for me, including understanding scale, interpreting contour lines, recognizing highs and lows, et cetera. I was also interested in geology: igneous, metamorphic, and sedimentary rocks, the various types of soils, and aquifers and artesian wells.

Subjects like chemistry and French, however, were mundane for me. They just did not stimulate my interest. I remember one occasion when I was trying to solve an algebra homework problem and I just didn't get it. When I asked my father for help, he said,

"Keep working and you'll figure it out." Another hour went by and I asked again. "Dad, I *can't* figure it out," I said. "Well, give it another try," he responded. Rather than helping me outright, I think my father was trying to get me to apply myself more—which might have been my biggest problem with school.

When I turned fifteen, my father and three partners set up their own engineering business and we moved 500 miles south to Brisbane. The Great Barrier Reef doesn't extend quite that far down, but here the surf beaches start. Forty miles south of Brisbane are the Gold Coast of Australia and the township of Surfers Paradise, and twenty miles north are Noosa and the Sunshine Coast. So it was around this time that I turned my attention to surfing.

I was a bit lonely after having left all my friends behind, so my mother suggested I go with her to play a quick nine holes of golf. I'd never tried it before, but Mum told me I had the basis of a reasonable swing. A couple of weeks later, she was playing in a tournament and I caddied for her (which, incidentally, was the one and only time I ever caddied for her). After her round, I asked if I could borrow her clubs and play by myself. She made golf look easy, and as I was fairly self-confident with my athletic abilities, I figured, If Mum can do it, why can't I? So I wandered onto the course and started whacking the ball around. A few went straight, but most were poorly hit. I even remember getting one ball stuck up in a pandanus tree and panicking. Back then in Australia, golf balls were expensive. Many came from the United States, and new ones were purchased in single packs. But the ball I hit into the pandanus tree was too high and too stuck for me to retrieve. It's probably still there.

And that's how I was introduced to golf: a simple invitation from my mother. Actually, she was an excellent athlete who played golf right up until the day before I was born. Perhaps that's how the sport got into my blood. Mum and I had a great relationship, and I always felt I could talk to her. Through our conversations, she instilled in me an emotional awareness about people and their feelings. My natural tendency was to be a little too up-front and in your face, which, of course, usually tends to make people recoil. My mother not only made me aware of that, she also taught me to care about others, to have an appreciation for good people, and to be loyal to my friends and family.

Over the years, Mum and I played a lot of golf together. She would educate me about the history of golf. And even though I wasn't very good yet, I told her that I wanted to one day win the British Open, because that's where golf was born. Never once did my mother tell me I couldn't do it. Rather, she told me I'd have to work exceptionally hard to achieve that particular dream. "I'll send you the trophy when I win, Mum," I would joke. "That'll be your reward for getting me started in golf."

CHAPTER TWO

IN BRISBANE, MY PARENTS joined the Virginia Golf Club and signed me up as a junior member, which meant I could play golf as often as I wanted, which I did. Mum would pick me up each day after school at 3:00 P.M. sharp and drive me to the course, where I'd stay until it got too dark to see the ball. Then we had a prearranged signal: When I was ready to come home, I would dial our telephone number, let it ring twice, and hang up. Mum would then come pick me up. It saved me the cost of a phone call, and, as often as I played, that allowed me to purchase golf balls and lessons. I can't exactly explain it, but there was just something about golf that captivated me. It seemed as though there were highs and lows all the time—on every shot, on every putt. It was spontaneous. It was here and now. It seemed so easy, but it was really so very complex. I loved the fact that you got out of the game only what you put into it. I also enjoyed the challenge of golf. It was the toughest sport of all to conquer. So every time I was out there, my determination, my passion, and my desire to improve drove me to become as good a golfer as I possibly could.

On August 8, 1970, when I was fifteen, my parents sprang for my first set of golf clubs. I'll never forget that date. I was so proud and so very grateful to them for the gift. After shooting my first official score of 108, the golf club assigned me the maximum allowed handicap of 27. Well, I was determined to reduce that number. Not only did I practice diligently, but I went out and bought two books

written by Jack Nicklaus. From *Golf My Way,* I learned Jack's fundamentals on how to play the game. And *My 55 Ways to Lower Your
Score* taught me quick tips on specific subjects. I remember being
impressed that Nicklaus said he wrote the books to give something
back to the game that had been so good to him. And I kept those
books with me all the time, marking them up and dog-earing pages.
In school, I'd practice my grip under the desk. And to this day, I still
have those books.

From there, I started going to junior golf clinics, but I knew that
in order to get better, I would need some more one-on-one coaching. So I started taking lessons (at twenty cents each) from John
Klatt, the golf professional at the club. During Saturday morning
classes, he drilled me in the basics, and after class I would spend
the rest of the day on the driving range. Around that time, I developed my own practice system of compartmentalizing things. First
I'd work on my short game, then back off. Second, I'd work on my
middle game, then back off. Next I'd work on my long game, then
back off. I realized that when I got tired, I'd start hitting bad shots
and get into bad habits. So I didn't go out there and hit until I got
tired. I backed off *before* I got tired.

My ability to compartmentalize things, I believe, led to some
early success. In essence, it's basic time management. If you know
how to manage your time, then you become a very productive manager of life, your own space, and the things around you.

My mother often recounts how hard I practiced, and that set
me apart from my peers. And my father reminds me that I seemed
to have an intuitive understanding about how the game was played,
with all its nuances and so forth. It didn't take long for my handicap
to go down, and I started playing in a few tournaments. In 1971 my
father and I teamed up in a tournament at Virginia Golf Club. I
think I surprised everybody, including myself, when I shot 15 under
my handicap and we blitzed the field. That was the first time I
brought home a trophy, and with that first taste of success, there
was no stopping me. I played every chance I got, most often with
my mother and father as partners, where we'd participate in club
competitions. There were ball comps, for example, where everybody would put ten cents into the cigar box and the top ten finish-

ers would win a golf ball in a single pack. And then there were the famous chook (chicken) comps. We'd contribute fifty cents and the top five finishers that day would win a frozen chicken.

My parents liked my progress in golf, but they were always trying to get me to throw away my wide-brimmed floppy hat. It wasn't like the hats I would wear later in my career. This one was a weathered straw hat that had been sat on, stepped on, and constantly abused. It really did look awful. Mum would hide it from me before we left the house. "That hat just isn't golf!" she'd say. But I'd find it and wear it anyway. My hat made me different from everybody else out there—and I wanted to be different. But there was really a more practical side to wearing it. It was a typical surfer's wide-brimmed straw hat, which I wore when I was fishing or boating, to keep the sun off my face and neck. Well, the same thing was true on the golf course. Not only that, I discovered that I was able to keep my eyes better focused on the ball—on the tee, in flight, and after landing—all without getting a horrible shot of sunlight in my eyes. In short, my unconventional hat worked for me. So I continued to wear it, despite what my mother thought.

During this period, I was still playing football, rugby, and squash. But a couple of things happened that would turn me away from those sports. Not surprisingly, I experienced several nasty injuries—one in particular that left me with a slightly bent nose. That happened during a rugby game when I got raked in a scrum by another player in an unsportsmanlike fashion. As soon as I could get up, I chased him off the field. But before I could catch him, we were both ejected from the game.

During this same period, I broke off my front teeth in an incident on the Barrier Reef. I was with my friends Peter and David Hay and their father, who was a local doctor. He owned a prawn trawler as a sideline business. During the off-season, the four of us and the captain of the boat would spend three to five weeks on the Barrier Reef fishing and diving. One afternoon I slipped on the deck and slammed my two front teeth into the wood coping on the freeboard. To this day, I still recall lifting myself off the deck and seeing pieces of my teeth embedded into the wood railing. We treasured the trips, and I didn't want to miss out on the experience, but my friends insisted that we go back to port immediately and get my teeth attended to. Because I was still growing, they could not be properly capped. The doctors therefore advised me to stop playing contact sports so that my teeth would not be permanently damaged.

After a while, I realized that no matter what the team sport, if I played well personally we could lose; conversely, if I played poorly we could win. It all depended on the entire team playing as one entity. At times that did not happen, much to my competitive dismay. I always believed in giving 100 percent of whatever I tasked myself—to be the best I could be, no matter what. I would rather play and lead by example than be a follower.

Another incident in team sports that affected me significantly occurred at a rugby practice while we were preparing for an interstate competition. As three of my teammates were running our normal circle of laps, my teammate right next to me suddenly fell down and lay motionless on the ground. A coach ran over, and four of us alternated performing mouth-to-mouth resuscitation. But there was nothing we could do to revive him. Later, we learned that he had suffered a massive heart attack. I traveled to the hospital in the ambulance, and when his mother arrived it was one of the worst moments of my young life. When she saw me, she knew: Her son was dead.

I thought a lot about that afterward. I realized how quickly life can end—and that it should be lived to the fullest. Hence my motto: "Attack life." I wondered, then, if I was really doing what I wanted to do in life. And I began thinking about the injuries I'd received in Aussie Rules and rugby, about getting angry at the guys who didn't give it their all, and about how much I loved the individuality of golf. Eventually, I came to the conclusion that playing golf was really what I wanted to do. So I moved away from team sports.

The time I spent by myself after my teammate died is pretty indicative of who I am. I'm an introvert by nature. I've always preferred to avoid crowds and spend time by myself, so golf actually fits my personality better than rugby, Aussie Rules, or cricket. But more than that, my tendency to be alone leads me to be more introspective than most. I think deeply on a variety of subjects. I search my inner soul and try to think things through to a conclusion. As a result, I tend to believe that I'm right until proven wrong. It's a great philosophy to have. It leads to an optimism and self-confidence that, I believe, results in success. Rather than always struggling to get uphill and wondering if I can make it, I just assume that I'm going to be successful. When I was a kid, for instance, I always thought life was like climbing a ladder. When I reached the top, I'd just set a couple of new goals that were represented by a few new rungs on the ladder, and I'd push myself to climb higher and higher. I still look at life that way today, and I believe it has helped me achieve a great many things.

Once I started concentrating on golf, I began to make some real progress. My club handicap dropped to 21, to 17, and then to 11. The senior members of the club predicted that I'd level off, but it didn't happen. From the time I picked up my first golf club, it was only eighteen months before I was playing scratch golf. In 1972 I won both the junior and adult Virginia Golf Club championships and followed that with a 5-stroke victory to claim the Queensland junior amateur title. In 1973 I did well in almost every tournament I entered, including wins in the Byrne Ford Junior Pro-Am, the Greenaway Ford Jacaranda Open, and the Gary Player Junior Golf Classic (by 9 strokes).

Both my mother and father caddied for me in those early tournaments. Mum is still fond of recalling the time I asked her advice on one particular shot. "You listened patiently to everything I said," she remembers, "and then you completely ignored what I said and did something different."

"That's because you were wrong, Mum," I'll say to her, with a wink and a smile.

During my senior year in high school, I was voted a prefect by the students and teachers. Back then, for the purposes of sports, academics, and camaraderie, seniors were divided into four different groups, or what were called "houses." A prefect was the leader of the house. Considering the fact that I was often truant, I was surprised when my name was announced, but it showed me that I had the ability to lead. To be perfectly honest, however, I was really somewhat irresponsible during my last few years of high school. I'd often leave at lunchtime, grab my surfboard, and head for Noosa Beach with my buddy Greg Lyons. Assessing the value of the big waves and then riding those great rollers certainly beat the dreariness of the classroom. It gave me a wonderful feeling of freedom and independence, which I needed at the time. Like the wide-brimmed straw hat I wore on the golf course, I chose to wear my watch on my right wrist even though I was right-handed because I wanted to be different. And when the high school needed some funds to finance a sports trip, I rented a roulette wheel and hosted a gambling party at my house (much to my father's dismay). But we raised the necessary dollars, even if it was in a somewhat unorthodox manner.

The first six months after I graduated from high school were aimless. I continued to play golf, but in between tournaments I headed for the surf. I let my hair grow down to my shoulders and, for the most part, spent my time on the beach. It didn't take long, though, for me to realize my life was going nowhere. The sheer repetitive nature of each day started to bore me, and I began to realize that the lifestyle I loved at the time would not give me the future I wanted. I knew life had more in store for me.

My father tried to help give me some direction. He was a partner in his own engineering firm and wanted me to follow in his footsteps. When I told him I didn't want to be an engineer he was disappointed—but he encouraged my second choice, which involved a perpetual interest in airplanes and flying. Part of the curriculum during my early school years included a choice between being an air force cadet or an army cadet. I chose the air force and, with time, became infatuated with the idea of becoming a pilot. I went on cadet bivouacs and learned about the military, received some basic training, and completed community service. I went to the local air shows and admired the skill of pilots who flew F-111s. So when it came time to choose a career, my dad and I talked about it and decided to explore a career in the military. We made it as far as the Royal Australian Air Force recruiting office in Brisbane. The papers were on the desk for me to sign, and the next day I would have been in the service. But I shocked my father (and the recruiter) by freezing. "Dad, I just can't do this," I said.

I never consulted anybody. I never asked anyone for advice. I just said no. I followed my gut and trusted my instincts. My feeling at the time was if I'd joined the air force, deep down inside, I'd have been doing something I really didn't want to do. Of equal importance, I didn't feel I had prepared for a career in the air force. I hadn't received good grades in school, nor did I have any formal flight training. Golf and surfing had taught me the value of preparation, of refining my skills, of being prepared. And quite frankly, I was all too aware that I was ill prepared to be a pilot in the air force. The next few days were awkward, to say the least—knowing that my father was upset and knowing that I had nowhere to go for work or a career. I think my dad's reaction, in part, had something to do with the fact that he himself once had a dream of being in the military. Later, he emphasized to me the importance of a good education and suggested I go to college. But I nixed that as well. I'd had enough of school, and besides, my mediocre grades would make it tough for me to get accepted.

My father is an interesting guy. He is short, stocky, strong as an ox—he was a great rugby player. I'm sure I inherited a lot of my athletic ability from him, along with his amazing tenacity, his drive to keep going, to never give up. He's also a man of high principles who taught me to always be honest. "Greg, if you ever get asked a question, just tell the truth," he said. "If you always tell the truth, you'll never get in a problem ten years down the line. You won't have to guess whether you lied or not."

I believe I can also trace my deep sense of right versus wrong back to my father. He was always hammering me about my behavior if he thought it was inappropriate. An incident I remember most vividly occurred during a tournament at the Virginia Golf Club. I'd made a bad shot, and in a fit of rage I sent my 7-iron sailing down the fairway. Well, Dad, who'd been following me, just turned abruptly and walked off the course. When I got home, he gave me a brief lecture. "Don't ever throw a club again," he said. "I do not believe in that sort of thing. No self-respecting golfer would ever think of doing what you did today. You have to respect the game." My father's words really sank in. Unlike other criticisms on less contentious topics, he used an economy of words. When he really wanted to make a point, he applied the "less is more" mantra, and that was very impactful. I learned to control my temper, and from that moment on, I managed my frustrations on the golf course.

Even though he gave me these pearls of wisdom from time to time, my father and I had a strained relationship. When I was young we were not very close. He did not compliment me very much, and I resented his constant criticism. When I let my hair grow long, I felt like he wanted to take our Victor lawn mower and run it right over my head. Did my father love me? Absolutely. He just had a tough time showing it. Dad, I later realized, was a product of the way he was raised and the way his parents treated him—which, I believe, was a product of the times. Communication is vital. But life and times are different today than they were fifty years ago. Back then I did not understand, nor did I appreciate, that my father simply did not communicate with me the way I do with my children.

When I finally decided to apply myself, it was partly because of that episode with the surf where I was nearly killed—and partly because I realized that the one thing in the world I *really* wanted to do was play golf. So I announced to my parents that I was going to become a professional golfer. My mom encouraged me, but my dad thought I was wasting my time. And for quite a while, things were a bit tense around the house.

At any rate, I began my long journey to the professional golf circuit by accepting a position in the Brisbane warehouse of Precision Golf Forgings (PGF). My job was to pack and box golf clubs, buggies (carts), and the whole range of equipment offered by the company, which were then shipped to pro shops and/or retail outlets. The head of the Queensland division of PGF, Sommie Mackay, allowed me to work special hours so that I could practice as much as possible (which I needed in order to be accepted into Australia's formal apprenticeship program with the PGA). I worked at PGF from 7:00 A.M. to 11:00 A.M. But when the time clock hit 11:00, I was out of there in a flash—dodging and weaving through Brisbane's main streets as I sprinted to the railway station to catch a train to Virginia Golf Club for my daily session on the practice range, which usually lasted until dark.

As a young amateur, I was picked to play on the pennant team representing Virginia Golf Club. My teammates—Lloyd Bode, Kevin Flanagan, Kevin Murphy—and I used to take a six-hour bus ride from Brisbane to Grafton, New South Wales, to play other golf clubs down there. During those trips we'd have a pretty rowdy time. On one occasion I made a shocking boast to my mates. "Before I'm thirty," I announced, "I'll be a millionaire and I'll be married to an American!"

After a moment of stunned silence, the guys really slanged me. "What in hell are you talking about?" they wanted to know. "Who do you think you are?"

"Well, my ultimate goal is to play on the American tour because that's where the best golfers play," I replied. "And since America is my ultimate goal, I think my chances of marrying an American are pretty high. You guys mark my words. When those two things happen, I'll call each of you from wherever I am and let you know they've happened."

"Don't be ridiculous," one of the guys said. "You're dreaming."

CHAPTER THREE

O<small>VER THE NEXT EIGHTEEN MONTHS</small> or so, my golf game continued to improve and I entered as many tournaments as I could manage. I cruised to a 5-shot victory in the Brisbane Golf Association Junior Championship, teamed up with my mother to capture the mixed doubles championship at Royal Queensland Golf Club, and won my second Gary Player Classic title (this time by 4 strokes).

In my first major national event as an amateur, the Australian Open (played at my home club, Royal Queensland), however, I didn't fare quite as well—largely due to an unexpected, somewhat freak occurrence. After having been granted a sponsor exemption, I had not disappointed by shooting three good rounds of 71, 76, and 71—which left me only a few shots off the lead. More important for me at that time, however, was that I shared the position of leading amateur with Terry Gale, a terrific golfer from Western Australia.

On the final day, Gale and I were paired up and became locked in a personal battle to claim the top amateur spot. He chipped in twice for birdies on the first 9 holes and, as we made the turn, I was trailing by a couple of strokes. One of my friends from the Virginia Golf Club, Roger Dwyer, volunteered to caddie for me, and when my second shot on the 10th found a front greenside bunker, he headed around to the back of the green where he left my golf buggy and moved a few yards away to see a friend in the gallery. Well, I dug in and blasted my shot out of the sand. The ball rolled across the green, passed the flag, and then trickled down the hill and hit the wheel of my buggy. That resulted in a 2-stroke penalty. I was seething with anger as I chipped the ball back up the slope and finally holed out for an 8 that wiped me out of contention for top amateur honors.

After I hit my tee shot on the next hole and began walking down the fairway, I couldn't hold back my rage any longer. "Do you know what you've cost me?" I said to Roger. "How could you have let that happen?"

"I'm sorry, Greg," Roger replied. "One day you are going to be a great player. Rome wasn't built in a day, and you will have many more bad breaks." But that didn't make me feel any better, and for the first and only time during a tournament, tears rolled down my cheeks. Then I grabbed the towel from my golf bag and draped it over my head. But Roger's statement was true, as time showed. I just had too much emotion in me at that moment. I would never forget that incident, because it taught me that emotion and business do not mix well. And in the future, I would constantly remind myself not to get emotional about a deal or get tied up in people's personal emotions. I double-bogeyed the 11th, closed with a final score of 77, and finished 5 shots behind Terry Gale. I was completely devastated by that misfortune and I did not handle it well on the golf course. I vowed never to let that happen again.

At this time, I was still representing Queensland in state amateur competitions, and our team would often practice together in preparation for interstate matches. My mates and I spent a lot of time together and became such close friends that, I'd venture to say, we would have done anything for each other. I recall a time when six or eight of us were playing on an amateur team competition, and during an afternoon break, we went over to one of the parents' houses. Suddenly Steve Perrin declared that he could swim six lengths of the pool underwater. Of course, we jeered at him. It was a kind of game we played with each other. It was a regular challenge to see how far we could push things. "I'll show you guys," he yelled— then he stripped down to his trunks and dove into the water.

Steve swam one, two, three lengths of the pool fairly comfortably as we lounged around and watched. But then he stopped face-down at the bottom of the deep end and remained motionless. I was on the first-floor balcony overlooking the pool and had been watching him fairly closely. "God, he's in trouble!" I yelled. And then, fully clothed, I instinctively jumped into the pool from the balcony while everybody else was waiting for him to move. I grabbed Steve off the bottom and hauled him to the surface. But he was such a big man, I screamed for the other guys to help me pull him out of the water. When we got him on the deck, I had all these memories of my teammate from high school who had dropped dead at rugby practice, and I was determined not to see that happen again. So while one of the guys ran to call an ambulance, I turned his head, got all the water out of his lungs, and then performed mouth-to-mouth resuscitation. Steve was unconscious, blue in the face, and he had obviously taken in a lot of water. I worked frantically with Bob Witcher to get him breathing. Finally the ambulance arrived and sped him off to the hospital, where he made a full recovery.

I think back on that incident from time to time, often wondering why it was me who jumped into the pool. To tell you the truth, I didn't even think about it. It was spontaneous. I assessed a bad situation fast and, I believe, reacted properly, friend or not.

Eventually I became convinced that my game had reached a plateau and that the only way to improve was to play on the harder courses in and around Sydney. I also believed it was time to take some concrete steps toward turning professional. Back then, however, you could not become a professional golfer just like that. In order to be eligible to play on tour, you first had to become a certified club professional. And in order to be a club pro, you had to go through a full apprenticeship program, which normally lasted three years and was very comprehensive. But a three-year apprenticeship seemed like an eternity to me. So, knowing that I needed to play in Sydney, I appealed to the New South Wales PGA for an exception that would allow me to play in tournaments and complete the training period in less than the allotted time. There had been a great deal of positive media coverage about my golfing performances, and I had heard that the NSW PGA sometimes made exceptions that allowed apprentices to play in professional tournaments. They were aware I had been called "Australia's next golfing superstar," that I'd been described as "a tall kid who hits the ball farther than Jack Nicklaus," and that other golfers who'd seen me play said that I "had the fighting quality and ability to play all shots under pressure that only the top golfers possess."

To my unbounded delight, the NSW PGA granted my request, and I arranged to apprentice under one of Australia's most famous golf instructors, Billy McWilliam, at the Beverly Park Golf Club in Sydney. So in March 1975, I loaded up my little Ford Cortina and drove south. Well, I was three hours down the road when I realized that I'd left my entire life savings of $2,000 resting on the kitchen counter at home. So I turned around and headed back. When I pulled into the driveway, my mother greeted me by saying: "You must have heard the broadcast."

"What broadcast?" I asked.

My mother then explained that shortly after I had driven out, she had discovered the cash and telephoned the local radio station. And she asked them to broadcast a message on the chance that I'd be listening. "Would Greg Norman, heading south to Sydney, please return home," the disc jockey had said. "He has forgotten his money."

The next day I reported to Billy McWilliam in Sydney to begin my apprenticeship. He was a very nice man who had coached both Bruce Crampton and Bruce Devlin to prominence. McWilliam wasted no time in putting me to work. Assistant professionals (as the apprentices were called) had to learn skills related to our profession: to clean, assemble, and repair golf clubs; give lessons to juniors; sell merchandise; close up the pro shop at night; manage inventory; interact professionally with members; and so on. David Graham later helped me refine my clubmaking skills, and to this day I still work on my own golf clubs. In fact, when I am playing in a tournament, I will occasionally wander into one of the equipment vans lining the practice fairway and repair one of my clubs or simply replace the grip. I've often been told that the equipment representatives say I'm one of the few pros who still choose to work on their own clubs and have the skills to perform such tasks.

As far as professional golf was concerned, the early 1970s

in Australia were like the 1950s in the United States. Having to become a club pro before you could become a touring pro was antiquated. Arnold Palmer, for instance, first had to be a club professional before he could go on tour. It wasn't until many years later that the Australian PGA and the PGA Tour of Australia split, so that members no longer had to be a club pro to be eligible to play on tour. Some people have referred to me as the "Last of the Mohicans" because I came up through the old system. For instance, my contemporaries on tour, such as Curtis Strange and Lanny Wadkins, played in college on scholarships and then immediately joined the PGA Tour. As a matter of fact, I may be the only active touring pro who knows how to whip a golf club. In those days, I had to learn how to craft a driver from a block of persimmon, shape it, melt lead into it for weight, fit it with a sole plate, put in an insert, add a shaft, whip nylon line around the hozzle, and put on a grip. Many years later, I would place my first handcrafted driver, which has my initials carved into the face insert, in my locker at the World Golf Hall of Fame.

My day-to-day routine as an apprentice under Billy McWilliam was grueling. I set my alarm every morning at 4:30, and by 5:00 A.M. I was hitting golf balls into the morning sunrise. At 7:30, I would unlock the pro shop, where I would work until 5:00 P.M. I also worked on the night driving range, selling buckets of balls to members. And when the lights were turned out at 10:30 P.M., I had to go out and pick up thousands of balls by hand and then clean and sort them so they'd be ready for the next day. It was not until after midnight that I was able to go to sleep. I remember plopping down in bed one night and thinking to myself: "I am really going nowhere fast."

After three months, Billy McWilliam informed me that the New South Wales PGA had reversed itself and would not release me to play in tournaments during the year. They said I would be held to my full three years as a trainee before I could play professional golf. I asked him why they had changed their mind. He didn't know. This turn of events devastated me, because I naturally assumed that a governing body of golf could be fully trusted. Surely they were held to a higher standard and weren't influenced by personal vagaries.

I guess I was naïve. I have since learned that institutions and governing bodies are often as mercurial as the people that run them.

I immediately put in a call to Charlie Earp, the head golf pro at Royal Queensland Golf Club in Brisbane, and explained the situation to him. "Come back to Queensland," said Charlie. "You can work for me as an assistant pro and I'll help you out with the Queensland PGA the best I can."

After hanging up with Charlie, I went back to speak with McWilliam. "Sir, I hope you don't take this the wrong way, but if I have to do a full three years as a trainee, I might as well do it back home in Queensland."

"That's okay with me, Greg," he replied. "Is that what you want me to tell the New South Wales PGA?"

"You know what, Mr. McWilliam? I was brought up to respect institutions, such as the NSW PGA, but I have learned a valuable lesson. You can tell them I don't respect their reversal and therefore don't intend to stay. How could I trust them?"

That night at ten o'clock, I set out on the 500-mile drive back to Brisbane, which back then was all two-lane roads through the country. I was so angry, so wound up, that I knew I could make the drive in one night. I figured I'd get home at around five or six in the morning, and I stewed about what had happened most of the way. It wasn't Billy McWilliam's fault. He was a nice guy. Why didn't the New South Wales PGA keep their word? How could they do this to me? Who did they think they were? I tell you one thing, when I get the chance, I'll . . . Whoaaaa! The kangaroo came out of nowhere. I slammed on the brakes and yanked the car hard left. My front grille hit a direction sign and I spun around twice before coming to rest on the opposite side of the road with the back of my car jammed into an embankment.

I paused for a moment to calm down and make sure I wasn't hurt. "What else could go wrong?" I wondered. I got out to inspect the damage, and from what I could see in the dark, the car seemed a bit banged up, but, fortunately, it was still running. So I got back on the road and drove the final hundred miles or so home.

The sun was just coming up as I pulled into the driveway of my parents' house. When I got out of the car and saw the damage in the cold light of day, my jaw just hit the ground. The back left of my Cortina was completely caved in, and the crash had apparently damaged the fuel tank, because gas was dripping into a pool on the cement. I realized at that moment that I could have been killed by an explosion from the ruptured gas tank. It taught me to always expect the unexpected. Although I was lucky I wasn't hurt, my car was in bad shape. Then I remembered that my professional golfing career seemed to be over before it had begun. And it all got to me. I broke down and just stood there in the driveway and sobbed.

As an interesting close to my damaged Cortina, Lloyd Bode, my pennant team partner, was able to fix the car. It took a considerable amount of bondo—or "bog," as we called it in Australia—for it to resemble its former shape. I have to admit, however, that I felt a little guilty when I sold that car to Jeff Senior, Peter Senior's brother, for a slight profit.

CHAPTER FOUR

....

NOW BACK IN BRISBANE, I went straightaway to see Charlie Earp. Even though he already had two trainees under his wing, he agreed to take me on. Charlie didn't have to say it, but I knew it was a stretch for him to add me to his roster. Charlie had a great partner in his wife, Margaret, who managed the retail operations of the pro shop. The two of them worked so seamlessly, and although it was a hardship taking on a third trainee, it was a sign of the shared commitment and belief of both Margaret and Charlie.

I was paid only twenty-eight dollars a week, so clearly I had to be very careful how I budgeted my money. I devised a system—the 30/30/30/10 rule—and stuck to it. I dedicated 30 percent of my earnings to pay my taxes; 30 percent went for my cost of living (which was kept down because my parents let me live at home rent-free); I put 30 percent into a savings account; the remaining 10 percent was my slush fund, which I used to reward myself when I felt it was deserved.

I started working in the pro shop and took care of the members and continued to assemble and repair clubs. I also learned how to balance a budget, decipher an income statement, and interact with the superintendent. And every other night, I had to pick up balls on the driving range. Back then they didn't have caged golf carts. Rather, I would grab a five-gallon bucket and pick up the balls by hand; as you might imagine, I took more than one golf ball to the back from the people still practicing. It was the worst job I ever had.

In my spare time, I hit the books because examinations were part of the curriculum. I was so charged up that, in the first six months back in Brisbane, I took and passed all the required tests that were normally reserved for the completion of the entire three-year apprenticeship. As a matter of fact, my test results were tops in the state. Not bad for a kid who didn't apply himself in school. I was proud of myself. It proved to me that when I did apply myself, my determination to succeed paid off.

I also developed a great relationship with Charlie Earp. We really connected—in part, I think, because he had such a strong work ethic. "Greg," Charlie said, "you've got to DIN and DIP."

"What is DIN and DIP?" I asked.

"Do It Now and Do It Proper—no matter what the task," he replied. "Even if you don't like it, you've got to do it."

Charlie worked directly with me every other afternoon (when I was free of my duties in the pro shop). He watched me hit thousands of shots, constantly encouraging me, and he helped me develop and refine my swing mechanics. He also taught me life lessons and respect for the game. And I really tried to listen to him, to not assume that I knew everything or had all the answers. At one point I asked Charlie for help in perfecting a low punch shot because I knew I would have to learn to hit the ball low if I ever hoped to achieve my dream of winning the British Open.

Charlie admired the fact that I not only had the long-term vision but wanted to learn a golf shot in preparation for achieving that vision. So he quickly grabbed my club, took one swing, and hit a perfect low punch. "Well," I said, "I guess if you can do it, I can too."

I worked on that shot for weeks and then asked him to take a look. "You've got it right, exactly right," he said.

And that's kind of how it went with Charlie. He worked me relentlessly, but we had a great connection.

I knew it would take a lot of hard work to make it as a professional, especially if I wanted to begin playing in less than three years. My commitment to practice was fanatical. As a matter of fact, I worked so hard that members of the club actually got angry with me because I took so many divots that, as Charlie said, it looked like pigs had come and rooted up the driving range. And I must say that Charlie made it interesting with his many unorthodox sayings. They were so unusual that I remember them. In addition to DIN and DIP, there was PPP: Patience, Pace, and Putting. "Patience: don't get greedy," said Charlie. "Pace: from the tee box until the ball is holed. Putting: have to putt well to have a chance." And there was BIG: Burn Into Gear. "Don't sit around, just do it," said Charlie. "You set the example because nobody is going to do it for you." This guy was certainly the Yogi Berra of Australia.

When I think back on my time with Charlie, I think his biggest and most important influence was directed toward motivating me, building on my already strong work ethic and giving me the confidence to be the best I could be. Charlie once said to me you have to first develop determination, then you can concentrate. Otherwise you're just concentrating on concentrating. He also told me, on more than one occasion, that I was never going to learn anything while I was talking! These and many other colloquialisms were sometimes a bit silly in isolation, but when said at the right time— and believe me, they were often part of Charlie's vernacular—they had great impact. And to this day I live by many of his life lessons, more so than his swing theories and fundamentals.

I realize that people like Charlie don't come along very often. He coached me well. He gave me the solid basis for a golf game that would last a lifetime. What I owe Charlie in terms of encouragement, friendship, and understanding cannot be measured. And when I reflect on it in later years, I realize how important it is to surround yourself with intelligent, decent people. Doing so can make all the difference in the world in determining whether you become a success or a failure. And, coincidentally, that was another of Charlie's lessons. "Young man, you are judged by the company you keep," he always said.

During my time as an assistant at Royal Queensland, a couple of days each week I was allowed to play with the members. Spending time with them really taught me a lot about life. One of my regular playing partners, Cyril King, for instance, was thirty years my senior. He was a contractor for small civil engineering projects for the state government. Sometimes when we were out on the course, we'd try to supplement our income by gambling with our opponents. And Cyril, who was calm, cool, and fearless, taught me to handle pressure and win. One situation I vividly remember occurred when we were teamed up in a four-ball match. Cyril and I were down about $800 with only a couple of holes to go. One of our cardinal rules was if we made a bet and lost, we always paid up. It was a matter of honor. Well, I knew I didn't have the money in my bank account. So as we were walking up to the 17th tee, I turned to Cyril and said, "If we lose, I can't afford to pay. Why don't we double down on our bets? At least that way we can get even and maybe make money." Cyril agreed, and I finished the last two holes eagle-birdie. We ended up making money that day!

But no matter who won or lost, no matter how fierce the rivalry on the golf course, it was all forgotten when we got together afterward. The winners would treat the losers to dinner. Then we'd go back to somebody's house and, around the snooker table, we would go through an almost ritualistic postmortem of the day's golf. "This is what you did wrong on the 6th hole, Greg. You should have used a 6-iron and hit it hard rather than use an easy 5." "That bunker shot on the 12th was really poor. You had too much weight on your front foot." We'd do that to each other until the wee morning hours. And I know it helped improve my game.

My relationship with Cyril King extended well beyond the golf course. He had grown up in the Australian outback—he knew it like the back of his hand and spent a lot of time there. When he found out I loved the outdoors as well, he invited me to go along with him and his two sons (who were slightly older than me) on a trip up to northern Queensland near the Gregory River. We jumped into two F-150 trucks with bunk beds in the back and drove for four or five days just to get that far into the outback. Once there, we camped on the bank of the river for a couple of weeks. Owners of the ranches (which are called "stations" in Australia and are often in excess of 5,000 square miles) gave us permission to hunt and fish on their land. Our time there was very much like a vacation, but we were also helping the owners.

We hunted the 300–400-pound wild boar that roamed the stations and constantly disrupted the cattle breeding areas. Then we'd round up as many of the little baby sucklings as we could find and give them to the families in the outback. The local residents had very little and were really in the middle of nowhere. There was very little communication with the outside world, except for maybe a Single Side Band (SSB) radio—and the Royal Flying Doctor Service met their medical needs. Back then there were no moratoriums on the shooting of kangaroos, so the station owners asked us to shoot as many as we could because the animals were always eating the feed (grass) and knocking down fences. The station owners and local farmers would then sell the furs and use the meat for pet food.

I loved being out there, and Cyril kept asking me back. I went as often as I could, partly because I was learning a great deal. Cyril taught me all the things about the outback that his father had taught him. He schooled me on nine of the ten most poisonous snakes in the world, which were indigenous to the area. He taught me how to avoid dangerous situations, how to collect firewood without being bitten by redback or funnel web spiders, how to navigate by the stars, how to find water where there was none, and how to live off the land, much as the indigenous people had for centuries. Cyril also taught me how to measure distances without using equipment. "Find out which is your dominant eye," he said. "Project out your arm full length and hold up your thumb. Focus on that tree over there. Close your dominant eye. Your thumb is now at a spot that is fifteen or twenty feet to the right of that tree. Multiply that by ten and that's how far you are from the tree: about 150 to 200 feet."

When I'd get home I'd relate all that I'd learned to my parents, which may have added to the strained relationship between me and my father. I spent a lot of time with Cyril doing things that my dad did not do with me. But I simply had to continue going to the outback. For me, it was the connection with the outdoors I could not resist. Seeing thousands of kangaroos taking off across the plains and running in what we called "mobs." It was mesmerizing. Hunting water buffalo and wild boar. Fishing for barramundi. Setting up traps in the Gregory River to catch mud crabs. Hearing crocodiles grunting and groaning. Being attacked by an aggressive ten-foot black snake that stands three feet high on its back quarter and charges—and then having to just stand there and shoot it before it got to you. And if you missed, you were likely to die in a matter of days. Being part of the outback absolutely thrilled me. It got my blood flowing and all my senses running at peak capacity. I couldn't get enough of it.

CHAPTER FIVE

Bᴇ THE SUMMER OF 1976, I was on a roll in golf. I'd won the Queensland trainee championship by 15 strokes, sailed to several other amateur victories, and completed the business management course that was required prior to becoming a full-fledged professional. It was at this point that both the Queensland PGA and the Australian PGA allowed me to join the Australian Tour—in less than two years.

I made my professional debut in the Queensland Open at Keperra Golf Club, finishing third and claiming $1,500 in prize money. Because I didn't want to borrow any money or be beholden to a sponsor who would take a large percentage of my earnings, I applied my winnings directly to expenses for upcoming tournaments. Doing so was an important step for me at the time, because I wanted to be master of my own destiny financially. The following week, I finished third again at the Bateman's Bay Open and then followed that up with a Top 10 finish in the New South Wales Open.

In October, I journeyed to Adelaide to play in the West Lakes Classic. This tournament was a really big deal for me. It had a very strong field, including Bruce Crampton, David Graham, Bruce Devlin, Graham Marsh, and a number of American players. I was also receiving a lot of press, so expectations were running fairly high when I teed it up in the first round. By the time I went off, it was late in the day and word was buzzing around that John Clifford had already completed his round and set the course record with a 67. I distinctly remember thinking to myself, "Wow, that's a pretty good score. I'll just have to go out and beat it."

And that's exactly what I did. I shot a 7-under-par round of 64, broke the hours-old course record, and ended up leading the field by 3 strokes after the first round. The next morning, I was thrust into the national spotlight as newspaper headlines labeled me the "Golden Boy," announcing that "Rookie Norman Upstages Stars." On the second day, I fired a 67 despite the fact that I incurred 3 penalty strokes—two shots lost in the water and one stuck in a tree. But that was good enough for a 5-stroke lead at the halfway point of the tournament. My 15 birdies in 36 holes really whipped the press into a frenzy, and newspapers everywhere had the words "Norman Conquest" plastered across their sports pages.

As I began the third round, my plan was to keep attacking the golf course rather than trying to play defensively. But I was starting to get nervous, especially as my playing partner was going to be the very serious, very intimidating, and very talented Bruce Crampton. I shot another excellent round despite an unusual occurrence at the short par-3 8th hole. My tee shot finished on the surface of a cart path from which I was entitled to a free drop. I picked up my ball and indicated to Bruce what I was going to do. But in his eyes, I had committed the cardinal sin of not marking the spot where my ball had originally lain. He advanced toward me and started to give me hell, demanding to know where my marker was. Rather than whimpering away, I pointed to the exact spot where the ball had been. But Bruce shook his head. "No, no, no. How would I know whether or not you are dropping nearer the hole unless there is a marker down?" he asked. Fortunately, an official stepped forward to support my case, and Bruce relented, satisfied with the outcome. But he had taught me a good lesson. I realized that, as a professional golfer, I was responsible for my own actions and thus I needed to understand the rules of the game. So in between tournaments, I started carefully reading the rule books of the R&A and USGA.

Despite that distraction with Crampton, I managed to shoot a 5-under 66. So I was heading into the final round at 16 under par

with an astounding 10-shot lead. After our round, Crampton congratulated me and then later told the press, "Greg is a fine player
and a fine gentleman."

Sunday dawned clear and warm and I had resolved to keep attacking the golf course. But I learned that day that, in both life
and a golf tournament, the toughest, loneliest place in the world
is out in front. My normal aggression quickly got me into trouble,
and then I became nervous and started to play defensively. I lost
3 strokes on the first 3 holes and then bogeyed the 8th and 10th.
Meanwhile, David Graham was having a great round and charging
hard.

After the bogey on 10, I had a talk with myself. "My God, you've
come all this way. You can't blow it now. Stay in the present. Play
your normal game." So I finally settled down and made some birdies. And when the last three holes rolled around, I had rebuilt my
lead back up to 7 or 8 strokes. At that point I knew I was going to
win, but my stomach started to get tied up in knots with nervousness. I bogeyed the 16th and 17th, and when I got to the 18th green
I was standing over a short tap-in for par and my first professional
victory. It was only a one-foot putt, but that hole was a million miles
away. I was so nervous, I actually missed the putt. Later, upon reflection, I realized that my emotions had gotten the better of me,
and I resolved to work on that and try to stay more focused and in
the moment. My tap-in bogey closed out my round with a 74, and I
finished at 13 under par—good enough to win by 5 shots. David
Graham and Graham Marsh finished second. Bruce Devlin came in
fourth.

I'll never forget seeing my best friend and roommate, Bryan
Smith, standing on the 18th green with a bottle of champagne,
ready to celebrate my first professional victory. He was a true friend
and has remained so to this day. My confidence was soaring as I
signed my scorecard and then walked into the clubhouse for the
presentation ceremony. But then I became nervous again. There
were a lot of people packed into one room, and my shy, introverted
nature began to take over. I had never liked being in crowded places.
So I went over and stood in a back corner with Bryan. I'll never forget that moment. I had on a big white belt, my hair was long and

blond, I was an immature twenty-one-year-old—and I did not want to step up and speak in front of that crowd, which, of course, was what they expected me to do.

At that moment, I made a snap decision. "You know what," I said to myself. "If you want to be successful in golf, you have to get out of this introverted feeling. You've *got* to change and get over it." That was the start of a process that would take some years to achieve.

When my name was finally called, I smiled and walked up to the podium amidst all the applause. They handed me the trophy and a check for $7,000. I couldn't believe it. That was more money than I'd ever seen in my life. I felt like the richest man in the world, as my earnings over the first month of my career were now $9,300.

I was next motioned to the podium to make an acceptance speech. I thanked the club president, thanked the directors of the tournament, thanked the volunteers, and thanked the fans. "This is my first professional victory," I said. "It was a great experience, but I really didn't think success would come so soon. I came to Adelaide not to win the tournament, but just to play four rounds so I could qualify for next week's Australian Open Championship in Sydney."

The audience chuckled at that last comment, and then several reporters raised their hands to ask questions. I pointed one out and he stood up. "Greg, we all know that you learned to play golf, in part, by reading two instruction books written by Jack Nicklaus."

"Yes, that's right," I responded.

"Well, what are you going to do if you find yourself paired with Nicklaus in the Open next week?"

That possibility had never even occurred to me. So I took a deep breath before responding. "You know," I said, "it would be one of the greatest moments of my life, but no doubt I'd be nervous standing on the first tee."

PART TWO

STARTING
TO SUCCEED

CHAPTER SIX

A̲FTER THE WEST LAKES CLASSIC, I flew from Adelaide to Sydney, but I was really on cloud nine. The euphoria from that first victory stuck with me a long time, although it was tempered a bit when I began thinking about the possibility of being paired with Jack Nicklaus during the Australian Open. My stomach was already churning with anxiety just knowing that I was going to meet him, let alone play a round with him.

Well, as fate would have it, when the pairings were drawn on the Tuesday of the tournament, the following three names were called: Greg Norman of Australia, John Lister of New Zealand, and Jack Nicklaus of the United States! I couldn't believe it! In the infancy of my pro career, I was going to have the opportunity of my life to play 36 holes with golf's greatest living icon, someone upon whose style I had molded my game since I was sixteen.

My nervousness carried over to the next morning on the first tee when I first met my hero, and he couldn't have been more gracious. "I heard about your great golf in Adelaide," Jack said. "Good luck this week."

I think I said, "Thank you." I don't know for sure. But I then promptly cold-topped my opening drive. The ball only went about thirty yards, hit a tree, and landed in some bushes. It was the most embarrassing moment of my life.

Jack clearly realized how nervous I was. A picture in the next day's paper showed us walking down the fairway with his hand on my left shoulder. It was Jack's way of telling me that everything would be okay, to just calm down. I finished with an 8-over-par 80 while he shot a 72. Afterward, at the press conference, I described my round as "bloody awful." But Nicklaus was more positive. "By his manner, you'd never know that Greg shot an 80 today," he said. "The score was not a reflection of his game. He's potentially a very good golfer."

We again played together the next day, and I rebounded with a 72 of my own. After that round, Jack invited me to sit down in the locker room for a chat. "Greg," he said, "you are definitely good enough to play on the PGA Tour in the United States."

"Really?" I replied.

"Absolutely. Why don't you think about doing that? Come on over to America. You'll be welcomed with open arms."

Over the next several minutes, we talked about a variety of things, ranging from overall golfing philosophy to swing mechanics. Specifically, I remember that Jack suggested I hit more delicately with longer clubs to gain additional control. He also recommended using a feathered 9-iron rather than a full wedge. Both were good suggestions that I would take to heart and practice over and over again in the coming weeks.

Within a month, I was selected (along with Bob Shearer) to represent Australia in the 1976 World Cup, to be played in Palm Springs, California, in December. The Australian PGA waived one of its rules to let me become the first trainee to receive the honor. But when I started getting visions of playing on the American PGA Tour, just as Jack Nicklaus had suggested, I was informed that, due to another obscure trainee rule, I would have to play all my golf in Australia for the next twelve months. Well, naturally, that upset me. If they'd let me represent my country at the World Cup, then why not a couple of pro tournaments while I was already in America? Fortunately, just before I left for California, Charlie Earp informed me that I could apply to have my final year of training waived. So I filed my formal application to do just that.

Charlie also pulled me aside before I boarded the plane and

said something that I will never forget. "Greg, everywhere you go, you're carrying the Australian flag with you," he said. "You're representing your country. Don't ever forget that." This life lesson would manifest itself nearly three decades later, when the American Australian Association honored me for my contributions to American-Australian relations.

As I look back on that piece of advice now, I realize how much it really affected me. Charlie could not have said that to a more receptive listener. For the rest of my life, wherever I traveled and whatever I did, I would hold Australia close to heart and try not to disappoint my country or the game of golf.

I did go to America and participate in the World Cup. Although I didn't play as well as I'd hoped, I believe my behavior and professionalism on the course did not let Charlie down. Afterward, I decided to stay in California for a month or so. I'd made some good friends there, so while waiting for the Australian PGA to rule on my application, I wanted to experience the United States. After all, it was the first time I'd ever traveled abroad, I was twenty-one years old, and the adventure of it all was too much to resist. So I spent Christmas and New Year's in California, saw the sights with my new friends, and drove their borrowed car on the "wrong" side of the road. I felt very fortunate to be able to visit the United States. I went to the Super Bowl in Pasadena. I saw the Lakers play basketball in Los Angeles and attended a tennis tournament in La Costa. From that time, I cultivated a number of relationships with professional athletes that have stayed with me to this day. And my new friend George Kelley invited me up to the Sonoma Valley, where I dined at some of the cellar door restaurants and first sampled California wines. Everything in California seemed bigger than life to me, and I remember thinking that America was right up my alley.

While there, I received word that the PGA had granted my request to drop the last training year and allow me to turn professional. But I surprised everybody by deciding not to join the American Tour. During that four-week period in California I had changed, becoming more open and less introverted than ever. I also sought the advice of others and then spent a great deal of time thinking about my future. My conclusion was that I simply wasn't yet good enough to play in America. A man's got to know his limitations.

I loved the success I'd achieved thus far, but I felt that to go out too fast would be a mistake. I needed more seasoning, more experience. So I made a decision to re-gear myself. First, I'd play the Australian, Japanese, and European Tours. After a few years I'd move on to America, but only when I felt ready. The reactions of other people, of course, were predictable. "What?" asked my friends. "You're not going to America?" "But why?" they inquired. "You can make extraordinary money in the U.S."

In spite of what other people thought, this was to be a pattern I would repeat again and again, in business and in other aspects of my life. To use a golf phrase, I was going to play my own game. Rather than look only at short-term gains, I would visualize myself over a longer period of time. Then I'd learn as I went along, gradually increasing my skills, reputation, and equity.

So in the spring of 1977, I used some of the $7,000 I'd won in Adelaide to cover travel costs for a trip to Japan. The first tournament I entered there was the Kuzaha International—which I won! My confidence was brimming, and when I was invited to play on the European Tour, I decided to give it a go. But before I left for England, I needed to figure out what to do with my winnings. The Japanese had paid me in cash, and I remember spreading it out on the bed of my hotel room. "What am I going to do with all this?" I remember asking myself. I was still just a kid, inexperienced in dealing with money. I loaded it into my briefcase and took it with me to London. When I arrived, I opened a foreign exchange account at an American Express office near Trafalgar Square.

I broke into the European victory column in my third tournament. At the 1977 Martini International in Blairgowie, Scotland, I fired a final-round 66 to beat the field by 3 strokes. I put my prize money straight into the bank and was off and running. Over the next eighteen months, I grossed more than $70,000 by entering as many tournaments around the world as I could. I usually placed in the money somewhere, and I was able to garner three victories in Australia (New South Wales Open, Traralgon Classic, Caltex Festival of Sydney Open) and one in Asia (South Seas Classic). I also played in my first two British Opens—missing the cut in 1977 but finishing 29th in 1978.

Around this time, I tried a new set of irons made by the Australian golf club maker Cobra. Called Mild Steel, they were cast in a softer black steel and chrome-plated for appearance and durability. The softer touch these irons provided was really impressive. So I made a cold call to Tom Crow, the owner and founder of Cobra. "You don't know me," I said to Tom. "My name is Greg Norman. I'm in England playing the European Tour, and I wonder if you might be interested in making up a set of your Mild Steel irons for me." Tom then took my specs (swing weight, club length, lie, loft, shaft flex, et cetera) and crafted a set for me. After eight or nine weeks, I called Tom again and asked that he make me a backup set.

"Did you like the first set?" asked Tom.

"You bet I did, mate," I replied. "I won four tournaments in seven weeks with them!"

As my victories mounted, people began taking notice. I won several "Best Young Golfer"–type awards. Members of the media began using words like "astonishing," "spellbinding," and "brilliant" to describe some of my victories, most of which I won by multiple shots. And then there were the inevitable comparisons with Jack Nicklaus. "With Norman's blond hair and Nicklaus hairstyle," wrote one reporter, "goes a lovely looping swing and a slide into the ball that generates enormous power with no effort." "Just like Jack Nicklaus, Greg Norman hits it very high and very long," wrote another. I was dubbed "A Young Jack Nicklaus," "The Golden Cub," and "The Silver Bear."

Even though I greatly admired Jack, I did not like all the comparisons with him. It made me feel like I was living in someone else's shadow rather than being known for who *I* was. For that reason, I consciously set out to establish my own identity as a golfer and as a person. I wanted to be known as somebody who worked hard and was always prepared, so I continued to dedicate long hours on the practice range. My philosophy was that if other pros were hitting 300 balls a day, I needed to hit 500. I wanted to be viewed as someone with a "never give up" mentality—so whether or not I was in the hunt or didn't have a chance to make the cut, I played every shot as if it were the most important shot of the tournament. It helped me avoid falling into negative thoughts from what might have happened on the previous shot. What's done is done. Never look back.

I also consulted frequently with Charlie Earp. "When you go out there on that golf course," he said, "everything you've got, everything you do, has to be right. Your presentation, knowledge of the rules, your demeanor. How you treat the spectators, your playing partners, your caddie, everything."

Heeding Charlie's advice, I worked very hard on my behavior, both on and off the golf course. I wanted to be the consummate professional, to be courteous, and to be thoughtful. I also tried to keep a clean image: dressing well, not smoking, and walking with my head high. And I resolved never to forget Charlie's enduring advice about my country. I represented the values of my homeland.

Charlie was instrumental in helping me understand that, instead of just making a living out of the game, I was representing ideals that were much more important: Australia and the great game of golf. He really instilled in me that I was an ambassador, a representative, and a role model. Charlie didn't know I was going to venture out and become very successful. He was instilling these values in me when I was an assistant professional making twenty-eight dollars a week. I'm not sure that even Charlie understood the magnitude of his teachings, and how they affected not only me but all those who worked under him.

CHAPTER SEVEN

Winning tournaments and receiving press coverage afforded me quite a number of business opportunities. All were pretty standard for an athlete. I would endorse their products, make appearances, and help promote their businesses. While this was the dawn of the soon to be burgeoning sports marketing industry, I always felt it important to find companies and products in which I believed. But more important, I took my responsibility as a spokesperson very seriously.

My very first commercial endorsement was with Qantas Airways, who initially gave me a ticket to fly down to Adelaide for the West Lakes Classic. After a while, I inked a promotional contract that has lasted some thirty years, during which time I've always had a Qantas logo on my golf bag. I'm told that this is the longest-standing sponsorship between an individual athlete and a corporation, eclipsing Sam Snead's relationship with Wilson Sporting Goods. In 1976, Qantas was one of only two Australian companies that were truly worldwide brands (the other was Foster's beer). To be associated with even one of them was, in my mind, a significant accomplishment.

Before the West Lakes Classic, I was also approached by Precision Golf Forgings (PGF), the company at which I used to pack boxes. As part of the endorsement, I would receive a small fee plus a $750 win bonus. Following one of my victories, I reminded them of the bonus. But several executives told me I would receive that money only if I entered into another, longer-term contract. Well, I viewed their demands as akin to blackmail. "My bonus for winning the tournament should have nothing whatsoever to do with an extension of my contract," I protested. "You owe me $750!"

"You can take it or leave it, young man," they said. "Well, there's no way I'm going to accept that," I replied. "Good-bye."

After that fiasco, I realized that I was not going to be successful if I represented myself. The fact is that I was naïve in business—and that naïveté could destroy me. So I sought the advice of Peter Thomson, the famous Australian golfer who was a generation ahead of me. He suggested that I sit down and talk with his good friend James Marshall, an independent agent who was a successful businessman in both England and the United States. After spending the day with Marshall, I asked him to manage my business and golfing career. He accepted the appointment, and, I must say, no more than two weeks passed before I had that $750 bonus check in my pocket.

My family and friends, especially Charlie Earp, were upset that I had made such an important decision so quickly. But I had little time, and I knew all too well that I needed to get some help. So I made my decision. I hired James Marshall and didn't look back.

Early on, things went very well. Marshall knew I had been drawing the attention of a number of big-name corporations. Wilson Sporting Goods, in particular, had been very impressed with my victories in Australia, Japan, and the UK. So Marshall contacted them and began some informal discussions. When the company indicated they were serious about negotiating a deal, a meeting was arranged in Los Angeles. Well, the Wilson executives were startled when I walked into the room alongside my agent. "This is the first time we've had a player at these sorts of business negotiations, Greg," one of them said. "We thought you were too busy to fly in from Australia. It's great to meet you and it's great to have you here."

By the time Marshall and I walked out of the room, we had a three-year contract with a base of $100,000 and incentives that, I believed, would easily allow me to double that amount without too much trouble. Needless to say, I was absolutely thrilled. And I learned later that this was the largest contract ever awarded to a Wilson staff player outside the United States.

When the golf season opened in 1979, I hit the world circuit with a lot of enthusiasm, and it paid off in four victories. I successfully defended my titles in both the Martini International (England) and the Traralgon Classic (Australia), won the Queensland PGA Championship (by 8 strokes), and then brought home $20,000 for winning the Cathay Pacific Hong Kong Open (which at the time had one of the larger purses outside the United States).

As I continued to gain experience, I began studying other golfers and thinking deeply about what set the winners apart from the rest of the crowd. It was the varying concentration and demeanor that seemed to make the most difference. On the course, a golfer has to be as cool and calm as possible. Otherwise, he or she will make mistakes. I also observed that many guys seemed to rush into shots without thinking of the consequences of missing their mark. And that all boiled down to the mental aspect of golf—which, I believe, is 85 percent of the game. It's your mind that tells your body what to do. If your thoughts are negative rather than positive, you're not going to perform well.

Golfers react differently to tense situations on the course, as I observed during my first few years as a professional. One guy I was paired with showed up six minutes late for his tee time and had to hit his first drive still dressed in street shoes. Giving him the benefit of the doubt, I'd say he was nursing a hangover, but in all likelihood he was still feeling the effects of the night before. When the officials approached him at the 4th tee box and informed him that his tardiness had cost him a 2-stroke penalty, he got so angry that he picked up a tee marker and hurled it over the fence into a garden adjacent to the course. "They could have at least waited until I'd finished my round!" he screamed. Later in the round, that same gentleman pulled a towel over his head, walked to the edge of a lake, and threw up. (At least he showed some discretion in front of the gallery.) The tournament's official statement on the incident, which I read in the press tent after our round, indicated that "he had been seen to react unfavorably to the ruling."

A different kind of player, however, reacted in a low-key, almost totally unpredictable manner when confronted with a frustrating situation. This particular European took 5 putts from within three feet of the hole—and he still hadn't knocked it in. Rather than stroking a 6th putt, he quietly said "thank you" to his marker, then picked up his ball and walked off the course. I never saw him again.

I must admit that, in those early days, I sometimes let my emotions get the best of me. If I sent a shot into the trees or missed a green, I might slam my club into the ground, swear, or simply not speak to anyone. Mind you, I never threw a club after that incident with my father years earlier. I was in my early twenties and volatile. I admit it. I tried to control my temper by being introspective and having a silent conversation with myself. If I hit a bad shot or wasn't playing particularly well, I might say, "What the hell's wrong with you today? Let's get it together." Before an important putt, I might say, "Do you see that swale on the green over there? Just hit that spot." Talking to myself was a way of keeping my emotions under control on the course. And in those early years, it helped me tremendously.

In a relatively brief period of time, I had established a good record in professional golf, but I still felt there were a few gaps that needed to be filled. For instance, my game wasn't well suited for the links golf courses of Britain and Ireland. When I missed the cut at Royal St. George's in 1978, I blamed the course. But later, I realized the problem rested with me. All players have to play the same course. So it was immaterial whether or not I liked it. If I was going to be successful and win major championships, I was going to have to find the key that unlocked seaside links.

With time, I also learned the value of preparation. In 1979 I achieved my first decent performance in the British Open, in part because I spent extra time getting ready for that tournament. I flew to Royal Lytham and St. Annes several weeks early so that I could familiarize myself with the course. I needed to solve its mysteries and develop in my mind the right strategy with which to play it. By the time the tournament started, I was ready. That year, the Open had a particularly strong field, including Jack Nicklaus, Lee Trevino, Hale Irwin, Gary Player, Seve Ballesteros, Tom Watson, and Isao Aoki. I was in the running until the final day, when I shot a disappointing 76, which left me tied for 10th place. Ballesteros won it that year, but I was pleased with my overall performance.

In 1979 I played in thirty-eight tournaments and flew the equivalent of five times around the world. And just about everywhere I went, people kept asking me why I wasn't on the American circuit. "I'm still learning my trade," I'd respond. "I'm going to keep playing in Australia, Japan, and Europe to pick up as much experience as possible." My thinking was that I could achieve a better balance to my game. Playing in Japan would teach me patience and time management. Playing the hard and fast courses of the Australian Tour would force me to use a variety of bump-and-run shots. And playing on the European Tour in poor weather would prepare me for rainy days in America. When people continued to bring up their belief that I could make far more money on the U.S. Tour, my comeback was consistent. "I'm determined to become one of the best golfers in the world," I'd say. "If I can do that, the money will eventually be there."

In 1980, I concentrated almost solely on the European Tour, and even though I missed the cut in the British Open, I won four other tournaments. One of the highlights was the Suntory World Match Play, where, in the second round, I outlasted England's Nick Faldo. We went all the way to a second sudden-death playoff hole in rain and bitter cold. It was almost total darkness when I finally sank a 15-foot birdie putt to win. The next day I beat Sandy Lyle and claimed a $60,000 paycheck, my largest to date.

Another highlight that year was the French Open in Paris. I went into the final round with a 4-stroke lead and a determination to finish strong. I wound up shooting a 67 to go to 20 under par and win by 10 strokes. Afterward, I told the press that I was dead beat after the strain of the win. Of course, they couldn't understand that even though I'd won going away, it had left me spent both physically and emotionally. And that is really the way I played every tournament. I gave it everything I had and believed it was a good sign if I was drained after the final round.

That type of physical commitment over an extended period of time, however, tends to have a cumulative effect. By the end of the year I had to withdraw from a tournament in Melbourne because I

had suffered a number of dizzy spells. My doctor said I was suffering from exhaustion and needed to rest. He put me on a special
diet, confined me to bed for a week, and insisted that I put away my
clubs for at least six weeks.

Although all my hard work was taking its toll on my body,
at least it was beginning to pay off. In Europe the newspapers
were starting to refer to me as "The Brisbane Bomber." Rather
than being compared with Jack Nicklaus, I was establishing my
own identity.

CHAPTER EIGHT

....

W<small>HILE MY DOCTOR</small> wanted me to rest for six weeks, taking it easy for me simply meant being away from the grind of playing professional golf. It did not mean sitting around watching television. So when James Marshall invited me to stay for a couple of months at his estate in Surrey, England, I accepted. As soon as I arrived, I made a conscious effort to upgrade my wardrobe, considering that my success on the golf course was now putting me in new social circles.

I began with suits, pants, shirts, and shoes. Realizing I had accumulated enough money, and staying within my 30/30/30/10 rule, I bought a used Ferrari 308 GTB. The Ferrari was my first real reward for my efforts, and it was unbearable to have to wait the requisite two days before I could take possession of the vehicle. I had long been a fan of the sleek lines, superior craftsmanship, and lineage of the Ferrari brand.

Unfortunately, the 308 and I quickly became all too visible to the authorities. I knew it wasn't wise, but I felt an insatiable need to test the power of that machine. I preferred to take the back roads of the English countryside, not just for the beauty of the scenery but to test the Ferrari as well as my skills on the tight, winding roads that were less traveled by the local police—although one policeman clocked me at 112 mph. After a while, I decided that the red Ferrari was too conspicuous, so I stored it and purchased a more powerful silver GTS model. Somehow, I was stopped only once in the GTS, but the policeman asked for my autograph and let me go with just a warning.

The Green Belt of Surrey, England, is an area set aside by the government for agriculture, forestry, and leisure. It was the perfect place for me to take some time away from golf. Often I would borrow a shotgun and take Marshall's dogs, Celia and Bruno, through the woods in search of game. The dogs loved these excursions as much as I did. Sometimes I'd just go for long walks in the backwoods. It reminded me of the times I was in the outback with Cyril King and his sons. I liked to be alone. I liked the outdoors. And I look back fondly on those long walks with Celia and Bruno by my side. I was finding new values and appreciating a broader canvas.

Overall, I learned a good lesson by taking that time away from golf. You can't indulge yourself in any endeavor one hundred percent for too long or you'll burn yourself out very quickly. You have to know when to walk away, when to take a break, when to rest and regroup. But how long you should stay away varies for each individual. For me, it was two to three weeks. For others, it might be longer. There are a million advisers in the world. But at the end of the day, everybody has to decide what works best for them.

By the time the summer of 1981 rolled around, I had decided to end my days as a young bachelor—not because I wasn't enjoying that life, but because I'd found the woman of my dreams. Laura Andrassy and I had met on an American Airlines flight from Detroit to New York two years earlier. She was a flight attendant who greeted James Marshall and me as we boarded the plane. I was immediately struck by both her beauty and her demeanor. "See that woman up there?" I whispered to Marshall shortly after we sat down. "I bet I end up marrying her."

Once we were airborne, Laura brought us drinks and Marshall immediately rose from his aisle seat, introduced me as Gregory Norman, and almost pushed her into his seat. Then Marshall went up to the galley and stood out of the way while Laura and I chatted. I had to talk fast, of course, because it was only a forty-minute flight and she had to work. "Will you have dinner with me when the flight lands?" I asked after a few minutes.

"Oh, no," she replied. "It will be far too late."

"But I'm catching a six A.M. flight to Bermuda, where I have to play in an exhibition match—so I won't be able to see you tomorrow. How about a late drink tonight?"

"I don't think so."

At this point, Laura went up into the cockpit and spoke with the pilot and copilot. "There's this cute guy back there who's been talking to me," she said, "and I think I'm in love."

"Again?" the pilot said jokingly.

"He's tall with blond hair and blue eyes, and he says he's a professional golfer."

"Well, I follow golf," said the copilot. "What's his name?"

"Greg Norman," replied Laura.

"Laura," said the copilot, "there is no professional golfer named Greg Norman. This guy is just giving you a line."

Fortunately for me, the skies that night were so crowded with planes that we had to remain in a holding pattern for another forty-five minutes before we could land. So that short flight turned into an hour and a half, which gave me more time to persuade Laura to meet me for a drink. If it hadn't been for the delay, we probably wouldn't have gotten to know each other.

After we landed, Laura still hadn't agreed to meet me. So I left for my hotel thinking I might never see her again. But as I was checking in, I received a page that there was a telephone call for me. It was Laura, who said that she'd reconsidered and agreed to go out for a drink. So right after I checked in, I rushed out to get a taxi, but it was the time of the energy crisis and a taxi wasn't to be found.

Just then a stretch limousine pulled up and let out its passengers. I offered the driver a hundred dollars to drive me over to Laura's hotel and then out for a drink. He agreed, and when I picked up Laura, she looked at me as though she was thinking, "Who the hell do you think you are?" After I explained the situation, she got in and off we went.

Due to the late hour, we had difficulty finding a quiet place for a drink. "Sorry, we have just called for last drinks," we were told at our first stop. We tried two more places and got the same answer.

Both of us could see the amusing side of the situation and we were content with our conversation and each other's company. When I finally dropped Laura back at her hotel, I had barely enough time to get to my hotel, shower, and head back to the airport to catch my flight.

I must admit that this wonderful woman had grabbed my attention, and I made up my mind to see her as often as I could. Ours was a kind of shuttle courtship because I was traveling to so many golf tournaments—and because Laura's job kept her on the go. I remember one time when I arranged to meet her in New York on my way from Tokyo to London. We spent the entire day together, and that night we enjoyed a long, romantic dinner at the restaurant at the top of the World Trade Center. Laura and I dated for two years before I finally popped the question. In mid-1981 we were married at St. Mary's Catholic Church in Old Town, Alexandria, Virginia, near where Laura lived.

Besides my marriage, 1981 was pivotal for me because it was the first year that I played in all four major golf tournaments. In addition to winning three other tournaments (the Australian Masters, the Martini International, and the Dunlop Masters), I finished 31st in the British Open, 33rd in the U.S. Open, and 4th in the PGA Championship. But my biggest thrill was playing in the U.S. Masters. I'll never forget my first look at Augusta National. It was the most beautiful course on the most beautiful expanse of real estate I had ever seen. The sense of history was very powerful. It was as though I were walking in the footsteps of past golfing greats. In short, I felt an overwhelming love for the game. And to this day, I still view the Masters as pure golf and the best-run tournament in professional golf, due in part to the absence of any commercialization.

Sometimes it's hard not to believe in destiny. But I can tell you, when I drew Jack Nicklaus as a playing partner for the first round of the tournament, all I could think about was that it was meant to be. Nine years earlier, I had been studying Jack's books and practicing my grip under the desk while in school. Now I was on the first tee at the Masters, and all my competitive juices were flowing. I was the last to hit, and when I went to address my ball, I avoided Jack's eyes and tried as hard as I could *not* to cold-top the ball again. Fortunately, I hit it down the center and then started walking with my eyes fixed straight ahead.

Looking back on it now, I'm sure Jack realized how tense I was, because he came up and draped his arm around my shoulder again. "I don't know about you, Greg, but I'm nervous as hell," he said. "By the time we reach the top of this hill, my feet will just about be back on the ground."

I looked over and saw Jack smiling at me. "Take a deep breath and let's enjoy the golf," he said.

What a kind, thoughtful, and decent gesture on his part. It really made me feel better—so much so, in fact, that I fired a 3-under-par 69 to tie for first place. Five other golfers also shot first-round 69s, including, you guessed it, Jack Nicklaus. After carding a 70 the next day, I went into Saturday's third round only 2 shots off the lead. Then I fired an even-par 72 to put me in Sunday's next-to-last group with Nicklaus. Tom Watson played in the final pairing with Johnny Miller.

As I began the back 9, I was still only 2 shots off the lead. But I hooked my tee shot on 10 into the trees and had to chip back into the fairway. After taking a double bogey, I was just unable to make up strokes. Watson ended up winning his second green jacket. Nicklaus and Miller tied for second, 2 shots back. And I finished by myself in fourth, 3 shots off the pace. It had been a magical beginning to my Masters ride, and twenty-one consecutive such rides were to follow.

For me the 1981 Masters will also be remembered for the nickname I was given by a headline writer working at the *Augusta Chronicle*. After my first-round 69, as one of the co-leaders, I was ushered into the press room for my post-round interview. I was tied for the lead, but nobody knew who I was. So they started delving into my past. I told them that I was an aggressive golfer with a fairly aggressive lifestyle, that I had grown up near the Great Barrier Reef, and that I enjoyed surfing, diving, and spearfishing. "Do you like sharks?" I was asked.

"No," I responded. "They would frequently feed from the fish I caught. Actually, I would love to shoot them."

Well, the next thing I knew, people were talking about how I used to shoot sharks when I was a kid. And Friday morning I picked up the paper and turned to the sports section to see the huge headline: "Great White Shark Leads Masters."

So now I had a new moniker, and unlike "The Brisbane Bomber," this one stuck. I was pleased at having established my own identity, but I was not overly enamored with the idea of being forever linked with a shark. After all, I didn't like sharks—nor had I ever shot one.

For the rest of the year, I stewed about that new nickname. Finally, when I returned to Australia, I decided to purge myself of the misrepresentation the media had created about my relationship with sharks—and, at the same time, ease my conscience. So I grabbed my .303 rifle, jumped into my thirty-one-foot boat named the *Divot,* and for several hours cruised along the coast until I was able to bait in an unusually large shark. Then I emptied my magazine and erased the myth created by the media.

CHAPTER NINE

As TIME WENT BY, more and more endorsement opportunities presented themselves. To be perfectly frank, however, I had begun to experience some problems with James Marshall's management of my affairs. For instance, when Laura and I decided to purchase a house, her first question was pretty commonsense. "Do you have enough money?" she asked.

"I think so," I replied. "But I really don't know."

When I contacted Marshall's secretary and asked for a printout of my account, she would not give it to me. At first I thought she was just following some sort of established protocol that Marshall had set in place. I respected that, but I also began asking questions, many of which went unanswered.

As I became used to the cut and thrust of business negotiations, I felt confident that I could take on more personal responsibility in my own affairs. So in early 1982, I resolved to tell Marshall that he would continue to handle my merchandising activities but no longer my financial affairs. From my viewpoint, it was a perfectly natural progression in my career.

Meanwhile, Laura and I were doing a lot of traveling. And when I wasn't playing golf, I was deep-sea fishing, scuba diving, or hunting. That was just my nature. I'd wake up at four-thirty in the morning, go all day until midnight, and then wake up again at four-thirty the next morning. I was just go, go, go—and it used to drive Laura nuts. "Look, Greg," she'd say to me, "nobody can keep up with you. You're burning out all your friends."

Fortunately, Laura was understanding of the demands I put on myself. We were very happy together as young newlyweds, and I must say, when we were in Hong Kong and she told me I was going to be a father, the feeling of joy that came over me is not something I could ever put into words. The first phone call I made to share the news was to the best man at my wedding, my friend and manager, James Marshall, who was in London.

"James, I've got some great news," I said.

"What's that?"

"Laura's pregnant. We're going to have a baby."

"Well," he responded, "I can see that is going to throw a spanner in the works."

I couldn't believe my ears. His first reaction was that my having a family was either going to take me away from him or be detrimental to my career.

"What the hell did you just say?" I asked.

When Marshall repeated himself, I ripped the phone out of its socket and threw it against the wall. "That son of a bitch!" I screamed.

As soon as I finished playing in the Hong Kong Open, I flew to London to tell Marshall face-to-face that I didn't want him to represent me anymore. Not merchandising, not my financial affairs, nothing. "The next time we speak will be through my lawyer," he said before walking out. And our relationship pretty much ended right then and there.

A short time thereafter, I received a notice from the Australian Taxation Office (ATO) saying that I owed it a considerable amount in back taxes. Almost in shock, I immediately called the accounting firm Marshall had appointed to handle my affairs in Australia. "What's going on?" I asked. "You told me my tax structure was completely legit and in compliance with the ATO."

It turns out my tournament earnings and endorsement funds had been transferred to a company that was not a tax haven for Australia, but in actuality was a tax haven from the UK.

Now the penny was starting to drop. Everything was coming

down around me. At this point in my career, I had no professional guidance and I felt very much like a ship without a rudder. Just when I was at the point when I felt I had nowhere to turn, the founder of International Management Group (IMG), the preeminent sports management company at that time, reached out to me. Mark McCormack had obviously heard of my difficulties with Marshall, and he saw it as an opportunity to recruit me as a client. McCormack said, "Greg, if you'd like to come onboard with IMG, we have the resources to help with any legal or accounting advice you might need."

McCormack had founded IMG back in the 1960s, representing first Arnold Palmer, then Jack Nicklaus and Gary Player, the big three. By the time I came along, IMG was a sports management powerhouse, representing hundreds of personalities and prestigious events around the world. It was obvious that IMG's reach was far superior to that of my previous representation. So when Mark reached out to me, I saw it as a positive step at that point in my career and signed on as a client.

True to McCormack's word, IMG did help me straighten out my tax liabilities and put me into a more efficient tax structure. Most of my money was tied up, some of it had been siphoned away, and I was in a predicament with the Australian government. In short order, I had to fly to Australia to speak directly with officials at the ATO. "Guys, don't shoot the messenger here," I said to them. "I'm an innocent bystander. Yes, it's me you're coming after. Yes, I haven't paid my taxes in Australia. But here's the evidence that shows I was unaware of this situation." I was between a rock and a hard place, so I made the ATO aware that if we weren't able to come to an agreeable accommodation, I would consider surrendering my Australian citizenship.

In the end, we worked out a settlement, and the Australian Tax Office treated me fairly. I paid my taxes and a minor penalty, but it took me two and a half years of legal battles to free up my funds and get the entire mess straightened out. I don't know what happened to the Australian accounting firm and I don't know what happened to James Marshall. To this day, I have not seen or spoken to him. It was a hard lesson to learn. I put a lot of trust into my relationship with James. After it ended, it took me quite a few years to give people the full benefit of the doubt that they rightly deserve.

Behind every dark cloud, however, I have learned that a silver lining does indeed exist. That traumatic experience turned me. It helped me think differently with respect to both business and my personal life. For instance, I never again allowed anybody to take total control of my finances. Even though IMG managed my money, I always made sure that there was a system of checks and balances.

Being represented by a large management company was an entirely new thing for me—a significant learning experience. I could see early on that IMG was not really interested in building equity in somebody else's brand. Their business model was built on garnering commissions on endorsement deals and appearance opportunities. And that's okay. I'm all for people making money as long as there is an understanding that commissions can often cloud people's judgment insofar as what is in the client's long-term best interests. When things are handled properly, endorsement deals can become a cash cow. And when your deal is up, you either renegotiate to extend or you say "Thanks very much, we enjoyed our time together."

Still, those early years with IMG increased my business acumen and created numerous opportunities for me. Hughes Norton was assigned to be my manager, and we developed a close personal relationship. Almost immediately, he began arranging a series of opportunities where I would be paid an appearance fee to play in an overseas tournament or special event. Interestingly enough, the U.S. PGA Tour did not allow tournaments to pay appearance fees to players. But appearance fees were paid by tournament promoters in every other country. So the more overseas appearances a pro took on, the more difficult it was to stay competitive. Back then, there was a balance between how well you played on the U.S. Tour and the appearance money you could make by playing overseas. Today the equation is quite different, as players on the U.S. Tour typically play for $5 million each week.

In addition, over the next several years, I signed endorsement deals with a number of high-profile companies, including Rolex, Spalding, Reebok, and McDonald's. For these products, and most others, my endorsement usually came in the form of wearing the company logo, making personal appearances, and appearing in their print advertising campaign. Several, however, also involved the filming of television commercials.

Epson printers and imaging products asked me to wear a coat and tie, which was the first time I was presented as a business executive. Swan Brewery in Australia shot a commercial where I was walking out of the ocean holding a surfboard, with a catchy little tune playing "They said you'd never make it, but you proved them wrong." And while filming a commercial for Campbell's Soup, the director told me that he wanted me to sound like a New Yorker. I tried to accommodate the guy, but after a few takes, I thought I sounded like an idiot. Finally I put a stop to it. "Listen, mate," I said. "This is ridiculous. If you want a New Yorker to do this, then you should bloody well get a New Yorker. I'm an Australian."

While these endorsements were lucrative and in many respects groundbreaking, I had the gut feeling that there was a lack of consistency in the messaging. After all, how did the Epson advertisement complement soup or, for that matter, beer? I sensed that while IMG was doing a commendable job presenting me with income-generating opportunities, they weren't helping me build a consistent message and equity in my own brand.

CHAPTER TEN

O N THE 17TH HOLE of the 1982 Martini International, I hooked my tee shot into the woods. I really didn't have a chance to win the tournament, but I was determined to get my ball back onto the fairway. Unfortunately, one bad shot led to another, then another, and then another. And as I swished away in the woods, I could hear the gallery laughing. After I finally knocked my ball back onto the fairway, I received a round of applause. Then I started laughing too. I figured I might as well keep my sense of humor about the whole thing and make the best of a bad situation. Besides, it really was pretty funny.

I took a 14 on that hole, finished with a closing round of 82, and ended up 19 shots behind the leader. The public never knew, but the night before that final round, I was informed that James Marshall threatened to file a lawsuit against me. All during that final round the next day, I was concerned about finding someone who could advise me on my best course of action.

The 1982 Martini International represented a low point in my career. It started me off in a pretty bad slump. My confidence had dropped to an all-time low, and I became irritable and moody, especially on the golf course. Bad bounces, bad breaks, and adversity in general all tended to increase my downward emotional spiral.

With time and introspection, I was able to figure out that the entire episode with my former agent (and the financial predicament

I found myself in as a result) had really taken its toll. I had not only lost my aggression on the golf course, but I was thinking negatively all the time. It also resulted in some bad habits with the mechanics of my swing. Somehow, I had to return to my natural tendencies because, after all, I thrived on aggression, on attacking a golf course. That's what had made me successful in golf, at least in part. So I hit the driving range day after day. I hit thousands of wedges and 9-irons until I achieved a greater control over this aspect of my golf game. And that helped balance my overall swing mechanics.

Emerging from my slump, I won three tournaments in Europe—the highlight being a 17-under-par, 8-shot victory in the Dunlop Masters. I also placed fifth in the PGA Championship—quite an improvement after finishing in the middle of the pack in both the Masters and British Open.

I might add that at the Australian Masters, I was looking for a caddie and ran across a kid who was looking for a job. Steve Williams was only fifteen years old, but he told me he was seventeen. I hired him, and he ended up working with me for a decade. Eventually, Steve moved on and is now caddying for Tiger Woods.

I really believe that my overall mental comeback was completed when Laura gave birth to our daughter, Morgan-Leigh, on October 5, 1982. When I held her in my arms for the first time, I realized what was really important in life. Golf was golf and business was business, but my family really, truly meant something much more. And I vowed at that moment to become the best father I could possibly be.

With my confidence back and my golf game on track again, I decided to work on some of the more subtle aspects of professional competition. I continued to study the other players: observing their mannerisms, their tendencies to be aggressive or reserved, and how they handled tense situations. Did they throw their clubs in frustration? Or did they simply shrug off bad breaks? Knowing these little things, I believed, would give me a bit of an edge when in direct competition with them.

I would take this very same thought process into the future when building a solid foundation for my businesses. It was a form of due diligence to learn as much as possible about your competition. And as in golf, that knowledge always seemed to give me an edge in business.

In studying players on the European Tour, I noticed similarities in behavior to what I had observed about the kids with whom I'd played team sports in high school. Many didn't seem to give it a hundred percent on the golf course. Nor did they work hard to improve their weaknesses. I saw a tendency, for example, to linger in the bars and shoot the breeze, to not concern themselves with continual improvement. It just seemed to me that many of the players on the European Tour were content with being second best. And that was simply contrary to my nature. I always strived to get the most out of myself, to be the best I could be. And as young as I was, I really couldn't understand why other people weren't the same way.

During the time I was thinking about all this, I made a few misplaced comments to the media. "The practice fairways are lonely over here," I said. "So many talented golfers on the Tour have not got the drive, have not got the guts or the inner strength needed to win when victory is in sight."

Essentially, I had called the players in Europe "gutless." What a mistake that was! I caught a lot of heat for my candor, and rightly so. I think my intent was correct, but my delivery was misguided. And looking back on it now, I really shouldn't have said anything at all.

"Greg, you can't just open your mouth and blurt out the first thing that comes into your head," one of my friends lectured.

"All I'm doing is being honest," I responded.

"Well, you can't do that!"

Speaking out so forthrightly was something for which I got the cane rapped across my knuckles when I was a kid in school. And I was still doing the same thing as an adult. It was something I knew I had to work on, especially now that I was getting close to joining the American Tour.

In 1983, after winning six tournaments (three in Australia, two in Europe, one in Asia) and running my victory total to 31, I felt I was ready to play on the U.S. Tour. And with this career move, I believe I became the first player to simultaneously retain membership in three of the world's premier golf tours: the U.S. PGA Tour, the European PGA Tour, and the Australian PGA Tour. And I am proud today to have a lifetime membership on all three of those tours.

While my career was following my script, I needed to find a home for my family. I was very fortunate that a few years earlier Arnold and Winnie Palmer had taken me under their wing. Thanks to them, I moved my family to Orlando, which proved to be an excellent base of operations for my first few years in the United States.

My first win on American soil was at the 1983 Kapalua International in Hawaii. Winning by 8 shots and garnering $100,000 in prize money sent my confidence soaring. So I charged onto the U.S. mainland, but one small incident caused me to think twice about my decision. In one of my first tournaments, I had just reached a long par 5 in 2 shots when one of the established American pros, J. C. Snead, who was my playing partner that day, walked over and scowled at me. "Son," he said, "you're not good enough to play over here. You should just pack up and go home." My reaction was to simply look down and keep on walking. But I have to admit that my first thought was "Welcome to America."

Although I didn't win that particular tournament, I did achieve a victory a few weeks later in June 1984 at the Kemper Open. Larry Mize and I finished regulation play in a tie and had to proceed to sudden death. We each parred the first 5 holes, but on the 6th play-off hole, Larry hit his approach shot way off the green while I was safely on in 2. At that point, I figured all I had to do was 2-putt to win the tournament. Larry tried to pull off a miracle shot, but instead, he bounced his ball off the green and into the water. I then made par and won my first fully sanctioned PGA Tour event in the U.S. I didn't know it at the time, of course, but I'd encounter Larry Mize some years later in nearly the exact same situation—with a vastly different outcome.

After the victory at the Kemper, I ventured north to play in the Canadian Open, where I posted 73, 68, and 70 for the first three rounds. The tournament was being played on a beautiful golf course designed by Jack Nicklaus (Glen Abbey in Oakville, Ontario). And

Jack and I happened to be paired together on Sunday. We were both chasing Nick Price, but I got hot and made up 4 strokes on the front 9. I went on to shoot a 5-under-par 67—good enough for a 2-shot victory over Nicklaus, who finished in second place. Just as with Larry Mize, however, a couple of years later, Jack and I would have a rendezvous with destiny where we'd be in a similar situation with a different result.

Perhaps my most vivid memory of my first full year on the PGA Tour occurred during the final round of the U.S. Open at the famed Winged Foot Golf Club in Mamaroneck, New York. I trailed the leader, Fuzzy Zoeller, most of the day. But after a late charge, I came to the 18th green having to make a 40-foot par putt to remain in a tie.

I can still remember lining up that putt. I knew it was going to break about ten feet. When I stood over that ball, I knew I was going to knock it in the hole. I could feel it in my hands.

Sure enough, halfway to the hole, the ball broke right at the apex of the pitch, and when the putt dropped, it was sure pandemonium. I ran around the green holding my putter high in the air. After calming down, I looked back down the fairway and saw Fuzzy Zoeller waving a white towel over his head in surrender. He thought I had made a birdie to seize the lead. I still believe that his gesture was one of the finest acts of sportsmanship I have ever witnessed on a golf course. After all, he was still in contention.

Fuzzy then parred the 18th and we finished in a tie at the end of regulation. The U.S. Open is the only one of the four majors that requires a full 18-hole playoff the next day in the event of a tie. But when I woke up on Monday morning, I was really tired. My energy, my adrenaline, my emotion—all were just gone. Normally, that would have been a good sign—that I had given it my all during the tournament. But in this instance, it was ill timed. And here's an entertaining twist that someone told me. Apparently Fuzzy was so nervous Sunday night that he kept lighting up cigarette after cigarette in his hotel room, so much that it set off the hotel smoke alarm. In reality, it was Fuzzy who got little or no sleep, but you would never have known that on Monday.

I never really did get it together for that round of golf. I shot a

75 to Fuzzy's 67. And on the 18th hole, I took a white towel out of my golf bag and waved it over my head in surrender, just as he had done the previous day. Then we walked off the green arm in arm with the fans chanting "Fuzzy! Fuzzy!" I was very happy for him.

My son, Gregory, was born September 19, 1985. Laura and I were thrilled. Our family was growing. We now had a daughter *and* a son. Life just didn't seem like it could get any better.

A few weeks after the birth, we had a family gathering in Orlando to celebrate Gregory's christening. Laura's younger brother, Jay, and I were being pulled on an inner tube when the boat that was towing us (driven by Laura's older brother, Richard) came hard around a corner and knocked us off the tube. Instinctively I let go, but Jay did not. The forward momentum carried him full force into me, his right foot hitting me in the face, nearly severing my lower lip, driving my teeth up into my jaw, and knocking me unconscious. If I hadn't had a life jacket on, I would have ended up at the bottom of Lake Tibet Butler. Richard got us safely to the shore, and when I came to, I remember hearing Laura screaming hysterically upon seeing the blood all over my face and the towel I was holding over my mouth. My first impulse was to reassure her. "Calm down," I said. "I'm okay."

I was rushed to the hospital, where I underwent a four-hour operation to pull the splintered teeth out of my upper mouth and sew up my partially severed lower lip. While the surgery proved successful, I would still have to undergo additional plastic surgeries.

When word of my accident reached the press, a number of reporters declared: "Greg Norman has a death wish." "Fast cars, swimming with sharks, and now high-speed boats," they wrote. "It was just a matter of time before Norman seriously injured himself."

Well, I've never had a death wish. I've always known my limitations. It's just that my limitations seem to exceed those of most others. Actually, I'd done a lot of things that could be considered more dangerous than this one boating accident. To me it was just an unfortunate mishap—and one from which I would make a fairly quick recovery.

As a matter of fact, not long after the plastic surgery, I flew across the Atlantic and teed it up at the inaugural Dunhill Cup at St. Andrews. And our Australian team, with David Graham and Roger Davis, won that event. The morning after the competition, doctors removed all the stitches from my mouth.

"You see?" I said to Laura with a big smile. "I told you I'd come out looking better than ever."

PART THREE

RISING TO NUMBER ONE

CHAPTER ELEVEN

As THE 1986 GOLF SEASON approached, I was thirty-one years old, married with two children, and far short of my golf and business goals. I had placed my faith in someone who turned out not to be trustworthy, and as a result, most of my resources were tied up in a complex maze of government bureaucracy and tax laws. I'm also sure that all these personal distractions negatively impacted my golfing performance in 1985 because I won only three tournaments, all of them in Australia.

The recovery period from plastic surgery, however, provided time for me to think, reflect, and determine what my next course of action should be. When I finally figured that out, I simply turned to Laura and said, "I have to go back to work."

This whole thing with Marshall had exacted a toll on me, and I needed to get back at it hard to recover what had been taken from me—pride, esteem, trust, money, and confidence in people and life. So with renewed vigor, I increased my playing schedule and started running hard—harder than usual. My participation in more than thirty tournaments yielded ten victories in 1986 (two in Europe, three in the United States, and five in Australia), including, at one point, six in a row. But many people viewed 1986 as a failure for me, largely due to my performance in the four majors. I did win my first major (the British Open), but because I led all four going into the final round, many felt that I should have won more, if not all of them.

I started off strong at the Masters in April. After rounds of 70, 72, and 68, I had sole possession of the lead (at 6 under par), but Seve Ballesteros, Tom Watson, Tom Kite, Nick Price, and Jack Nicklaus were all within striking distance. But Sunday's final round turned out to be a free-for-all. I was holding my own on the first 6 or 7 holes when I began to hear roars from the galleries up ahead. They were for Nicklaus, who, despite having begun the round 4 shots off the pace, birdied the 9th, 10th, and 11th holes to put himself in contention.

I was still tied for the lead at the turn. On 10, however, I hooked my drive; it bounced off a tree and wound up a long way from the green. Revved up, I then smoked my second shot, but the ball came to rest behind a pine tree just left of the green. With a restricted swing, I punched my third shot into a bunker, blasted out from there, and 2-putted for a double-bogey 6. That left me tied with Nicklaus at 5 under par, 2 shots off the lead held by Seve Ballesteros. Jack then proceeded to birdie the 14th, eagle the 15th, and birdie the 17th. He walked off the 18th green with a magnificent 65, good enough to take sole possession of the lead.

I heard the screams and yells up ahead, I saw the scoreboard, and I knew that I had to make some birdies if I was to have any chance at all to win the tournament. So I made a big charge. I birdied the 14th, 15th, 16th, and 17th holes to tie Jack for the lead. And when I walked up to the 18th tee, I was determined to get my fifth birdie in a row and win the Masters.

I used a 3-wood off the tee to make sure I hit the fairway, which I did. Now I was faced with a 186-yard, uphill approach to the green. All day long, I had been pulling out the right club and hitting it hard. Initially, I believed this situation called for a hard 5-iron. But I talked myself out of it. "Okay, the pin is cut middle back right," my thought process went. "I generally hit the ball left to right. This is 186 with a four- or five-degree slope. It's the end of the day and hard to fire your hips up the hill. Rather than hitting a real hard 5-iron, I'm better off going in there with an easy 4. That should provide me with a bit more accuracy and allow me to get the ball close to the hole. I need to make birdie on this hole. Worst-case scenario, I'll 2-putt for par and I'm in a playoff."

Unfortunately, I was so pumped up that I hit the ball too hard and pushed it fifty feet to the right, into the gallery. As a result, I ended up bogeying the hole and finished in second place. You can't take anything away from Jack Nicklaus, though. He fired a magnificent 30 on the back 9 and earned his sixth green jacket and his eighteenth professional major, and at age forty-six, Jack became the oldest-ever Masters champion.

As painful as it was for me to lose that tournament, I waited around for Jack to complete all his interviews and then personally congratulated him. After all, it was by studying Jack Nicklaus's storied career that I had learned sportsmanship on the golf course. And that it was far more important to be gracious in defeat than to celebrate your victory. It was not only a symbolic moment for me personally, it was also the right thing to do.

The next day I performed a postmortem of the entire tournament, because I wanted to know what had prevented me from winning. Was my putting poor that week? Was it left-to-righters? Was it my bunker play? Was it this? Was it that? Whatever it was, I wanted to know so that I could go out and improve that particular facet of my game. My swing was akin to a mechanical engine. Once in a while something was going to break down, and the thing to do was fix it right away. Not a lot of people will take the time to conduct a postmortem. Most don't like to admit they failed, let alone try to analyze why they did. But I believe that those of us who can face failure, learn from it, and move on will succeed in the long run. That is called determination and drive.

In the case of the 1986 Masters, everybody remembers my bogey on the last hole, but nobody remembers the four birdies in a row that allowed me to get to that point. After analyzing things, however, I realized that everything did, indeed, come down to my approach on 18. I could have been more conservative and played for the tie rather than go for the win. But that was not in my nature, nor do I believe it was the reason I lost the Masters. The real mistake I made was in my choice of clubs. Rather than trying to finesse a longer club, I should have stayed in attack mode and hit the hard 5. That's what had been working for me all day. "Never again will I do that," I vowed. "When I get in another similar situation, I'm going at the hole hard."

Of course, the irony of all ironies is that Jack Nicklaus had advised me to do the very thing that cost me the Masters. Back during our locker-room conversation at the Australian Open a decade previously, after playing two rounds together, Jack suggested I hit more delicately with longer clubs to gain additional control. And I had worked hard on my game to perfect that shot.

A month later at the U.S. Open (played at Shinnecock Hills on Long Island), I fired rounds of 71, 68, and 71 to again take a one-stroke lead into the final day of a major. I had been feeling under the weather, however, and that morning I went to see a doctor, who promptly diagnosed walking pneumonia. "You shouldn't play today, Mr. Norman," he advised.

"Doc, you don't understand," I said. "I'm leading the U.S. Open! I've got to play!"

I was on the driving range, loaded up with a variety of medications, when a couple of tournament officials pulled me aside to explain that someone had made a death threat against me. "Why would anybody do that?" I asked incredulously.

"We don't know, Greg," they replied. "But we're going to place plainclothes security guards in the galleries today, and they'll be armed."

"Well, that's just great!" I remember thinking.

I did not play a great round of golf that Sunday, but I didn't surrender the lead until I took a double bogey on the 13th hole. And as if that wasn't bad enough, some clown in the crowd started harassing me. "Are you choking, Norman?" he shouted. "Are you choking just like you did in the Masters?"

Without thinking, I stormed into the gallery and wagged my finger under that guy's nose. "Look, if you want to say something to me," I said, "say it in the car park afterward when I can do something about it."

The spectator walked away, so I turned around and headed back to the fairway. I immediately regretted going after that guy, because it violated a lot of the things Charlie Earp taught me. It was a bad image to portray. But I'm the type of person who has to get that sort of thing off my chest. Even if my behavior was wrong, at least I was able to get the anger out of my system right then and there.

The truth is that I find it frustrating to be on public display and not be able to fight back. I wish I could have done what my mother did a few years earlier at Royal Melbourne Golf Club in Australia. Hole after hole, a spectator kept harassing me. Finally, on the 18th tee, he shouted: "Norman, you're playing like crap. I didn't pay good money to come out here and watch crap golf!" The next thing I know, I heard this *whack*. My mum had hit the guy with her umbrella. "Go watch somebody else!" she snapped.

Unfortunately, I was not able to turn around my golf game in this U.S. Open. I faded over the last six holes and was defeated by my good friend Raymond Floyd, who (at age forty-three) became the oldest player ever to win a U.S. Open. I don't know if you can call these things coincidences or not, but I had carried the lead into the final round of the first two majors that year and ended up losing to the oldest-ever champions of both events. Go figure.

In July, I journeyed to Scotland to play in the British Open (held at the famous links golf course at Turnberry). After I shot a 4-over-par 74 in an opening round where nobody was under par, the wind let up a bit on the second day. That morning I woke up feeling pretty good, and on the way to the first tee, I kept saying over and over in my mind, "Blue skies and a 65. Blue skies and a 65." I'd made up my mind to be as aggressive as possible and aim directly at the pin on every approach shot. After birdying two of the first three holes, I knew I was on my way. That day, I could do little wrong: I shot a 63, still tied for the record for the lowest score ever recorded in a major championship. Carrying a 2-shot lead into the third round, I ended up shooting another 74 in the wind and rain, but that was good enough to maintain a one-shot lead over Tommy Nakajima at the end of play on Saturday. So now, for three major tournaments in a row, I held the lead outright going into the final round.

That evening, as I sat in the restaurant at the Turnberry hotel, a number of players came up and offered words of encouragement. Fuzzy Zoeller, John Mahaffey, and Hubert Green all said they wanted me to win this one. And then, just after I finished the last bite on my plate, Jack Nicklaus walked over and asked if he could pull up a chair. "Absolutely," I responded.

"Greg, there's no one in the world who wants you to win this tournament more than I do," he said. "You deserve to win."

I was moved by Jack's sincerity. We spoke for a few minutes and he offered me some advice. "Just concentrate on the pressure of your grip," he said. "That will orchestrate your tempo. Everything else should fall in place."

I woke up on Sunday morning having great anticipation for the day ahead. Before I left for the course, my three-and-a-half-year-old daughter, Morgan-Leigh, came up and gave me a huge hug and kiss, and said, "Good luck, Dad!" That was all I needed.

On the golf course that Sunday, everything went my way. I steadily increased my lead so that, by the time I knocked my approach shot to within six feet of the 17th pin, I was nursing a 5-shot lead. I held back my excitement for the walk up to the 18th green. As was tradition with the British Open, the spectators were allowed to fall in around the final group to walk up the fairway. As is normal, thousands of people flooded around us, creating mayhem for the players, caddies, and officials. As the fans rushed ahead of me, I had to force my way through the crowd by following the BBC remote television cart as it made its way up to the green. And when some of the British fans performed a traditional rugby scrum in the middle of the 18th fairway, I knew I had won my first major golf tournament. It was the British Open, no less—the fulfillment of my childhood dream.

After I putted out on the 18th green, my caddie, Pete Bender, was the first person to congratulate me. Next came Laura, who hugged me as I walked toward the scorer's tent. And then Jack Nicklaus came down out of the television booth, leaned over the bleacher railing, and extended his hand. "Congratulations, Greg," he said. "I knew you could do it." That was an incredibly classy and kind thing for Jack to do, and it was one of the proudest moments of my professional career.

Shortly before I left the course, a Concorde chartered to fly many of the American players back to the States flew by on its way to the local airport. The Concorde flew in low over the sea, straight up the 18th fairway, stuck on its heels, put on the afterburners, and lifted up over the clubhouse. It was a salute from my friend Captain John Cook, lead pilot for the British Airways Concorde.

As soon as Laura and I got back to our hotel room, I placed a call to Australia. It was six o'clock in the morning in Brisbane, and both Mum and Dad had been up all night watching the television coverage. My mother said she was proud of me, and my father commented that he was pleased to see "the knockers" finally put in their place. I learned later that Mum was so pumped up, she went out that morning and played in the Royal Queensland Women's Club Championship—and won! She didn't know it at the time, but my mother really won two trophies that day, because I later presented her with the Claret Jug, just as I had pledged to do years earlier.

Four weeks later, I competed in the fourth and final major tournament of 1986: the PGA Championship at Inverness Club in Toledo, Ohio. A course-record 65 in the first round gave me a 2-stroke lead right off the bat. After a 68 and 69 on Friday and Saturday, I carried a 4-shot lead into the final day. Although I felt like I was swinging the club fairly well on Sunday, I kept missing shots by a foot here or a foot there and, as a result, drifted back toward the pack. In the meantime, my playing partner, Bob Tway, was on fire, and by the time we reached the 18th tee, he had forced himself into a tie for the lead.

I drove my ball into the middle of the fairway on 18, but Bob pushed his ball to the right and it became buried in deep grass halfway up an embankment. He ended up in more trouble by hitting his second shot into a greenside bunker. Meanwhile, I hit my approach shot into the deep fringe on the edge of the green. Feeling pretty good at this point, I considered that the most likely scenario was that my opponent would bogey the hole and all I would have to do was get down in 2 from eighteen feet for the win.

I was standing to the side, lining up my chip, when Bob Tway blasted his third shot out of the sand. His ball landed a few feet from the flag and rolled right into the cup for a birdie 3. I have to admit that it was an absolutely perfect shot.

Of course, now I had to regroup. My first thought was matter-of-fact. "Well, I guess I just have to chip this ball in the hole," I thought.

I hit an aggressive chip that came close, but the ball rolled by the hole a good ways and I missed the par putt coming back. I wound up in second place, and it was a tough loss for me to swallow. Bob really earned that victory, though—and it was his first major.

The next day, several newspaper reporters noted that I was the first golfer since Ben Hogan to have led all four majors going into the final round. But then I was blasted for winning only one of those tournaments. I should have won all four, they said, which would have made me the first player to win the single-season Grand Slam.

My performance in the 1986 majors was eventually labeled by most as "The Saturday Slam." A few referred to it as "The Choker's Slam." Naturally, I would like to have garnered victories in more than one of those majors. But when it was all said and done, I was proud to have won the British Open and nine other tournaments that year.

CHAPTER TWELVE

A MONTH AFTER the '86 PGA Championship, I flew back across the Atlantic to compete at the European Open in Sunningdale, England. Rounds of 67, 67, 69, and 66 were good enough to get me into a sudden-death playoff with Scotland's Ken Brown, which I won on the first hole. That victory earned me the biggest individual payout in British golfing history. I received $83,913 for the win, but also collected a bonus of $119,875 for adding this victory to that in the British Open. Not only did my 1986 earnings on the American Tour pass the $1 million mark, I also took over the number one spot on the Sony Rankings.

The Sony Rankings were first published prior to the 1986 Masters, with the top six golfers being Bernhard Langer, Seve Ballesteros, Sandy Lyle, Tom Watson, Mark O'Meara, and myself. The system was created by IMG in conjunction with the Championship Committee of the Royal & Ancient Golf Club of St. Andrews. It was devised principally because there was no consistent method to rank the best players in the world. Additionally, it was thought (correctly so) that the governing bodies of certain events, including the R&A, would use the rankings as a form of qualifying criterion. As it was specific to the British Open, some of the game's most talented players were not exempt under the old criteria and many were hesitant to fly across the Atlantic to prequalify. Eventually, the system was adopted by each of the major tours.

From the time the rankings were first published until Septem-

ber 14, 1986 (when I first took over the top spot), the top six players
rotated quite a bit. I recall, for example, that it was nip and tuck
among Ballesteros, Langer, and me for a number of months. But
after the European Open, I remained number one for the next 62
weeks, 130 out of 132 weeks, and a total of 331 weeks over the next
decade.

The international media were somewhat critical of the Sony
Rankings, accusing IMG of crafting the point system to favor its
own clients. But early on, I became a staunch advocate for modify-
ing the three-year rolling average calculations to give more weight
to current performance, rather than giving equal weight to the
three-year sliding scale. Even though I didn't create this ranking
system, I felt it was my duty to take the responsibility of being the
number-one-ranked player seriously. It was my duty to help move
the game of golf forward, to give other people the opportunity to
view and experience the sport personally rather than just watching
it on television.

Over the years, I participated in numerous events and activities
that would help promote the game of golf. Additionally, with my
father's assistance, I took some of my earnings and endowed the
Greg Norman Golf Foundation (GNGF) in Queensland so that kids
of all ages and abilities could participate in golf camps and tournaments. Over the past twenty years, the GNGF has fostered and promoted the game of golf by taking it to the bush (rural areas), to
minority groups, and to the disabled. We also created a junior program for elite players, with both coaching and regional tournaments. And I am proud to say golfers such as Karrie Webb and
Adam Scott came through some of these programs. In fact, the annual Greg Norman Junior Masters, which is now entering its fif-
teenth year, was very much modeled after the Gary Player Masters,
which I won as a junior. And wherever I traveled, whether to Australia, Europe, America, Asia, or South Africa, I tried to make time
for exhibitions and clinics to help promote the game.

Over the next several years, golf's international movement
picked up speed. This was a period of transition in our sport, and as
a player who was bridging the domestic and international sides
of golf, I was blazing new territory. Inevitably, I encountered things

that were outdated and needed to change. As a result, I became somewhat of an outspoken advocate for individual player rights. Take the U.S. PGA Tour, for instance. I had to play a minimum number of tournaments each year to maintain membership in the organization. I understood the rationale: The Tour needed to have the players commit to a certain number of events if it was to extract the greatest television rights fees through collective bargaining. But I took the view that if I played in that minimum number, I could then participate in other tournaments at my discretion. However, PGA Tour administrators mandated that tournaments held opposite PGA Tour events were deemed "conflicting events," and therefore I was forced to apply in writing for a release. Often, when I would apply for such a release, the Tour would try to negotiate a trade-off by granting it subject to my playing one of the weaker tournaments on the PGA Tour to bolster its television ratings. I objected. Surely I should be able to determine which events I played, so long as I played the minimum.

It became so onerous, in fact, that I needed to submit an application to play tournaments in Australia. "Nonsense!" I responded. "That violates the Sherman Antitrust Act." I wasn't going to stand idly by while the rights of players were being infringed upon. So I pushed the PGA Tour to the point where they finally created the home-circuit exemption, which basically states that if you want to play in a tournament on your home circuit (in my case, the Australian Tour), you wouldn't need a conflicting-event release, and the minimum number of tournaments required to maintain your PGA Tour membership was reduced from fifteen to twelve. Informally, this home-circuit exemption became known as the Greg Norman Rule. At the same time, Seve Ballesteros, a proud member of the European Tour, was pushing for similar change.

I also fought for players' rights when it came to the Sony Rankings themselves. Sony was paying IMG a considerable retainer to run the ranking system, which many construed as an implied endorsement by the players of Sony, given that the Sony name was so inextricably linked to the world's best golfers. I helped create a monetary pool whereby players would receive a year-end bonus based on their ranking.

There were a number of issues I tackled that, in the long run, benefited my fellow professionals. Of course, as with any institutional change, it was a struggle to get things going, to stand up and speak out. As a matter of fact, I got the distinct impression that a lot of administrators didn't particularly like hearing my thoughts, because they knew I had issues that I wanted to discuss and invariably changes would be required.

As time went by, I began to see that along with the responsibility of being number one came a certain number of problems. First of all, I was under such a microscope that whatever I said could be and often was taken out of context. Second, I found that a number of players took exception to my standing. And third, I learned that some people don't like the number one guy whoever he is. I periodically experienced negative reactions from the players, the fans, and, of course, the media.

It was the response of some players that I had the toughest time dealing with. There was quite an undercurrent for a long time. I knew some of the guys were talking behind my back and saying things that they wouldn't say to me personally. Eventually, I came to realize that my personality probably didn't help. "You're a very confident person," Laura told me. "Some people interpret that as arrogance. You're also very busy, intense, and tough to get to know. When you add being number one to all of that, you're bound to have some people react negatively. It's just human nature." Well, human nature or not, I just could not comprehend being jealous of someone else. When I was climbing the ladder, I admired Jack Nicklaus. But I wasn't jealous of him. I wanted to emulate him and learn from him, not diminish him through envy.

Negativity from the fans also started almost immediately after it was announced that the Sony Rankings had listed me number one. At the end of the World Match Play Championships in England, I felt more like I'd won a war than a golf tournament. When I missed a putt, people would clap and yell "Good! Good!" They made noises in the middle of my backswing and booed when I made a nice shot. Now, granted, I was playing against Sam Torrance, a British favorite and the hometown hero. I had played against local favorites before but never experienced this sort of thing. Sam, by the way, was a real gentleman about the entire thing, both apologizing to me and, at one point, telling the gallery to back off.

It didn't take long for the media to start in. After all, it was good fodder. I half expected it, though. After the Bob Tway chip-in at the PGA, the press was suggesting that the monkey was on me for not winning more majors. "Are you guys kidding?" I asked. "I won the British Open and nine other tournaments in '86!" Constant bombardment from the media really does get to you after a while. And I must admit that there was a time when I refused to talk to the press about anything except my round of golf. I attempted to emulate what politicians often do when handling the media, which is sometimes saying quite a lot without really saying much at all. But that didn't work. As a public figure, I didn't have the luxury of setting parameters for what the media might say. There's an old expression in Australia that refers to "knocking down the tall poppy." In agricultural terms, if one of the poppies in a field gets too high, you take a sickle and lop it off. In social terms, if someone tends to pop up too high too fast, whether a politician, a sports figure, or a businessperson, they tend to get cut down. This is most often associated with the media. It creates something of an ebb and flow between the subject and the media. While it's most prevalent in Australia, I also experienced it in other countries. Interestingly, the media in the United States are least prone to the tall poppy syndrome, which is one of the many things I admire about America. If you work hard and are fortunate enough to reap the rewards of your success, people—and the media—tend to applaud your success. I must say, however, that the worse the criticism got in the media, the more the public supported me. It was a wonderful reverse balance. A good example is what happened after I got in the face of that unruly fan at the 1986 U.S. Open at Shinnecock. That guy had bought into the media's negativity. But the next time I played in New York, I was a fan favorite, because the public liked the fact that I stood up for myself.

Of course, I didn't understand the tall poppy syndrome when I was young. But over the years, I've spoken with quite a few sports figures, businessmen, and politicians who have experienced it. One person with whom I found particular solace and perspective was my good friend Kerry Packer, one of Australia's most successful businessmen and a great philanthropist, who recently passed away. Kerry was very generous with his time, and we had many thought-provoking conversations. Regarding the tall poppy syndrome, he would often say that it didn't matter what he did, people would still resent him for his wealth. "You have to be thick-skinned and resilient, Greg," Kerry would say. "You have to accept the fact that the media is going to build you up and cut you down. That's just the way it is."

I believe the tall poppy syndrome is just a reflection of one element of human nature. If you find yourself placed on a pedestal, at one time or another, some people are going to resent you. And often, the more outspoken you are, the more severe the reaction will be. Sometimes the perception of the masses, no matter where you go in the world, is simply wrong. Because of the way they interpret what you say or the way they perceive your actions, people may think you are arrogant when, in reality, you're merely confident.

The interesting thing to me about all this is that I never really wanted to be number one. My goal was always to be the best I could be. If you think about it, there is a finality in reaching the top spot. Not only is it hard to get there, but you can't stay forever on that perch. But being the best you can be is infinite. There's always room to grow. There's always something new to learn. And there's always something new to do.

In the end, I really never felt that I had anything to prove to anybody—except to myself and, maybe, to my father.

CHAPTER THIRTEEN

S<small>UNDAY, APRIL 12, 1987</small>, at Augusta National Golf Club was cloudy and windy. After opening rounds of 73 and 74, I shot my way back into contention at the Masters with a 66, good enough to be only one shot back going into this final day. Ben Crenshaw and Roger Maltbie were tied for the lead at 4 under par. Bernhard Langer and I would be playing just in front of them in the next-to-last pairing.

Early in the day, the wind was wreaking havoc and everybody seemed to be just hanging on or backing up considerably. By the time I made the turn, I was at 2 under par, 2 shots behind Maltbie. Besides Crenshaw and Langer, also in the mix were Seve Ballesteros, Jodie Mudd, T. C. Chen, and Larry Mize, a hometown favorite who had grown up in Augusta, Georgia. Things began to look bleak for me when I bogeyed the 10th and 11th holes, putting me 4 over par for the previous seven holes. I knew if I didn't turn things around quick, I could kiss another chance at the green jacket good-bye. Revving myself up, I knocked my tee shot on 12 within six feet of the pin and sank the putt for a much-needed birdie. Then, after making a couple of good pars at 13 and 14, a birdie at 15 tied me with Crenshaw. But things were changing rapidly, and when I bogeyed 16, I found myself in second place, a shot behind Crenshaw, Ballesteros, and Mize. On 17, I made a twenty-foot putt to pull back into a tie for the lead.

When I walked to the 18th tee, I had a chance to win the Masters outright if I could only make one more birdie. I was so charged up that I drove the ball 305 yards, over both bunkers and through the fairway. I had a good lie, though, and was able to hit my approach shot on the green pin high and only sixteen feet from the hole. Mize and Ballesteros were in the clubhouse watching on television, and Crenshaw bogeyed the 17th behind me. As I lined up my putt, I knew I had a good chance to win the tournament. I had practiced this putt many times before and knew what it was going to do. I made a solid stroke, and when the ball was halfway to the hole, I thought I had made it. Uncharacteristically, though, the ball did not break its normal inch and a half toward Rae's Creek. Instead, it stayed straight for the final twenty inches and rolled over the right side of the cup with perfect speed. I was stunned that it did not drop. And, I must admit, I've thought about those last twenty inches many times over the years. I just don't know how that ball stayed out of the hole. My tap-in par left me in a tie for the lead after regulation, and when Crenshaw missed his birdie attempt at 18, Ballesteros, Mize, and I headed to the 10th tee to begin a sudden-death playoff.

All three of us drove our ball onto the fairway at 10, all three of us had birdie putts, and all three of us missed those putts. Unfortunately, Ballesteros missed his par attempt and was knocked out of the playoff. So while Larry and I headed to the 11th tee, Seve (with tears streaming down his face) began the long, lonely walk back up the 10th fairway to the clubhouse. On the second sudden-death hole, Mize and I both had decent drives. But on our approach shots, Larry pushed his 194-yard iron shot out to the right, and I hit a 7-iron 164 yards onto the fringe.

While I walked around the green scoping out my long putt (about 50 feet) from all directions, Mize hiked 140 feet off the green down into a little swale where his ball had come to rest. At this point, I was feeling pretty good about my chances. My opponent was going to have a tough time getting down in 2 for a par. Actually, odds were that he'd most likely bogey the hole. So I decided to concentrate on making par. "Four, worst case, I go on to the next hole," I thought. "Four, best case, I'm going to be Masters champion."

As Mize prepared for his pitch, I concentrated on my putt. I was down on my haunches and trying to put myself in as positive a frame of mind as possible. "Okay, visualize this putt. It has a big, soft break. Just cozy it down to within two feet of the hole. Then I'll tap it in for par and win the Masters."

I never even saw Larry hit his shot.

The ball punched into the hill, bounced up on the green, and rolled down toward the pin. It was moving at a nice speed, and I could tell it was a good shot. But I was absolutely stunned when the ball fell into the hole for a birdie 3.

I couldn't believe it!

One of the most powerful moments I have ever experienced occurred when the enormity of the decibels made by the gallery hit me. The 11th green sits down in one of the low points of the golf course and is surrounded by large pine trees. When that ball disappeared into the hole, the roar of the crowd was so loud that the noise reverberated into the ground like an earthquake. It was bad enough that I had probably just lost the Masters, but those reverberations, quite literally, shook me.

The next forty-five seconds, of course, were just pandemonium. Everybody was going crazy. Larry was running up and down in excitement. The crowd was delirious. And all I could do was just wait there and take it. It was the hardest forty-five seconds of my life.

I have to give Larry Mize a lot of credit, though. He clearly realized that I still had a chance. So he pulled his ball out of the hole, held up his hands to ask for quiet, and then stood off to the side of the green. It was a classy thing for him to do.

Now I had to regroup. As usual, I remained calm as I thought about how I was going to make this long putt. Everything I had done previously—lining the ball up, getting ready, lagging the ball up to the hole, making a four, all of that—was out the window now. So I went back into my routine. I walked around the green and looked at the putt from all angles.

When I lined up that putt, I was determined not to leave it short. I told myself that I had made longer putts before and I could make this one too. I gave it my best shot. But the ball missed a bit to the left and drifted past the hole. Then I went straight over and shook Larry Mize's hand. "Great shot, Larry," I said. "Congratulations."

In the clubhouse, I joked with the media. "I didn't think Larry would get down in two from there," I said. "And I was right—he got down in one." I tried to put on a good face, but the truth is that, in my heart, I was dying. I felt like somebody had just ripped that green jacket right off my back. With the putt on 18 and Larry's chip, destiny showed its powerful head. And I didn't think there was anything anyone could say or do to make me feel any better.

But as I walked out of the media center, my four-year-old daughter, Morgan-Leigh, slipped her hand in mine. "Daddy," she said, "I know you didn't win today, but we can still have a party. And I'm very proud of you." I cannot put into words how much that meant to me at that moment.

Of all the things I would go through in my career, this was the toughest. It *really* rocked me. After I got the emotion out of my system (which I really needed to do), I started to analyze what had happened. First I thought about all the shots I could have picked up here or there over the previous four rounds. And then I relived the 11th over and over again. But the conclusion I came to was that I had executed everything correctly on that hole. In all honesty, I told myself, I had done nothing wrong to lose that tournament. Larry Mize had won it. And I had no control over what he did. I remember reading that one reporter wrote that "Norman had again snatched defeat from the jaws of victory." But that was wrong. It was Mize who really did snatch victory from the jaws of defeat. He hit a phenomenal chip shot. It truly was magnificent. It was maybe one in ten thousand that it would actually go in the hole. But, you know what, he did it—and he did it under tremendous pressure in a tough situation. You have to give the guy credit.

I also started thinking more deeply about the game of golf in general. Because golf is an individual sport, you can really only control what *you* do. Sometimes you'll be the best out there. Sometimes you'll miss the cut. In other words, you'll win some and you'll lose some. That is just the nature of the game. Victory is great. But I believe how you handle yourself in defeat is just as important, perhaps more so. I think it's like that in any profession. Sometimes you take a body blow, but you pick yourself up and move on. You become more determined with every defeat. That's the nature of a true champion.

In many ways, golf is very much like life. You have your highs and you have your lows. But things seem to even out in the long haul. All you can do is play your own game and use your gifts to the best of your ability. I do, however, take a bit of comfort in something Lee Trevino once said. "God never gave golfers everything, He always held something back," noted Lee. "Jack Nicklaus didn't get a sand wedge and Greg Norman didn't get any luck."

I would not be telling the truth if I did not acknowledge that it took me much longer to get over that loss than I would care to admit. For the longest time, I would tell everybody that I could take it all and keep going. But I was only kidding myself. The truth is that I tried to bury it deep within myself. But the longer I held it in, the deeper it buried itself inside me. And the deeper something like that gets inside you, the more it harms you.

Adversity can be a negative if you allow it to be a negative. But adversity can also be a positive if you analyze it, understand it, and learn from it. Looking back on it now, I believe those eighteen months were beneficial for me, because I learned some very important lessons.

I learned, for example, how to put tough breaks behind me and move on.

I learned that, deep down, I am a resilient individual, and that nothing can keep me down forever.

Because of those eighteen months, I developed a new mantra: The next minute is the most important minute of your life. The minute that just went by—it's gone.

There is also one very practical lesson I took away from the 1987 Masters. While Larry Mize was lining up his shot, in all my preparations on the green, I never for a moment considered that he would make that shot. I never thought, "Oh, he might just chip this in."

But now I always expect the unexpected.

CHAPTER FOURTEEN

O<small>NE OF THE BENEFITS</small>—or curses—of being number one is the fact that everyone wants a piece of the action. Not surprisingly, there were countless endorsement opportunities presented to me. Of course, it was just a matter of time before I was asked to consult on a golf course design. Initially I balked. "I have zero interest at this time," I said. I felt golf course design would be an unnecessary distraction at this point in my career.

When I was presented with an opportunity to act as a consultant or co-designer, I usually declined. However, one project in particular did pique my interest. It was a pristine tract of land on the island of Lanai in Hawaii being developed by David Murdoch as part of an exclusive resort. I knew that at some point I would eventually experiment with golf course design, and what better project to take on than something that would be this iconic? What's more, the lead designer, Ted Robinson, had an excellent reputation for being the consummate professional, which was what I wanted in a partner.

At first, I wasn't involved in the details of the process, but I was present at various stages to see the bulk earthworks, drainage, and final contouring. Initially, I restricted my comments to the point of view of golfers playing the course. "Ted, why would you place houses so close to the right side of this fairway and green?" I'd ask. "Most golfers are right-handed and they slice the ball."

After a while, though, I began to observe more closely and ask more detailed questions about the design and construction of the course. Ted and his engineers were generous with their time in helping me understand the entire process. They educated me on the land planning, design layout, documentation, and technical specifications. When we reviewed the topographic maps and contour plans in greater detail, I surprised both them and myself with an ability to understand exactly what was going on with the topography, the flow, and geography. These were the very things that interested me when I was a kid in school. Now I was surprising myself with how much knowledge I had retained. In addition, I began to realize that I might have inherited some of my father's gift for engineering. The civil works, earthworks, and hydrology—preventing sheet flow into a bunker, green, or tee, for example—all interested me. In the end, I enjoyed working with Ted on the project in Hawaii as well as another golf course we worked on together in Chicago.

In similar fashion, I was presented with a number of opportunities to consult with various designers in Australia. While I had a very positive experience with Ted, I felt that the most successful golf course designers had what I referred to as a dedicated approach, meaning that if you have a true passion for the business, then you should establish a company and resource it appropriately. I viewed this from the perspective of the golf course owner: Would there be more credibility working with Greg Norman Golf Course Design, or Greg Norman acting as a consultant to Ted Robinson, Fred Bolton, or some other designer? Knowing that I wanted to first establish this business in Australia in order to gain experience before taking on the United States, and understanding the tyranny of distance, I floated the idea of creating Greg Norman Golf Course Design as a joint venture with IMG in Australia in October 1987. James Erskine, who headed IMG Australia, was a bit more entrepreneurial and understood that IMG had missed the opportunity of creating businesses with its clients in the past. Otherwise they would have formed such a venture with Arnold Palmer or Jack Nicklaus. In very short order we agreed on the basic framework for the partnership. IMG dedicated a portion of Bart Collins's time to administer and run business development, and we hired Bob

Harrison, an engineer turned golf course architect who designed a course in Tamworth that I had reviewed and liked.

Right away, we picked up a couple of projects in Australia (the Grand, Pimpama, and the Vintage), received some recognition—and then the bug hit me. This, I realized, was something I really wanted to do.

While I had already made an important first step in determining that I would have a dedicated approach, I needed to give careful consideration to what Greg Norman Golf Course Design would represent and how we would go about becoming best of breed. Accordingly, I spent some time studying several of the great golf course architects, namely A. W. Tillinghast and Alister MacKenzie. For me, it was relatively easy to identify with the old masters. After all, my favorite golf courses include Royal Melbourne, Augusta National, St. Andrews, Winged Foot, Shinnecock, and Cypress Point.

Tillinghast interested me in part because of his commitment to the environment. "The creator of golf holes must not only possess imagination, but a keen appreciation of the offerings of nature," he once wrote. "And the art of landscaping must be allied closely with that of the architect." In addition, some of the golf courses he designed and built are simply timeless, including Baltusrol, Winged Foot, Newport Country Club, and San Francisco Golf Club. The overall balance and flow of Winged Foot is perfect. And San Francisco Golf Club is one of the most underrated golf courses ever built, largely because professional events are seldom played there.

MacKenzie fascinated me for a variety of reasons. First of all, I was surprised to learn that this Scotsman had originally been a doctor. He had served in the Boer War as a field surgeon and done double duty in setting up battlefield camouflage. Later, he helped design the trenches used during World War I. After that, MacKenzie left the field of medicine to pursue his combined passion for architectural design and the game of golf.

In becoming one of history's most respected golf course architects, MacKenzie immersed himself in all aspects of the business. And the time he put into each and every golf course was awe-inspiring. First of all, he worked in an era that was before jet travel; he traveled instead by steamship and stayed on site for weeks or months at a time. By spending that amount of time, he was able to understand how a course would play under different weather conditions, and he was able to give a tremendous amount of thought to the strategy of each and every hole. In studying his methods, I got the impression that MacKenzie liked to engage in a game of chess with the golfer who was going to play his courses.

A great example of his thinking, for instance, comes through in the 14th hole at St. Andrews. The longest hole on the old course, it is a 581-yard par-5 that features the famous "Hell Bunker." In the Royal & Ancient clubhouse, there is a hand-drawn diagram by MacKenzie that shows how he designed the hole to be played in five different ways. When I started thinking about that, I realized that he was truly a genius.

I love all of MacKenzie's golf courses I have played, in part because you have to play them in reverse. What I mean by that is that before you hit your tee shot on the hole (whether it's a par-3, -4, or -5), you must first know the pin placement on the green, because that knowledge dictates how you play the hole (where you place your drive and how you hit your approach shot). The 312-yard par-4 3rd hole at Royal Melbourne is a great example. Normally, it is a drivable hole. But when they place the flag in the front right portion of the green, the only way you can get at it is to drive the ball long and left—even if it's in the rough, past the green, or in the greenside bunker. Otherwise there's absolutely no way you can get the ball close to the hole off the downslope of the fairway. Some players might hate a hole like that. But I love it because I feel it is a great challenge and a true masterpiece of thought and design.

MacKenzie, similar to Tillinghast, strived to be at one with the landscape. Neither man pushed a lot of dirt. Not only did they lack the tools or resources to move a large volume of earth, but they built most courses with a horse-drawn box plow. They chose to work with the topography of the land, which, in my opinion, made for a more interesting challenge. Given that both worked with the land, essentially their philosophy was unique to each course they designed, which is a premise I adopted into my own philosophy. Rather than impose artificial features on the landscape, I believe it's best to work with what the land has to offer.

After studying the great golf course architects of the past, I set out to get some experience under my belt. The late 1980s and early 1990s are today looked back upon as the halcyon days of golf course development. The game of golf was booming, real estate was exploding, and new markets were emerging all over the globe. My general strategy was to begin in Australia (where I was both known and felt comfortable), expand to Asia, and eventually move into the United States and Europe. This plan was not unlike the way I approached my golf career in the early days. I wanted to first prepare myself before I entered the major leagues. I did not want to enter America and Europe without sufficient experience.

After our early success in Australia, we recognized that the burgeoning economies in Southeast Asia held great promise and we chose to capitalize on these emerging markets. While most signature design groups were focused on the United States, we pursued projects that often paid larger design fees and had larger construction budgets; and, most important, we were able to design golf courses on spectacular tracts of land. We began following the "nomadic bubble," first in Japan and Thailand in the late 1980s. Then, over the next several years, we took on additional work in Malaysia, Indonesia, the Philippines, Saipan, India, South Korea, and China. Overall, I take great pride in pioneering emerging markets, which, to this day, is one of the stronger principles of growing my business. Moreover, I immersed myself in the details of all phases of the business. In a relatively short period of time we completed sixteen projects, and I gained an extraordinary amount of experience.

During this period, I developed several basic principles that set the foundation for what our approach to golf course design is today. First and foremost, I was going to respect and preserve the environment. I'd done plenty of traveling and had enough experience to observe the negative impacts of human development on the environment. I'd seen desecration of wildlife, forestry, and fishing. I had viewed entire sections of reefs bleached out. And I'd witnessed the slash-and-burn techniques of a number of unsavory developers. Because of all that, I resolved to take the opposite approach and be a good steward of the environment. After all, the Earth doesn't belong to us, we belong to the Earth.

GOLF COURSE DESIGN PRINCIPLE #1: LEAST DISTURBANCE

I learned from studying the designs of the classic architects that each golf course has its own personality and character that is determined, in a large way, by the property on which it is located. When starting the design process on a new course, I spend a considerable amount of time finding the most desirable natural features of a site (streams, rock features, vegetation, and undulating topography) and incorporate them into the routing. I also go to great lengths to preserve and maintain as many of those natural features as possible. If a magnificent tree is on the edge of a fairway corridor, then we simply shift that corridor so the tree is not disturbed. During my self-imposed golf course design apprenticeship, I learned a lot about many different types of trees and how they survive. For example, the drip line is defined by the outer edges of the leaves where the rain falls to the ground. In turn, the drip line most often delineates the maximum root spread for that tree. Well, a hundred-year-old tree may have a 15,000-square-foot canopy—and I must not, and will not, go within that canopy, because the tree could be destroyed.

In Australia, I was fortunate to work on several pristine tracts of land. The Moonah Course, at Cape Schank, south of Melbourne, is one such example. Because the course was on the undulating sand hills of the Mornington Peninsula, it was apparent that we would not have to move a lot of earth to create a dramatic golf course. Yet we were still challenged to find a golf course routing that made the best use of natural topography. On that particular project, we must have considered more than thirty different routings, not one of which moved more than 15,000 cubic meters of dirt. Sometimes the greatest challenge is to have a perfect bit of land and extract the most from it. Several years later I would be fortunate enough to have this same challenge at Doonbeg, a seaside course on the southwest coast of Ireland.

I also had the good fortune to build a golf course for Kerry Packer in Australia at his private estate in Scone, north of Sydney. For the two of us, it was a wonderful pet project, as we were not constrained by land planners or local authorities, and I had the opportunity to have free rein in designing a golf course on an 80,000-acre estate. Kerry and I had many animated discussions, many of which revolved around my holding the line on least disturbance. In a very short period of time, the Ellerston course has been ranked the second best course in Australia. When considering the pedigree of Melbourne's Sand Belt courses, that is an accomplishment I am very proud of. One interesting point I remember about the project is that I conceded to Kerry's wish that there be no women's tees. This is a course that may receive ten rounds of golf a week, and it's very much a bloke's retreat.

GOLF COURSE DESIGN PRINCIPLE #2: BEGIN WITH THE END IN MIND

If there is a principle that I feel distinguishes me from my design colleagues, it's that, from the beginning, I imagine what the golf course should be like upon completion. To this day, I think I'm one of the few signature designers who treats the initial layout phase as something more than just a land-planning exercise. I insist on walking the property before the golf course routing is finalized. Going to the untouched site of each and every project is one of the most important things I do. During that first visit, I try to paint a picture in my mind of what the golf course will look like when we're finished. You might see a nuance with a rock face here, or a creek bed might be gentler over there. If you walk through the tall timbers, you might come across a large specimen tree. "Make sure we incorporate that tree into the design," I'll say. For projects that have these unique features, I work diligently to preserve and incorporate them into the overall concept for the golf course. On projects that do not have such distinguishing characteristics, however, I strive to create shape and undulation on a broad scale over the entire site in addition to crafting the individual holes. I'll also look out as far as the eye can see and try to incorporate the mountain, desert, or seascape vistas and tie them into the course. I want the golfer to have the sense that we were fortunate to find a beautiful piece of land. In many respects, my insistence on walking the virgin site before the design corridors are finalized limits my workload. But to me, it is of critical importance.

In the late 1980s, we were commissioned to design a golf course just west of Melbourne, which had been used as a salt mine, where saltwater was pumped in and evaporation took place. As a result, there were layers and layers of salt, the property was flat as can be, and there wasn't a tree to be seen anywhere. On my first visit to the site with Bob Harrison, I almost couldn't believe my eyes. "Bob, what have we got here?" I asked.

"Greg, we've got salt," he replied.

"How does the drainage look?"

"We've got no drainage. Zero."

"And just exactly what do the developers want out here?" I asked.

"They want a residential community with a golf course," he replied.

Bob and I looked at each other and started laughing. "What are they, crazy?" I said. "They bought this property and they expect people to live out here?"

"Yes, sir!" said Bob. "And they want us to be the guys who build the golf course."

"Okay, Bob," I said, clasping my hands together and rubbing them. "I love it! It's relatively easy to build a golf course on a great piece of land. But this . . . *this* is a real challenge!"

Clearly, this was a very complicated project from both an aesthetic and a technical standpoint. By creating saltwater wetlands and large water features through cut and fill, we were able to tie the contouring of the golf course into the overall master plan for the community. Now, I must admit, it was a struggle to achieve this vision. It took several years to get the pH of the water and the soils just right. We experienced some problems with leaching, and excessive rainfall altered the salinities. But through hard work and patience, and with a good on-site superintendent, we finished the job. And guess what? People bought everything the developers built. The project sold out in a very short period of time. Today, I enjoy visiting Sanctuary Lakes because to me it's not only a classic example of beginning with the end in mind, but the course is a masterpiece of engineering. Few people would know the site was originally a salt mine.

GOLF COURSE DESIGN PRINCIPLE #3: SUBSTANCE OVER STYLE

Many designers incorporate water features, artificial landscaping, or other man-made formations they believe will add to the aesthetic value of a golf course. But that doesn't resonate with me. A great golf course incorporates as much of the natural surroundings and terrain as possible—even when you have little to work with. A great golf course design is also about interesting shot-making, clever course management, and challenging the golfer.

One of my favorite golf courses along these lines is Melbourne's Kingston Heath. This course is consistently ranked among the top five in Australia and has hosted a number of prestigious tournaments, including the Australian Open. While the 1932 course is built on sand, which is easy to sculpt, it is also built on a 105-acre site that had featureless topography and was devoid of all vegetation. But today, it is one of the most thought-provoking and aesthetic golf courses in the world. I have total respect for Alister MacKenzie and what he did with Kingston Heath. I have seen fortunes spent to create parkland courses with man-made features, nonindigenous vegetation, and manicured landscaping where nobody can remember the holes. Employing a "substance over style" principle not only maintains the traditions of the game but also creates golf courses that members will be challenged to play time and time again.

A good example of a project I did in later years is the Great White Course at Doral (Miami, Florida). It was my first redesign of an already existing course, and we were boxed in with a limited amount of real estate. There were high-rise buildings on the north end of the property and major power lines to the east side. We had easements from roads on several sides, and of the total 90-acre site, approximately 27 acres were made up of lakes. In the end, we took a golf course that was 6,600 yards, made it 7,200 yards, and added a first-class hotel. But most important, we created a quality experience for the golfer that is unique in Florida.

As the demand for my golf course design services grew, and as my knowledge of the industry expanded, I decided to open an office in the United States sooner than I had anticipated. My original plan had been to give it seven years. But by early 1993, I knew we were ready to compete in the United States. So we created Greg Norman Golf Course Design in Jupiter, Florida, which would handle the U.S. market. Unlike our competition, we adopted a decentralized approach, with two offices 10,000 miles apart. One group handled Asia-Pacific and the other handled the Americas. This arrangement means that "supply lines" between the office and the client are short—and that allows us to be more responsive and more hands-on in serving our customers. I still use the decentralized approach today, and even though I have to work hard at making sure our two offices have a high degree of communication, I believe it has served GNGCD well.

CHAPTER FIFTEEN

In THE MIDST of building my golf course design business, I was still playing a full schedule of professional golf in the United States, Europe, and Australia. Laura and I had also purchased a home not far from where Jack and Barbara Nicklaus lived in southern Florida. Now that we had kids, we were thinking about putting down some roots, and the Nicklauses convinced us that the school district in their area was superior to that where we were currently living. With our children's education a priority, we decided to move.

Close to Christmas, I went over to the Nicklaus house to drop off some presents. Jack was out in the front yard when I got there, and we ended up talking in his driveway for a good hour or so. I remember Jack telling me that he admired how hard I had worked on my game and that he thought Seve Ballesteros and I were head and shoulders above anybody else in the game. I also recall mentioning to him my frustration with losing tournaments by miracle shots at the last hole. Jack's response was initially very kind and soothing. But then he told me something that sticks with me to this day. "Greg, you are one of the best—number one, in fact," he said. "When you walk out on that first tee, people are going to try to elevate their games to your level just to beat you. And sometimes they will, whether it's with a phenomenal round or a miracle shot."

"Do you think so?" I asked.

"Absolutely," Jack replied. "It's happened to me. I've been through it. It took me a while, but I finally realized that I should take it as a compliment. And I think you should too."

Just then Barbara came out of the house. "What are you guys doing?" she asked. "Don't you know it's raining? You're getting wet. Come into the house."

We were so absorbed in our conversation that neither of us had any idea it had begun to rain. As I turned to go home, Jack walked back toward the front door, waved good-bye, and said: "Remember, Greg, with the glory goes the pressure!"

We had a number of conversations like that, often speaking about the mechanics and nuances of our golf swings. Taking some of Jack's advice into the 1988 season, I won several early tournaments in Australia, including the Palm Meadows Cup, the PGA National TPC, and the ESP Open at Royal Canberra (where I shot an opening round 62 and ended up winning by 7 shots).

From there, I flew back to the United States to participate in a couple of events before going on to Europe. I was preparing for the Heritage Classic on Hilton Head Island in South Carolina when I received an unusual request. I didn't know it at the time, but it would involve one of the most memorable (and important) events of my life.

"Greg, we've received a call from Thursday's Child," I was told by an IMG representative. "It's an organization that helps kids."

"Okay," I responded. "What are they asking for, memorabilia?"

"No, it's more than that. There's a kid, seventeen years old, from Wisconsin, who's had Crohn's disease since he was seven. Just a few months ago, he was diagnosed with leukemia. They said it's a thirty-million-to-one shot that he'd have two unrelated diseases like this."

"What can I do to help?" I asked.

"Greg, his dream is to watch you play a tournament—and win."

"And win?" I asked.

"Yes, and win."

"Well, let's see if we can get him down here for the Heritage," I said. "We can do at least that much. I don't know about the winning, though."

Just before the tournament began, I was informed that Jamie

Hutton and his mother would arrive sometime on Thursday after the first round. They'd probably stay only a day or two, I was told, because Jamie had to get back home to prepare for a bone-marrow transplant. There were some delays at the airports, however, and they didn't arrive until fairly late at night. I was actually asleep when the telephone rang in my hotel room.

"Mr. Norman, it's Jamie," said the soft voice on the other end of the line. "I'm sorry to call so late, but I wanted you to know that my mom and I just got here."

"That's great, Jamie," I said. "I'm glad you called. What do you say we meet for breakfast downstairs tomorrow morning at nine. Then we'll spend the day together."

"Okay. I heard you shot a 65 and are tied for the lead with Paul Azinger."

"Yeah, I had a good opening round. Tell you what, when we go out on the practice range, I'll introduce you to Zinger and some of the other players. How does that sound?"

"Great, Mr. Norman."

"Okay, Jamie. But just one thing. Call me 'Greg.' Okay?"

"Okay, Greg. See you in the morning."

When we sat down to breakfast the next day and I met Jamie and his mom for the first time, I was struck by the openness with which they discussed the illness confronting them. Jamie showed no sign of being despondent, but I clearly detected the worry in his mom's eyes. We had a good leisurely chat and, after eating, took a stroll along the beach. When Jamie saw the Atlantic Ocean, he said, "My God, it's so big!"

"What? Have you never seen the ocean before?" I asked.

"No, this is my first time," he said. "And that's the first palm tree I've ever seen too."

Now, that really gave me pause. I had grown up with the ocean as my backdrop and had always taken it for granted. And here this young man had never even *seen* the ocean before, let alone experienced it.

"Well, we're going to have to find a way for you to get on the water before you leave," I promised.

At the practice range before my round began, I introduced

Jamie to Azinger, Curtis Strange, Sandy Lyle, Tom Watson, and Lanny Wadkins, among others, and they couldn't have been more accommodating. It made me proud to be a professional golfer. I remember that Tom Watson, especially, spent an unusual amount of time talking to Jamie while I took some practice swings.

I shot a 69 during the second round, good enough to finish only one shot out of the lead. As Jamie and his mom followed us around the course that day, Lawrence Levy (a professional photographer, good friend, and godfather to my daughter) took a special interest in them and became their unofficial escort. After the round, Lawrence and I asked them to join us for dinner, but Jamie was just too tired. Besides, he said, he wanted to get to sleep early so he could cram in every moment with us on Saturday's round.

At breakfast the next morning, I asked Jamie and his mom if they really had to fly back home on Sunday morning. "Well, I have to go to the hospital Monday to begin tests for my bone-marrow transplant," Jamie replied.

"We have to drive to the Savannah airport," said Mrs. Hutton, "change planes in Atlanta, and then make a change in Chicago to get us home to Wisconsin. It'll take us all day."

"Tell you what," I said. "If you'd like to change your plans, Lawrence and I have tentatively chartered a private plane that will fly you direct from Hilton Head to Madison after Sunday's final round. Why don't you give it some thought?"

After his mom gave the thumbs-up, Jamie grinned and said, "We can change our plans!"

"Great," I said. "Now we have another option for you. Since this is your first time near the ocean, we've lined up a powerboat to take you and your mom out on the water after breakfast. You'll have plenty of time to do that and get back to join us on the practice tee and walk the course with us."

During Saturday's third round, Lawrence gave Jamie some camera equipment and arranged for him to walk inside the gallery ropes. "He's my assistant," Lawrence told the marshals. So Jamie was there every step of the way. I must admit that I was a bit distracted at first. I shot a 71 that day, which left me 4 shots off the lead going into Sunday's final round.

Jamie retired early that evening. His knees were aching from a second day of walking. That night Mrs. Hutton had to rub down her son's legs to help ease the pain. But come Sunday morning, Jamie was right there at breakfast with a bright smile on his face.

On the driving range, I gave Jamie a few tips on his swing and then we went over to roll some around on the practice green before I teed off. "You know, I really haven't been putting very well this week," I said. "What do you think? Should I be more aggressive today?"

"I think that would be a good idea," replied Jamie. "You need to start making some putts."

Well, Jamie was right. On the front 9, I was aggressive on the greens, and the putts started rolling in. I birdied the 5th and 8th, then began the back 9 with a birdie on 10. The leaders were not making any real moves. In fact, some of them were backing up. And when I walked onto the 14th tee, I learned that I was leading the tournament by one stroke. Fired up upon hearing that news, I rolled in a long putt for birdie on 15. Now I had a 2-stroke lead with 3 holes to go. When I reached the 18th green, I had about a six-foot putt for par. Not being in the last group, I knew that those behind me would have to make a few birdies to catch me. So if I could sink this last putt, my chances would be fairly good that I'd hold on to win the tournament.

As I lined up that final six feet, I was thinking not so much about making the shot as I was about Jamie. If I missed, I knew it would break his heart because, after all, part of his dream was to see me *win* a tournament. Never before when I played golf had my mind been on something other than executing the stroke at hand, particularly with a shot as important as this. I couldn't believe how much pressure I felt as I stood over that putt. On the other hand, I was as calm and as focused as I'd ever been on a golf course.

As I walked up to address my putt, I whispered to myself, "This one's for Jamie." The ball rolled right into the center of the cup, giving me a final-round 66 and a 13-under-par total of 271 and the victory.

I don't know if I've ever seen anyone as happy as Jamie Hutton was at that moment. At the awards ceremony, a female official gave him the red plaid jacket right off her back. A similar jacket was presented to me as the tournament's winner. But I felt that Jamie was the real champion that day. So when I was presented the victor's trophy, I turned and handed it to my young friend. "This is for you, Jamie," I said. "I'd like you to have it and keep it with you in your hospital room."

After the press conference, Lawrence and I accompanied the Huttons to the airport to see them off, and I made it a point to keep in touch with them over the next several months. Unfortunately, things got rougher for Jamie. His bone-marrow transplant had to be postponed for almost a month because he came down with chicken pox and had to be quarantined for six days. Magically, Jamie received autographed basketballs from Larry Bird and Michael Jordan—and a new set of golf clubs. Each club was engraved: "To Jamie, from Greg."

In June, just before Jamie had his successful bone-marrow transplant, I was at a banquet in New York receiving an award from the Metropolitan Golf Writers Association. When they called my name, I stepped up to the microphone to make a brief acceptance speech. I mentioned to the audience that I had spoken to Jamie, that he was in good spirits, and that his condition was improving. "I don't believe many people realize what goes on in the life of a sick child," I said.

Before my victory at the Heritage Classic, I had not won a tournament on the American tour in two seasons. The truth is that Jamie helped me more than I helped him. His courage in the face of such a devastating disease actually inspired me on the golf course. More than that, however, I realized that losing the PGA Championship or the Masters by last-second miracle shots really didn't mean a lot in the larger game of life. My time with Jamie taught me to have a greater appreciation for what is happening around me and to enjoy life to the fullest while you can. And that awareness will stay with me for the rest of my life. By the way, I'm very happy to note that today Jamie is a happy, successful, and healthy adult.

PART FOUR

BUSINESS IN A BIGGER WAY

CHAPTER SIXTEEN

THE LATE 1980s were, for me, a time of study, planning, reflection, and action—all at the same time. By trying to be the best I could possibly be at golf, I had become the number-one-ranked player in the world. Realistically, I figured it was just a matter of time before my age and the great young players coming up displaced me. But then what? Was I going to end up retired with nothing but social activities and travel to keep me occupied? That wasn't me. I needed greater stimuli. In thinking ahead, I sat back and asked myself three very important questions: (1) Do I enjoy the prospect of building businesses around myself? (2) How can I use the status I've attained in golf to solidify my position in the business world? And (3) Where do I want to be in fifteen to twenty years?

The answer to the first question was clearly "yes."

To answer the second question, I reflected on two of the most successful golfers/businessmen of all time: Arnold Palmer and Jack Nicklaus. Arnold mostly went the endorsement-related route, licensing his name extensively and becoming a spokesperson for other people's products. He stayed affiliated with IMG, which brought him ample opportunities but did not build long-term enterprise value. Palmer adopted an umbrella as his logo, which didn't resonate well with the consumer and was too easily confused with the logo used by Traveler's Insurance.

Jack, on the other hand, broke away from IMG in 1971 and

structured his own business. He almost single-handedly created the concept of a signature golf course design and created a very powerful logo. Like me, he had a moniker. A journalist, Don Lawrence from Australia, labeled him "The Golden Bear." As with a "call sign" for a fighter pilot, you can't give yourself a nickname. It needs to be bestowed upon you by others. Overall, Jack's model appealed to me, but I noticed that from time to time he would assume risk that I considered unnecessary, whether with ownership of MacGregor Golf or possible exposure in various real estate ventures. I came to the conclusion that I would need to develop my own model, borrowing on the most successful elements of what Arnold and Jack had established.

I also sought the advice of a few successful businessmen. Kerry Packer made two observations that really stuck with me. "Most successful businessmen not only cater to the masses," he said, "but have identified a niche (or void) and filled it." The other key thing Kerry advised was something I already did naturally. "Every successful businessperson I know," he said, "forges strategic and long-term relationships."

Years later, I met Nelson Peltz, a highly successful American businessman who made his fortune in finance and leveraged buyouts. He advised me on general business and investment banking strategies. One of the best pieces of advice he ever related was from his father: Sell more and keep costs down. Over the years, Nelson has been a constant sounding board for me. Many times I have called to seek his advice. And Nelson was always glad to help me. To this day, we are very close friends.

Once I'd accumulated enough information and firmed up my ideas, I established a blueprint and stuck to it. It was short and easy to remember, the type of thing I didn't have to carry around in a briefcase:

(1) Take control of my business.
(2) Develop equity in my own brand.
(3) Identify a niche and fill it.
(4) Forge strategic and long-term relationships.

(5) Do not heavily invest my own capital. My currency is my name, my likeness, and my personal exertion.

(6) Separate business interests from personal wealth management.

Clearly, I would have to terminate my relationship with IMG. I found it interesting that Arnold had stayed with a management company but Jack had not. I later learned that Arnold had an equity stake in IMG, which certainly helped explain his rationale for staying with them—and perhaps explained why Jack had left.

I also performed some mental arithmetic about my financial relationship with IMG. At that time I was paying them a 20 percent commission on my merchandising deals. That was a considerable amount of money. Would I be better served if I invested that same amount of money into building my own enterprise, rather than paying commissions on short-term merchandising and appearance-related activities?

Leaving IMG would take time. Some years earlier, I had already taken the first step toward controlling my finances by hiring the financial executive who had been administering my account and moving my portfolio to Bessemer Trust. Now I needed to build a foundation. The next step was to create a parent group, under which my various businesses and merchandising agreements would be domiciled. It was relatively easy to select a corporate name. I created Great White Shark Enterprises, and I instructed IMG to put all my merchandising agreements in that company.

During this period, we were in the midst of negotiating a renewal of a contract I had signed in the 1980s with Spalding. While I enjoyed working with Spalding's executives, Jacques Henrick and Chuck Yash in particular, I always viewed this endorsement with a sense of trepidation. Spalding had significant market share in the golf ball industry but had never posed a serious threat in the high-end or performance-ball market. To this end, Spalding developed the Tour Edition golf ball, the forerunner of today's two-piece premium ball technology. Despite their best efforts, the Tour Edition ball had some unique characteristics. In particular it had a lot of action (spin), and many in the golf industry believed that the ball was not well suited for my game. While I cannot blame the Spalding arrangement on IMG, we were all motivated to change when my experience in assembling golf clubs came in handy. Upon receiving a new set of irons, I proceeded to disassemble them, only to be shocked to find lead plugs jammed in the hozzle as a balance. But in reality, as precise as I was with my game, I knew that this type of balance was not what I needed to perform at my best. I knew then that both the ball and the clubs I was using were inferior equipment. Soon I was approached with a new opportunity that, I believed, better fit my business plan.

Tom Crow, the founder of Cobra Golf, called me personally to inquire whether I'd be interested in signing an endorsement deal and become a shareholder of his company. My relationship with Tom went back to the late 1970s, when he built me that original set of Mild Steel clubs. Tom also invented a golf club called the Baffler: a 3-wood with two bars on the sole that allowed a golfer to swing through the rough. The Baffler's success elevated Cobra to the next level in both sales and prestige. The fact that Tom and I had stayed in touch all these years and remained close instantly made me think of Kerry Packer's advice about forging strategic and long-term relationships.

I knew both Tom and his partner, Gary Biszantz, very well. Tom was a former Australian amateur golf champion and Gary a California businessman. They had teamed up to tap into the American market by setting up an office in Carlsbad, California. Both were outstanding entrepreneurs, both were great guys, and both were aggressive. They wanted to build Cobra up to a level where they could rival industry leaders. I knew that. I could see that. We were on the same wavelength.

"What have you got in mind, Tom?" I asked.

"Well, Greg, we know your contract with Spalding is up," he replied. "So we'd like you to come on board with us. We'd like to offer you a multiyear endorsement deal, but I'm sure you can appreciate that we can't match Spalding's offer."

"And you'd like me to invest in Cobra as well?" I asked.

"Yes, I would. What do you say?"

Tom and I then worked out a deal where I would both endorse

their products and become an equity partner. Cobra would pay me an amount close to my old deal with Spalding for product endorsements, and I would purchase a 12 percent stake in the company. In addition, I would receive a seat on the board of directors. The only thing I asked in addition to this arrangement was that a significant amount of the money I invested be spent in research and development. When Tom and Gary agreed, I remember blurting out, "Let's get going. We have a lot of work to do."

It was a no-brainer in my mind. The endorsement agreement would match my investment in three years. After that, it was blue sky. And to top it off, by being an active member of the board, I was going to become strategically involved and learn about an entirely new aspect of the business world. Overall, I thought this was a great opportunity. IMG, however, did not. In fact, they advised me not to sign, which was perhaps motivated by the size of the commission they would have earned had I gone with Spalding. Personally, I thought I was being fairly generous because as part owner I was effectively paying 12 percent of my own contract, yet still allowing IMG to take their commission. What's more, I offered to let them in for a piece of the action. They declined, saying that it was not a good investment. I could understand IMG's reasoning, of course. I was at the zenith of my career. Spalding was offering me a ten-year contract for what at the time was a record endorsement fee. It was easy money. "Take it!" they said. Well, I *didn't* take it because I wanted a more strategic investment and I wanted to play the best equipment available. In addition, because Cobra was not a ball manufacturer, I would be free to enter into a separate contract with a ball manufacturer whose product better suited my game. So I wrote out the check and never looked back.

Once I took a seat on Cobra's board, I worked hard to connect with each of the directors. They were glad to use my expertise as the number one player in the world, and I was pleased to soak up as much information and knowledge as they were willing to impart. I learned the intricacies of product development, sales, marketing, and the administrative functions of human resources, finance, and accounting. I soon discovered that I enjoyed the entire process. I liked starting something new, I liked learning as I went along, and I especially liked building something to the point where it began to yield strong dividends. I became a sponge for information.

Along the way, Cobra was able to identify the niche I'd been looking for. It turned out that when our major competitor, Callaway, came out with their oversized Big Bertha driver, they ignored the other clubs in a golfer's bag. So we immediately designed, built, and introduced King Cobra oversized irons. No other company had anything like them. We followed up on that coup by identifying the untapped markets for women and seniors and introducing new technologies, such as lighter swing weights and graphite shafts.

As a company, we also ratcheted up our advertising. It got so that whether you were in the United States or the UK, if a golfer walked into a golf shop and asked the salesperson what the best clubs were, the answer would invariably be "Cobra."

"Why Cobra?"

The answer was varied, based on a number of success factors, including the quality of the product, my validation of the company as an investor, our protection of the green-grass (pro shops) distribution channel, and, finally, enhanced margins for the retailer.

As a result, our sales shot through the roof. We grew from $38 million to more than $220 million.

Not long after I made the investment in Cobra, I cultivated another opportunity, which I would later come to categorize as an "adjacent space opportunity." Knowing that Cobra had not reached its full potential in my home country, I purchased a 50 percent interest in the Australian distribution rights. To give you some kind of idea of the market, Australia had a population at the time of approximately 18 million. Of those, approximately 1.2 million were registered golfers!

Operating a distributorship gave me an entirely different perspective on the business, not that of an original equipment manufacturer (OEM), but as a wholesaler needing to understand import duties, quotas, parallel importing, assembly, foreign-exchange hedging, stock programs, licensing and managing subdistributors, et cetera. All presented their own unique challenges and rounded out my education on an entirely different aspect of the business. We instituted policies and procedures that the Australian hard goods market had never seen. We were hard-nosed but fair, and we soon ran the most efficient distributorship in Australia, taking Cobra's sales from $2 million annually to $16 million. My father sat on the board of this entity, Cobra Golf Australia (CGA), and had a great deal to do with the company's success. It was a wonderful father-son project for us.

I also learned another hard lesson, one that I hoped would never repeat itself. A number of my friends in Australia were shareholders in this venture. I consider myself a very loyal friend, so I provided opportunities to a number who asked. But one situation with Roger Dwyer did not turn out well.

Roger had caddied for me during my very first Australian Open back in 1973. He was the guy who left my buggy on the wrong side of the green and I was subsequently penalized 2 strokes when my ball hit it. Well, all these years later, he was a shareholder in CGA and the subdistributor in Queensland for Cobra and other brands. But in the late '80s Roger committed what the industry considers to be a cardinal sin, that of opening a retail store. Obviously, it's difficult to be loyal to your clients as a wholesaler when you are competing with them as a retailer. What's more, Roger took a liberal view on using my name and likeness in promoting his storefront, which amounted to an implied endorsement by me of his store.

"Roger, you can't do that," I told him. "You don't have the right to use my name. You only have the right to buy inventory through my distribution business. This other stuff you're doing is wrong. You're taking advantage of our friendship."

Well, Roger argued and argued with me. And when I finally realized that I wasn't going to bring him around, I just exploded. "You know what, Roger?" I said. "You're an idiot! You've just thrown away our friendship. And over what? Maybe five or six grand profit?" So I cut Roger off right then and there. Unfortunately, we have not spoken since.

CHAPTER SEVENTEEN

I WAS SCUBA DIVING at Riding Rock, one of my favorite spots in the Bahamas, at a depth of eighty-eight feet, when I ran out of air. I had damaged the first stage of my regulator as I chased a grouper into a hole. Now I was gasping for air and knew I was in trouble. At that moment, everything seemed to move in slow motion. I didn't panic but thought through what I was going to do next. I was still in the hole, and my diving buddy, Charlie Stuve, seemed too far away. So I had to make a calculated decision: either get to Charlie or try to get to the surface. My last breath was like putting your hand over your mouth—you try to inhale, but you just can't. "I'm going to the surface," I thought. "I need to avoid an air embolism, so I have to be very deliberate and gradually exhale whatever air I have left. I also need to control my buoyancy compensator to avoid ascending too quickly."

Slowly, methodically, and almost in a trance, I started toward the surface. Kick your legs easily, not too fast. Let out a little bit of air, not too much. Don't ascend faster than the bubbles you are exhaling. Keep your finger on the BC inflation valve to capture any expanded air that might be left in the tank. Keep moving. Don't stop. Stay alert. Don't pass out. I don't know how long it took me to breach the surface, but it seemed like forever. When I finally did take the first gulp of fresh air, I almost blacked out. My boat captain, Gary

Stuve, Charlie's dad, was nearby when I surfaced. It did not take long for him to get to me and help me into the cockpit of my boat, *Aussie Rules*. I lay there motionless with my gear on, starting to feel the minor effects of the bends. It was not pleasant. My joints felt as though they were being squeezed in a vise, but fortunately I didn't have to go through the agonizing process of recompression.

I think of that event often and have come to view it as something of a metaphor for my golfing career, especially the previous two years. I was doing something I really loved to do, but it was always up and down, up and down. Down to the depths, gasping for air. Up to the surface and new life.

The 1989 and 1990 seasons were typical. In the '89 Masters, I finished tied for third, one shot out of a playoff between Scott Hoch and Nick Faldo (the eventual winner). At the press conference somebody said I'd win the Masters sooner or later, but I was incredibly disappointed, incredibly down. "Sooner or later?" I responded. "How much later is it going to be?"

I did manage to rise back to the surface that year by winning five tournaments (two in Australia, two in the United States, and one in Asia). I also found great satisfaction in creating my own golf tournament, the Shark Shootout. My buddy Lawrence Levy and I used to organize a mini-tournament at Bay Hill in Orlando. We'd team up a pro with three amateurs and play a mixed format of alternate shot, better ball, and scramble. We usually had four or five groups and everybody had a great time.

I thought that was a great format for a charity golf tournament, so I approached Arnold Palmer and together we started a shoot-out to benefit his children's hospital in Orlando. It began with only four players (Palmer, Nicklaus, Raymond Floyd, and me) and was originally played as a one-day event. Eventually the idea morphed into a PGA Tour–sanctioned team event that is broadcast on national television. The week starts with a two-day pro-am, a unique attribute the amateur participants have really embraced. The tournament proper starts Friday, and we maintain the same format: alternate shot in the first round, better ball on Saturday, and a final-round scramble. Over the years, the Shark Shootout would benefit several charities, including Ronald McDonald House and the National

Childhood Cancer Foundation, and the event would be played at a number of different courses. Today the Shark Shootout is held regularly at Tiburon Golf Club in Naples, Florida. Two dozen professional golfers participate. We've had two ideal corporate partners over the years, Franklin Templeton Investments and Merrill Lynch, and we continue to raise much-needed funds and awareness for children's charities.

If the Shark Shootout breathed new life into me, the 1989 British Open brought me back down to the depths of disappointment. I began the final day at Royal Troon 7 shots off the lead, but then I got hot. At one point, I made 6 birdies in a row, then holed a chip shot at 17 to save par. My 64 set a course record and, more important, put me in a three-way tie for the lead at the end of regulation. Normally, Mark Calcavecchia, Wayne Grady, and I would have moved to sudden death. But this was the first year that the tournament instituted a 4-hole, total-stroke, playoff format, which I endorsed as an appropriate format for the playoff in a major championship. In the age of network television and viewers wanting to have an immediate result, an 18-hole playoff the following day, as is the case with the U.S. Open, just isn't satisfying. At the same time, a sudden-death playoff often doesn't yield the best result, as anything can happen on one hole. The 4-hole cumulative playoff is like a mini-tournament in and of itself.

I birdied the first playoff hole for a 1-stroke lead, birdied the second hole for a 2-stroke lead, but then took a bogey on the third hole. So when I came to the fourth and final playoff hole (18), I still led by one shot over Calcavecchia. I took out a driver and hit an adrenaline-powered, flawless fade that landed in the middle of the fairway, but on the downslope of a subtle mound, and it kicked forward into a deep pot bunker that nobody had reached all week. The tee shot measured 320 yards, which in 1989 was a monster drive! Unfortunately, my ball came to rest right up against the lip of that bunker. As I stood there trying to figure out how in the world I was going to get the ball anywhere near the green, Calcavecchia hit an impressive 205-yard second shot from the right rough to within six feet of the hole.

Just as I was addressing my ball in the bunker, a most unusual

My father, Merv; my mother, Toini; my sister, Janis; and me in a 1963 family portrait.

Suited up and ready for air force cadet training (1969).

My father, Janis, and I
with *Peter Pan*, the sabot
we handcrafted under
our home in Townsville.

Throughout my
school years,
I spent a great
deal of time
aboard the
Hays' prawn
trawler on the
Great Barrier
Reef.

The floppy surfer's hat that my mother constantly tried to hide from me.

Celebrating my first professional victory, the 1976 West Lakes Classic, at the Grange Golf Club in Adelaide.

I was paired with Jack
Nicklaus at the 1976
Australian Open, the
week after my West
Lakes victory.

My coach, mentor, and
close friend Charlie
Earp caddied for me
at the 1984 U.S. Open.
Charlie was always
teaching me, both on
and off the golf course.

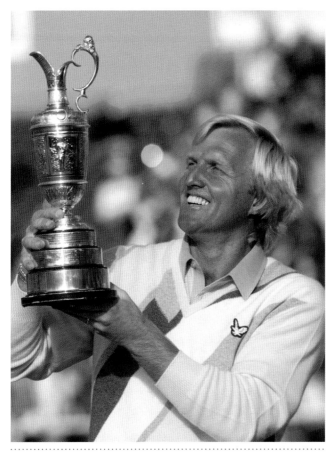

Hoisting the Claret Jug for the first time at Turnberry in 1986.

Morgan and Gregory share in the trophy presentation after my victory at the 1986 Suntory World Match Play.

A final-round 64 at Royal St. George's in 1993 propelled me to my second British Open victory.

A captive audience watches me prepare for the 1993 British Open. From left: my caddie, Tony Navarro; Butch Harmon; Gregory; and Tom Crow.

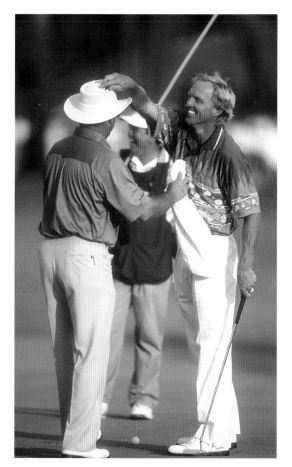

Reminiscent of his gesture nine years earlier at the U.S. Open, Fuzzy Zoeller pulls out a towel to cool me off after my record-setting performance at the 1994 Players Championship.

Spending time with Nelson Mandela meant a great deal to me. This photo, with my friend Nick Price, was taken at the 1995 Alfred Dunhill Challenge.

Three generations of Normans aboard my Jetstar in December 1991.

A family of straw hats! Sharing a moment with my mother and father during the 1993 Doral Ryder Open.

On the flight deck of the U.S.S. *Carl Vinson*. In two days I would have eight hops aboard F-14s and F-18s. An incredible experience!

thing happened. Somebody flicked a switch on the public address system, and the voice of Peter Allis (who was commenting for the BBC) was suddenly booming across the links of Royal Troon. "Norman has absolutely no chance. I think he has a 9-iron and he needs to pick the ball cleanly. I just don't think he can reach the green from there."

The distraction caused me to back off the shot while, in the broadcasting booth, Allis realized what was happening and immediately stopped speaking. I blasted out of the bunker and left my second shot in a greenside trap. I caught the ball thin on my third shot, airmailed the green, and ended up out of bounds. End of story. My official score on that hole was an X.

When Calcavecchia made his putt to win the British Open, I went over and sincerely congratulated him. But another major had gotten away from me. And when I walked off that green, I was thinking, "Man, I should have won."

I really hate failure. I don't fear failure, mind you. I've *never* feared it. But the idea of failing at anything has always been a driving force for me. I'm sure it's one reason I won fifty tournaments in the 1980s worldwide, and I know it has helped me achieve success in the business world. Still, failure is something we all have to contend with, and for me, 1990 on the golf course was no exception. I missed the cut in the Masters that year and didn't really come close to winning the other three majors. And then I had victories snatched away from me by two more extraordinary shots, the kind that seem to have defined my career. At the USF&G Classic in New Orleans, David Frost holed a 50-foot bunker shot on the 72nd hole to beat me by one stroke. That one really hurt because I was already on the green and basically had a tap-in for par. And then, on the 72nd hole at the Nestlé Invitational, Robert Gamez holed a miracle 7-iron to beat me by one stroke. It was a 176-yard shot from the middle of the fairway that rolled into the hole for an eagle 2. I just couldn't believe I'd lost another tournament on so improbable a shot.

My morale rebounded as I claimed four victories that year (one in Australia and three in the United States). The victory at the Doral-Ryder Open was particularly gratifying. I began well off the pace on Sunday but got on the move quickly. I had just made a couple of birdies when I came to the par-5 8th hole. My drive found the fairway but came to rest in a divot, which significantly decreased my chances of reaching the green in 2—especially because there was a lake in front of the green. But not wanting to lose the momentum I had generated, I pulled out a 3-wood, knocked it onto the green, and made another birdie. I shot 10 under par for the final 12 holes, ended with a scorching 62, and wound up in a four-way sudden-death playoff with Mark Calcavecchia, Paul Azinger, and Tim Simpson. We all hit good drives on the short par-5 first hole and then placed our second shots on or around the green. Well, lo and behold, I chipped in for an eagle 3. Finally, I had made a shot at the end that would seize victory. Calcavecchia and Simpson missed their eagle attempts, and that left it up to Azinger, who had a long putt to tie me and send us to a second playoff hole. As Paul was lining up his putt, Mark walked over to him and said something to the effect of "Hole this putt. Don't let the fucker win!"

I don't know if that comment was anything more than one made in the heat of competition, but it bothered me at the time. This came on the heels of my congratulating Calcavecchia after winning the British Open at Troon, and wrongly or rightly, I felt there might have been some element of jealousy because I was the number one player in the world at the time. Or perhaps it was because I was a foreigner who, unlike previous international stars, had set up shop in the United States and made good on the American Tour. Either way, when Azinger missed his eagle putt, I walked away with that sudden-death win.

During the 1991 golf season, however, any momentum I had built up over the previous twelve months left me. I missed the cut again at the Masters and had to withdraw from the U.S. Open due to an injury, and although I had respectable showings at both the British Open and PGA Championship, I still was not able to pull out victories. As a matter of fact, even though I played a fairly aggressive schedule, I did not win a single tournament anywhere in the world that year. I was in a slump.

Also in 1991, I started sparring again with the PGA Tour. It started when I was asked by Tour organizers to participate in a

Shell's Wonderful World of Golf match, which was played internationally but televised in the United States. "I'll play if I get residuals," I responded.

"What are you talking about?" they asked.

"Well, like the original Shell matches, you're going to sell this program for years to come," I said. "I believe the players should be paid every time the program is aired. Just like a songwriter or an actor, we should receive residuals."

"No," came the response. "When you joined the PGA Tour, you signed over your name, image, and likeness to us. We own them in perpetuity."

"But this isn't a full-field tournament. It's a made-for-TV exhibition match," I replied. "Just what is your jurisdiction for players' rights?!" In the end I didn't win, but my campaign was far from over.

Television rights were just one of a number of concerns I had with the PGA Tour. While I had yet to study the history, corporate governance, and structure of the Tour, I had an innate sense that the Tour had morphed into something much more than what the original charter had intended when it broke away from the PGA of America in 1968. More and more, I observed that as a number of top players developed our own businesses, we were competing with the very Tour that represented our interests. At a time when Jack, Arnold, and I all had our own apparel brands, the Tour had its own golf apparel brand under license with Van Heusen, which we were forced to compete against. The same can be said for golf course design, real estate development, event management, sponsorship sales, and, in later years, the Internet. When I first joined the Tour, the players would cede their rights for television and print media; sometime later, the Tour included Internet rights.

To this day we're still competing against the Tour online, in database management, e-commerce, and so on. Over the years, the Tour has phased out some of the activities that were clearly in conflict with its players'. For instance, the Tour no longer has its own apparel line or its own golf course design division. But still the conflicts exist. Today, my wine label competes against PGA Tour

Wines, and in fact my Reserve selection competes against the Commissioner's Private Reserve. Isn't that ironic! What started in the late 1980s would become an ongoing campaign for me not only to protect my own rights but also to keep the Tour in check and in some small way blaze a trail for others.

In 1991 the press combined the fact that I was arguing with the PGA Tour with my lack of victories and really let me have it. I was labeled "The Great White Carp," "The Toothless Shark," and "The Great White Minnow." In addition, I was alleged to have been on drugs, to have been stricken with cancer, and to have been fighting with the people closest to me. There was not an ounce of truth in any of it, but the damage was done. The public developed a false impression of me based on what they read or heard. And even if someone wrote a retraction, it came too late to make a difference.

It was the tall poppy syndrome all over again, and I knew that all this negativity simply came with being a successful public figure. So I had to find a way to deal with it. I did that, in part, by keeping physically fit. Staying in good physical condition is very important to me. It helps me relax, unwind, and purge negative emotions. I have always worked out with weights or different cardiovascular exercises, such as long rides on my road bike. I also watch what I eat, which makes a significant difference in my mental outlook. In August 1991, for instance, while competing in the PGA Championship at Crooked Stick, I was trying my best to stay hydrated like all players in the humid conditions in Indiana. Throughout the round I was drinking soft drinks, since that was the only beverage offered on each tee. By the time I got to the 17th hole, I had a severe headache and felt just awful. I committed myself then and there to never drink another carbonated beverage—other than beer!

As an early advocate of physical fitness, I realized that the Tour could gain a lot of ground by providing an environment in which the players could maintain a consistent level of health and fitness. If the Tour couldn't get water or isotonic drinks on the tees, then clearly they were a long way from supporting other health-conscious regimens. Some years later, the Tour had a fitness trailer and a qualified physical therapist on site each week. While the Tour has gained ground, I think more can be done with respect to providing a safe workplace. In particular, I'm currently advocating the Tour putting in place covered structures over the driving range so players have the option to practice in the shade.

Amidst some of the flak that I was getting from the media over my perceived poor play, one or two incidents occurred that were a bit more in your face than simply an unruly fan shouting at me. One such incident occurred when I was playing in Peter Jacobsen's charity tournament, the Fred Meyer Challenge in Portland, Oregon—and apparently all the negative publicity was having an impact on some members of the public. My fellow Australian Steve Elkington and I were hanging out with our Pro-Am Partners, and on the way back to the hotel, somebody suggested that we stop for a beer. So we pulled into a local tavern and ordered a round. It turned out that only Elkington and I could drink because the two guys assigned to us were not allowed to partake (due to tournament rules): They were our designated drivers.

Steve and I had a couple of beers and were sitting at a table minding our own business when four guys who recognized me came up and tried to make trouble. They were all in their twenties or thirties, about my height, and dressed in blue jeans. "You're Greg Norman, aren't you?" one of them asked. After I indicated that I was, they started in on me.

"You're a choker, Norman," one of them said.

"Why don't you go back where you came from?"

It was pretty clear that these guys were drunk and spoiling for a fight. I was angry, and normally I would have accommodated them in this situation. But we were in town for a charity event and did not want to create an incident. So Steve and I decided to take the high road and just walk away. "We're outta here," I said.

But that didn't dissuade the four of them. They followed us out to the parking lot, and their verbal assault continued. Even though we kept trying to walk away, they eventually confronted us between two cars, covering our exit from front and aft. It was really me they were after, and just as one of them was about to throw the first punch and I, in turn, was about to attack, Steve stepped in. "Hey, why don't you guys just move on," he said to them. "We just came in for a couple of beers and now we're leaving."

Steve's action caused them to back off for a moment. As we drove away, they proceeded to follow us, throwing beer bottles at our car along the way. So we exited and doubled back, but they maintained the course this time, trying to run us off the road! At that point we used a cell phone to call the police, and the next thing we knew, there were squad cars all over the place.

The cops walked back and forth for several minutes, getting both sides of the story. Fortunately for us, we had two guys in the car who had not had a drop to drink, so they were believable. Finally, one of the policemen came back and told us that he was certain we were telling the truth. "Here's the situation," he said. "If you want to file an arrest warrant on these guys, we'll take them down to the station and book them. I know you guys are up here for the tournament, so there's something you should know. Once we book them, this entire incident becomes public information. The press will get ahold of it and you can bet your life that it'll be in the papers tomorrow morning. So what do you want me to do?"

The other guys looked at me and said, "It's your decision, Greg. We're with you whatever you decide."

I thought about it for a minute or two. I could have buried these guys, but doing so could have tarnished Jacobsen and the Fred Meyer Challenge. So I turned to the policeman and said: "I'll tell you what you do, Officer. You go back over there and you tell those clowns that if they give an apology to me, Steve, and our two friends here, then we won't file charges. But if they don't apologize, they're going to jail. And you might ask them to think about what that will do to their families, their employers, and their friends."

The policeman then went over and explained the choice they had, and I guess when they realized the magnitude of what they were facing, those guys sobered up pretty quickly. The four of them came over and apologized to each and every one of us. The whole thing ended right then and there.

Overall, I felt pretty good about having taken the high road in that situation. I could have sent those guys to jail, and believe me, I wanted to. But I think that in some small way it would have been a reaction to all the negative things that had been happening to me recently. And it would not have been the right thing to do.

At that moment I also felt pretty good about life. Why? Because I realized that my mate Steve Elkington would stand shoulder to shoulder with me no matter what. You don't come by friends like that very often.

CHAPTER EIGHTEEN

GREAT WHITE SHARK ENTERPRISES gained a great deal of momentum in 1991. While I hadn't yet separated from IMG (that would happen two years later), I was now controlling the shape and content of my merchandising deals. I hadn't really delineated specific business opportunities but, rather, the path I wanted to pursue. That path, of course, was the development of my own brand.

In searching for business opportunities, I paid particular attention to corporations with like-minded values. I wanted partners who were interested in using golf as a platform from which to promote their brand while at the same time assisting me in building the equity of my own brand.

Once again, using Australia as a springboard, I had begun to promote my own logo in conjunction with several endorsement deals. Niblick golf shoes, with whom I'd had a long-standing relationship, helped promote the creation of a shark-branded shoe utilizing a brass-enameled button in the shape of a shark, which they used on a signature line of footwear. Then we cut a deal with a Melbourne-based clothing company that placed a shark logo on a high-end variety of wool sweaters. But it was the deal we cut with Akubra, the iconic Australian hat company, that really validated the prospect of creating shark-logo merchandise.

Akubra was Australia's equivalent of Stetson, manufacturing cattlemen's hats made of felt and rabbit fur. I liked them and started wearing them before we established a formal affiliation. I then cultivated a relationship with the managing director, Steve Keir, and offered the prospect of creating a hat to my design, which would be branded Great White Shark and would display the same enameled shark logo that we had used with Niblick.

In structuring the terms of the agreement, we did something unique, which to this day I try to incorporate into most of my licensing agreements. I would receive a royalty on gross sales with a minimum guarantee. This arrangement included a provision whereby the minimum royalty for each year would be that which was stated in the agreement or the equivalent of the largest royalty paid in any one year of the agreement, whichever was higher. I don't believe Akubra anticipated that their Great White Shark model would sell so well. For a period of time, it seemed like everybody in Australia wanted that particular hat. It was very, very popular, and my minimum royalty rose tenfold.

As is the case with the advent of new products in the fashion industry, sales either plateau or decline after the first year. But given the structure of the agreement, Akubra was obligated to pay on the highest threshold. Obviously I had no desire to bankrupt an iconic Australian company, so we agreed to certain accommodations for the ensuing years. More important, the entire exercise clearly demonstrated that we could build a merchandising program around the strength of my identity and the creation of a shark logo.

Not long thereafter, I received a phone call from Paul Fireman, CEO of Reebok, that would ignite a very exciting chain of events. A few years earlier, I had secured a three-year endorsement to wear Reebok golf apparel (which, at first, was made by another manufacturer). Shortly thereafter, the company created Reebok Golf and began manufacturing their own apparel.

When Paul called, he suggested that we consider creating shark-branded clothing that would have appeal on a much wider scale. "Greg, you have conclusively demonstrated in Australia the value of creating the shark logo," he said. "Selling tens of thousands of your shark hats at forty dollars a throw is simply amazing. I think it's time to capitalize on your image. I think we should create your own line of apparel—eventually wean ourselves of the Reebok imprint and make the shark icon the center of attention."

Well, of course, that was music to my ears. Paul and I had always had that connection. We saw opportunities in much the same light. So I invited Paul down to Florida to discuss our relationship in greater detail. A couple of guys from IMG joined me, and Paul had brought along a few of his people from Reebok. Early on, Paul and I exchanged ideas on how we could create the brand. Being a shoe manufacturer, he liked drifting into the soft goods side of the business. Creating Greg Norman Collection would be a real boon to both Reebok and GWSE. We could refine the shark logo, work out a deal on how best to license it, and figure out various methods of distribution. There were many ways to structure a mutually beneficial deal, Paul explained.

As the meeting progressed, we all became more and more enamored with the idea. But the IMG guys were pressing hard for a three- or five-year term, which Paul was resisting, and I instinctively sensed that the deal was in jeopardy of being scuttled. I could easily understand both parties' positions. IMG was protecting my interests by setting parameters around the terms of the agreement, which is part and parcel of virtually every licensing deal. By the same token, I could also see things from Reebok's perspective. They were going to invest tens of millions of dollars in creating a brand, and they didn't want to put themselves in a position where it could then be taken from them. Like Paul, I was certain that an arrangement could be established that would protect everyone's interests, so Paul and I excused ourselves from the meeting to discuss the more salient points of what would become a very important partnership.

Paul had mentioned, and I agreed, that we would need to refine the look of the shark logo. Through my activities in Australia, and in the lead-up to our renegotiation, both parties knew that the shark logo was already a registered trademark of Dama (the parent company of Paul & Shark) in more than thirty countries. We would need to figure out how we were going to deal with Dama. We agreed that I would own the logo and that Reebok would accept the financial responsibility to register, defend, and settle any trademark-related issues in my name. Knowing of the Dama registration, I felt this was a show of good faith by Reebok. We also came to an arrangement whereby the term of the Reebok agreement would be lifetime—so long as Reebok continued to build the business and reach certain milestones. If they didn't perform, I would be given the right to take back the brand. Additionally, Reebok could not sell or assign the license to a third party without my consent, which, coupled with the realization that ultimately the brand would require my own involvement and support, gave me the comfort of knowing I had sufficient control. Given that both Paul and I gave birth to the concept, we also agreed that if Paul should ever exit the business, I would be given the opportunity to purchase the business from Reebok.

We also agreed that it would be important for me to be "clean skin"—meaning that I would not wear other corporate logos. At that time, I was in the third year of a five-year contract with McDonald's that was paying me good money. I contacted the McDonald's representatives and spoke honestly with them. I explained to them why I wanted to discontinue our arrangement and reassured them that it had nothing to do with the corporation, its products, or its people. Overall, this was a conscious decision on my part to take money off the table. But I knew in the long run it would help me to better craft my future direction.

In the early years, we were extremely bold with our designs, as it was important to establish the look and the visualization of the shark icon. To this day, most everyone remembers the first generation of shirts, which had the "wraparound shark." The logo was literally three feet long, wrapped around my body.

In the early stages of developing Greg Norman Collection, I immersed myself in the business. I made recommendations on the designs, the materials used, collateral, advertising, everything. When I played in golf tournaments, I wore early mock-up designs and provided feedback to the design team. I also had a hand in designing a new version of the wide-brimmed hat that had become my trademark over the years. And because the Akubra arrangement was unique to Australia, the only hat that featured the new shark logo was manufactured by Greg Norman Collection. In those early years, we sold an amazing number of those trademark straw hats.

As the new business got rolling, everything ran smoothly. Reebok's muscle, capital, and distribution helped get the new business off the ground. With time, however, it became apparent that the people within Reebok who were running Greg Norman Collection did not have the requisite experience in either the golf industry or the apparel business. Moreover, the pitfalls of a large company began coming into play. Competition from other divisions, delay in the chain of command, and other inefficiencies started to be a major liability. When I came to the realization that Greg Norman Collection was not going to be a success while being run by a large athletic footwear company, I went to see Paul.

"Paul, this is not working," I said. "If we are going to be a major apparel brand, we need to be autonomous. We need to resource this differently."

After reviewing the situation, Paul agreed that changes needed to be made. So we morphed Greg Norman Collection into a separate division of Reebok. Rather than being run under the auspices of Reebok Golf in Boston, it would be headquartered in New York, in the heart of the fashion district. We would bring on experienced "rag trade" executives to help us build the business. We would develop our own design and sourcing capabilities, and we would appoint our own sales representatives, who would focus on Greg Norman Collection alone.

Although this arrangement was technically a licensing deal, in a practical sense it was run as a partnership. And that was because Paul Fireman and I had a very close personal relationship, one that centered around mutual trust and respect. As a result, Greg Norman Collection became what I consider to be the third prong of Great White Shark Enterprises, sitting alongside Greg Norman Golf Course Design and Cobra.

For the next seven years (1991–1997) I was hot, the golf industry was hot, and retail was buoyant. As a result, our sales escalated from an initial yearly total of $15 million up to $78 million. Everybody's reaction was, quite naturally, euphoric. "Wow!" we thought. "Maybe we can surpass the magic $100 million mark." We studied Tommy Hilfiger, Ralph Lauren, and Donna Karan, who at that time had just gone public with great fanfare. "That's the model," we all said. "Let's go deeper into retail and build our business on licensing. By concentrating on department store chains, we can open up two thousand doors in addition to the golf channel." So we decided to go for the brass ring. We hired the necessary people and expanded our licensing activities into myriad products. It was just a matter of time, we believed, before we would achieve our full potential as a lifestyle apparel company.

Unfortunately, our dreams were dashed. Not only did we underperform, but a major correction took place in the industry. Competition increased exponentially, while major department stores not only went soft on golf, but their terms were horrendous and some even introduced their own private labels. And when that happened, many dropped Greg Norman Collection. Of course, with each department store loss, two hundred or more doors closed. As a result, our business suffered. From 1997 to 2002, we dropped to just under $50 million. There was a sense of panic, and all kinds of excuses were voiced. "Greg's not playing well." "Retail is soft." "Golf is on the outs!" Finally, I pulled the team together.

"Guys, I am not going to listen to all these excuses," I said. "We need to do what Jack Welch does: Sell it, fix it, or shut it down. Well, we're not going to sell because the price would be too low. And we're sure as hell not going to shut it down, because I believe we have a winner here. So the only other option is to right this ship. We're going to conduct a serious review. We're going to look at our business, see where we went wrong, develop a blueprint for success, and we're going to execute. *We are going to make some changes!*"

After reviewing our entire business, Paul and I sat down and agreed on the necessary changes to the company's strategy and direction. Just as it was for Cobra in the late 1980s, the remedy was quite simple. We needed to protect the golf channel, giving the green-grass operator the best possible margins and product that delivered on its promise. Such a program would require a lot of hard work. After all, green-grass accounts have to be secured one at a time, but if you should lose an account, you don't need to close two hundred doors as you do in the retail business.

Paul and I also had to make some tough decisions on personnel. We admitted to ourselves that we'd made some mistakes. We had put some people in executive positions for which they were not well suited. Some had not been as strong at merchandising or team building or building a sales force as we had at first believed. Consequently, there had been some poor execution. So the question for us became: Do we make an attempt to re-educate and redirect the executive, or do we hire somebody else?

"Don't change the people," I told Paul. "*Change* the people."

"What?"

"We should not try to improve a failed executive," I said. "We cannot change the internal workings of an individual who has risen to such a high level. Rather, we should dismiss the failed executive and hire somebody with the right skill set. Besides, the people who got us to first base are probably not the ones who will get us home. Don't change the people; *change* the people."

As fate would have it, in 2001 Paul recruited Suzy Biszantz to take the reins of Greg Norman Collection. Suzy came to us having achieved a great deal of success launching Ashworth's women's line, and yes, Suzy is the daughter of Gary Biszantz, my business partner with Cobra. While the recruitment was purely coincidental, it was a welcome surprise.

At the same time, we had to contend with the looming Dama trademark opposition. Five years earlier, when Paul and I agreed to launch Greg Norman Collection, we adopted the strategy that "it's better to beg for forgiveness than ask for permission," but it was now time to negotiate with Dama for the cohabitation of our respective logos. Notwithstanding the fact that our sales had dropped off, Greg Norman Collection's sales had eclipsed those of Dama, which potentially made for an expensive settlement. Dama was privately held by an Italian family, and not surprisingly a great deal of emotion crept into the negotiations. At the same time, they played us masterfully, with the son of the founder leading the negotiations.

Each time we felt we had reached a resolution, the patriarch of the family would move the goalpost a bit farther back. Clearly the cash settlement was going to be sizable, but the specific terms of the cohabitation were almost comical. For instance, their shark swam from left to right, so our shark would have to swim from right to left. Because their shark was monochromatic, ours had to remain as a four-colored emblem; and although we could use our logo in yachting, we could not use it in sailing. We also agreed to refrain from selling Greg Norman Collection in Italy, Spain, or Taiwan, as these were major markets for Paul & Shark. In return for more market concessions and a lump-sum fee we were granted cohabitation rights to the shark logo for apparel in a variety of trademark classes.

The serious review we conducted when our business was facing challenges reminded me of the postmortems I conducted when I lost a golf tournament. After the 1986 Masters, for example, I boiled everything down to that approach shot on 18. All day long, I had been hitting my irons hard, and that had served me well. But for that last shot, I opted for a softer swing with more club in an effort to ensure accuracy. It was a mistake that cost me the green jacket. So I resolved to go back to my natural tendencies. And that's what we did with Greg Norman Collection. We went back to basics—back to what had helped us succeed in the first place. From 2002 to 2006, our sales consistently improved. In fact, Greg Norman Collection posted 11 consecutive quarters of double-digit growth over that period of time and significantly improved profitability.

As part of our turnaround, Greg Norman Collection introduced some very creative and innovative products. A new fabric called PlayDry is a good example. Greg Norman Collection was one of the pioneers of what the industry today refers to as moisture-wicking technology, whereby perspiration is carried away from the skin over a wider surface area, where it evaporates quickly. We launched a full complement of women's apparel in 2003, which filled a very important niche, as there are relatively few good alternatives available to the female golfer. More recently, Greg Norman Collection launched a Signature Series to capture the most discerning buyer and offer the highest-end green-grass shops, resorts, and specialty shops a product line that is truly unique. Today, I'm proud to say, Greg Norman Collection is the global leader in golf-inspired sportswear that combines performance, luxury, and style.

The personal relationship I maintained with Paul Fireman was valuable in achieving our success. While I was traveling around the world playing golf, I would schedule visits with our sales associates wherever I could. If I saw something that wasn't working well and needed to be changed—or something that was right and needed to be expanded upon—I'd just pick up the phone and call Paul. And he knew that when I called, it wasn't to gripe. It was about something important.

While there's no doubt that my relationship with Paul helped Great White Shark Enterprises, I also believe the success of Greg Norman Collection has been of some benefit to Reebok. In 2002, for instance, Reebok made a conscious decision to focus on becoming a master licensee for the National Football League, National Basketball Association, and National Hockey League. The success of Greg Norman Collection helped add credibility to Reebok's presentation, showing the administrators of these leagues that Reebok was not just an athletic footwear company but a legitimate lifestyle fashion resource. After all, the owners of many of the teams were already wearing our product on the golf course!

In March 2006, adidas purchased Reebok for $3.4 billion. Out of that, Paul Fireman would walk away with a small fortune. I was very happy for him. Given that our success over the years in no small measure resulted from our unique partnership, we will go through a learning curve in becoming acquainted with adidas. While integration is always a challenge, adidas already owns TaylorMade and has a very hot brand with adidas Golf. In fact, other than Greg Norman Collection, adidas Golf is probably the other growth brand in the golf industry. Fortunately it is sold at a different price point and targets a slightly different audience. Already I've had several positive discussions with the adidas CEO, Herbert Hainer, and CFO, Robin Stalker, and I look forward to exploring the options and opportunities that will exist with adidas.

Over the years, I've learned that no business can stand still. There are always changes in ownership and personnel, and invariably challenges with keeping your product or service relevant and in demand.

The reality is that businesses change, they evolve. Greg Norman Collection is going to be creative, it's going to adapt, and it's going to keep moving—just like a shark.

CHAPTER NINETEEN

WHAT DO YOU want to do?

"Do you want to give up the game?

"Or do you want to fight back and be the best you can be?

"Are you willing to do the hard work it will take to get back on top again?"

I was standing in front of a mirror asking myself these questions. It was just after I'd missed a three-foot putt and lost a playoff to Nick Faldo. Once again I had shaken Nick's hand after a crushing defeat. I had gone through the media interviews, offered no excuses, and held my head up high yet again. And you know what? I was getting *sick* of it.

I had not won a tournament anywhere in the world in more than two years. I'd been thinking about giving up the game altogether and just concentrating on business. I was as low as I have ever been. I was ready to quit.

So I stood in front of the mirror and asked myself these questions. Why? Because you can't lie to yourself.

"I love to play golf!" I answered back. "It would be easy to walk away, but that would be quitting—and I've never thought of myself as a quitter."

The truth was that I liked the Sunday afternoon competitions. I liked the feeling of being in the hunt. Even if I didn't win, just being there felt great. But winning was better, much better. I knew I still had the ability to win more golf tournaments. I just wasn't working hard enough. I felt as though I wasn't applying myself, and it was time to get back to work.

"The question of success will be decided by your own level of commitment," I said, pointing to myself in the mirror. "If you get back on top, it will be the best feeling you've ever had in golf. That's what makes failure so great: You can't really appreciate success—I mean *really* appreciate it—until you've failed. So let's get after it."

When I walked away from that mirror, I rededicated myself to being the best I could be at golf. One of the first things I did was call Butch Harmon, a well-known golf instructor. Butch was working out of the Lochinvar Club in Houston, and Steve Elkington had introduced me to him some months earlier at the Houston Open. I wanted to step up my efforts to improve my game, and Butch wasted no time in helping me. Together we completely overhauled my game, my mechanics, everything. He helped me tighten up my body rotation so that it was more in sync with my swing. In turn, that gave me more control over distance, flight, and accuracy. And I worked hard, very hard—as hard as or harder than I did when I was twenty-one or twenty-two.

My relationship with Butch was special. We were friends, and we enjoyed each other's company. It was very much a partnership. In addition to the assistance he gave me on swing mechanics, he was very good at putting me in a positive frame of mind. And in some instances, the teacher became the pupil. I think Butch would credit me for giving him some tips and theories on the short game, particularly shots from inside 60 yards and bunker play. In fact, at the 2005 Players Championship, Butch was working with Adam Scott on the practice green and he called me over to work with Adam on some of the short-game aspects he was struggling with at the time. That session proved effective, as Adam got it up and down from about 20 yards on the 72nd hole to secure a one-shot victory.

I have also worked with David Leadbetter over the years, and we have maintained a strong relationship. In fact, when I need someone to take a look at my swing, I will occasionally make the trip to Orlando for a quick session with David, who, at my suggestion, established his world headquarters at ChampionsGate Golf

Club, which is home to two courses I designed. Interestingly, a few years ago David introduced me to Joaquin Gari de Sentmenat, which led to me winning the design contract for Real El Prat Golf Club, a magnificent 45-hole facility in Barcelona.

By the time the Canadian Open rolled around in 1992, I was feeling pretty good about my game again, so I ventured up to Oakville, Ontario, to play at the Jack Nicklaus–designed Glen Abbey course, where I had been victorious back in 1984. I posted a 73 in the first round but quickly followed it up with a 66, which left me tied for the lead with Nick Price at the halfway point. Going into the final day, Nick and I were bunched up with Corey Pavin, Fred Couples, and Bruce Lietzke. It was a wild run down the stretch, with each of us taking and giving back the lead at one point or another. But during a stretch on the back 9, I started clicking. On the final three or four holes, it was like somebody put a coin in the jukebox and the right song started playing. I mean, I hit the ball perfectly on every swing. And there's no better golf experience in the world than when your caddy gives you yardage of 185.5 and you're able to hit the ball within a foot and a half of where you want to hit it. Feeling in total control of my game, and with my adrenaline really surging, I birdied the 18th hole to finish in a tie (at 8 under par) with Bruce Lietzke at the end of regulation. Then, on the second playoff hole, a par-5, I blasted a 3-wood 240 yards over water into the back bunker. I blasted out to about two feet, made the birdie putt, and had my first tournament victory in twenty-seven months.

That was a big step for me. A huge step. I had almost forgotten what it was like to win. Now I was getting to where I wanted to be. My experience at the Canadian Open made me realize that I had been lacking my old aggression. But now the Shark was back on the attack. And by the time I started the 1993 season, I was really on top of my game. My first tournament that year was the Doral-Ryder Open in Miami. After shooting a course-record 62 in the 3rd round, I cruised home on Sunday with a 4-stroke victory over Paul Azinger and Mark McCumber.

There were some ups and downs as the season progressed. I finished in 33rd place in the Masters, in second place at the Western Open, and missed the cut in the U.S. Open. Still, I was feeling pretty solid as I crossed the Atlantic to play in the 122nd British Open at Royal St. George's in Kent, England. When I arrived, everybody was talking about how the seven-week drought had made the fairways rock hard and that, when combined with knee-high rough and the wind whipping across the great sand dunes, we'd likely be in for a high-scoring tournament. That all changed, however, when the unpredictable weather from the English Channel unleashed some fearsome rain just in time for our practice rounds. It poured both Tuesday and Wednesday nights, so by the time we began the tournament on Thursday, the entire golf course was soft. Golf balls would no longer roll forever in the fairways, and once brick-hard greens became more receptive.

I began the tournament inauspiciously by hitting my first drive into the deep rough. It took me another 3 shots to reach the green, where I 2-putted from nine feet for a double-bogey 6. "Okay," I said to myself, "you still have 71 more holes to play. Just start making some birdies and work your way back to even par." I immediately got one of those strokes back with a birdie on the 2nd, then sank a 9-foot putt on 5 for another birdie. I made the turn at even par, and when I got to the 13th hole, I really caught fire. A pitch to within 18 inches resulted in a birdie. On 14, I holed a 45-foot sand wedge—birdie! On 15, I hit a 6-iron to within two feet of the flag—birdie! I sank a 24-foot putt on 16—birdie! On 17, I hit a 5-iron to within 5 feet—birdie! And I finished my round by holing a 15-foot putt for par on the 18th. I'd shot a 31 on the back 9 to finish with a 66—good enough for a share of the lead after round one.

The media was reporting that this year's tournament had the chance to be one of the best British Opens in history, simply because many of the game's best players were bunched together at the top. Bernhard Langer, who had just won his second Masters, was one stroke back after shooting a 67. Lee Janzen, the current U.S. Open champ, was only 3 back, at 69. Nick Faldo, the defending British Open champion and number-one-ranked player in the world (I had dropped to number four), also shot a 69. Fred Couples and Nick Price were at 68. And then there were all those familiar names who had, at one time or another, beaten me in the final round of key tournaments. Seve Ballesteros, who'd won the 1979 British Open, was only a few shots back. Jack Nicklaus, to whom I'd lost the 1986 Masters, shot a 69. The Australian golfer Peter Senior, who beat me on the last hole of the 1991 Australian Masters after I hooked my tee shot, fired a 66 and was tied with me for the lead. Also shooting a 66 that day were Mark Calcavecchia (who beat me in a playoff at the 1989 British Open) and Fuzzy Zoeller (to whom I lost the 1984 U.S. Open in a playoff). It was like old home week. Hell, even Larry Mize was only a few shots off the pace.

Things really got going during the second round, where the big story was Nick Faldo. Despite a torrential rainstorm the night before, Nick went out there and seized the lead by firing an amazing round of 63, which tied the course record. I managed a 68 to stay within 2 shots, but nearly all the other guys were bunched around me, including Langer, Couples, Senior, Zoeller, Mize, Ballesteros, and the hard-charging Corey Pavin. Unfortunately, Nicklaus had a poor second round and missed the cut, as did Gary Player, Tony Jacklin, and Tom Watson. After the third round, I found myself tied for second with Langer at 8 under par, one shot behind Faldo and Pavin.

On Sunday morning, as I drove over to the golf course, the main thought I had was to make love to my hands and be sensitive to their feelings. "That will orchestrate your tempo, and everything else should fall in place." So I gently caressed the steering wheel with both hands. I felt the movement of the automobile through my fingertips. I contemplated every turn, every bump, every stop and go. And the drive was tough that morning, because it poured along the coastline. The rain gradually tapered off, though, and by the time the last few groups were ready to go, it had stopped completely. Patches of blue sky were visible through the low-hanging clouds, but there was still a chilly and 20- to 30-mile-per-hour wind blustering the course. On the practice putting green before I teed off, I remember my putts rolling dead center into the hole. That was a loud signal of good things to come.

As I stepped up to the first tee, I was calm, in total control of my feelings, and I could feel the sensitivity in my hands. I sent my drive down the middle of the fairway, lofted an easy 9-iron to within about 9 feet, and made the putt for a birdie. I don't think I looked at a leaderboard until after I tapped in for my fourth birdie at 9 and was walking to the 10th tee. I had gone out in 31 and had a 2-shot lead over Faldo and Langer. Everybody else seemed to be having trouble with the wind. It was at that point that I recalled something that Larry Bird, the great professional basketball player, had said to me. "If we're down a point with two seconds left, I want the ball," he said. "I want to control the situation and take the shot that is going to decide the game." When that thought popped into my head, I took stock of my situation heading into the back 9. "Good, I want the lead," I thought to myself. "They're going to have a tough time catching me the way I'm feeling right now."

A sense of excitement permeated the air on the back 9, and the crowd broke into two groups, one following Langer and me, the other sticking with Pavin and home-country favorite Faldo. I birdied the 12th and 14th holes to go to 11 under par, but Faldo stayed right with me. Langer, unfortunately, had a double bogey and dropped 5 strokes off the pace. One of the most important things for me was staying very focused, never even watching Langer's tee shot going out of bounds. I picked my spot on the horizon for my drive, stepped up, and executed it perfectly. I started walking off the tee, not realizing that he had to hit another tee shot.

Another birdie at 16 put me 3 shots ahead, but then I made a mental mistake at the 17th hole. Reaching the back of the green in two, I lagged my first putt to within a foot and a half. But then my tap-in lipped out of the cup. I couldn't believe it! I hadn't missed a putt that short since the 1976 West Lakes Classic! It was a blessing in disguise, though, because it really kicked me into gear. It was my only bogey in an otherwise flawless round, and I would be damned if I'd make another one.

Standing on the 18th tee, I had a 2-stroke lead over Faldo and was 3 ahead of Langer, who had stormed back over the last several holes. Just like on the first tee, I hit a solid drive down the middle of the fairway. And for my second shot, I hit a beautiful 4-iron to within 18 feet of the flagstick. And that was it. I knew I was going to win my second British Open Championship.

As I made the long walk up to the 18th green, Langer joined in with the applause of the fans who lined the fairway and crowded the grandstands. Then, just as I stepped onto the green, he came up to me, put his arm around my shoulder, and congratulated me. "Greg, that was the greatest round of golf I've ever seen," he said. "You deserve to win."

I 2-putted for par, posting a final-round 64, and won the tournament by 2 strokes. As soon as I pulled my ball out of the hole, I walked toward the gallery and pointed to my friend Tom Crow, whom I had told before the round that I thought I would win. Faldo and Langer both shot 67 and finished second and third, respectively. Unfortunately for them, they caught me on a good day. Except for the hiccup on 17, I did not miss-hit a single shot. I hit 14 of 14 fairways, and every long iron, short iron, and wedge was executed flawlessly. It was as close to a perfect round of golf as I would ever shoot. And apparently other people agreed. The great champion Gene Sarazen said, "It was the most awesome display of golf I've seen in seventy years."

During the press conference afterward, people informed me that I had set a couple of records. "Greg, did you know you were the first Open champion to shoot all four rounds in the 60s? You also set the record, at 267, for lowest aggregate score, beating Tom Watson's mark by one stroke. And you fired the lowest final round ever recorded by a champion in British Open history."

To win that championship, and to win against the quality of the competition that day, meant everything to me. I was choked up, emotional, and physically spent. And it wasn't all just because I'd won my second major. It was also for having climbed out of the deep valley I'd been in during the previous two years. I'd once again reached the pinnacle and reestablished myself as a winner. And just as I'd said to myself in the mirror, it was the best feeling I'd ever experienced in golf.

Several weeks later, I flew to Japan to play in the Taiheiyo Masters, where I stayed hot. I won that tournament by one shot after making an eagle at the par-5 18th hole. It seemed like nothing could stop this hot streak, which actually continued right through the entire four rounds of the 1993 PGA Championship. On the 18th hole, I had another 18-foot putt for birdie to win the tournament in regulation. When the ball was 2 feet from the hole, I thought it was going in, but it lipped out, sending me into a sudden-death playoff, this time with Paul Azinger. On the first extra hole, however, I 3-putted for bogey to hand Paul his first career major victory. The dejected feeling I had after that loss was short-lived, though, because a short time later, I won the Grand Slam of Golf by 2 strokes and picked up a check for $400,000, the largest single payoff of my golfing career to that point.

At the end of the season, somebody asked me to describe the 1993 golf season, and I responded by saying: "It was like a mackerel in the moonlight: shiny one minute and smelly the next." It might have been that same interview when I was informed that I had become the only professional golfer to lose all four major championships in a playoff.

I thought a lot about that statistic and came to the conclusion that it was okay. I may have lost all four majors in a playoff, but I'm glad I was in those playoffs. What makes golf so thrilling is not so much the wins as *the losses*, which put a man's humanity and grace on public display. Besides, at the age of thirty-eight, I had a sense that I understood what was really important and meaningful in life. Golf was hugely important, but I sensed I was finding the right overall balance to many other things that were equally important.

CHAPTER TWENTY

$\mathbf{B}$EING NATURALLY INTROVERTED helps me in business. I'm not a Wharton Business School graduate, but I'll sometimes sit on an airplane and stare out the window for hours on end thinking about nothing but business. I'll contemplate where I want to go or what I want to do, and I'll keep thinking until I map something out. I like to be on my own time, in my own space, with my own thoughts.

In 1993 I started thinking very seriously about the future. I realized, for instance, that my body was trying to tell me something. It was getting harder and harder for me to maintain the top physical condition required to play world-class golf. I'd fallen from number one after not having won a tournament in over two years, and although I had climbed out of that hole, I knew it was just a matter of time before my performance would drop off again. I had some injuries that I knew would get the better of me with time. I began thinking about golfers who were past their prime. Tom Watson (who'd won eight majors) had recently lost his putting stroke. Jack and Arnold were playing on the senior tour. All three had graduated from idols to icons in golf. But could they have done more, I wondered, in leveraging their success in golf to achieve something far greater in business? Hmmm. That was an interesting question. Perhaps they had never really wanted to do that. But I did. I wanted to put myself in a position where golf would not be everything to me once my prime playing days were over. I wanted to give myself an opportunity to make a choice: business or golf. More important than that, though, when I looked at myself in the mirror at age sixty and asked how I did at life—family, friends, business, golf—I wanted the answer to be that it was more than just winning tournaments.

Still, though, the question remained: What do I have to do *now* in order to be ready *later*? In order for an entrepreneur to become successful, he or she has to have vision. It's as simple as that. Just like one of my Golf Course Design Principles, you have to begin with the end in mind. As a matter of fact, I think that applies to all aspects of business. If you go into something with no vision for the future, you are destined to fail in the long run. Furthermore, in viewing the future, you should prepare an exit strategy. How long is it going to take you to get where you want to be? Once you build up your business, what are you going to do with it? What is your exit strategy?

As I sat back and thought about everything, it dawned on me that the new millennium was seven years away. When the year 2000 rolled around, I was going to be forty-five years old. That would be a good time to step back and reevaluate things. Seven years would be ample time to structure and achieve a plan that would put me in a position to make the choice of either staying with golf or leaving it altogether. Okay, now I felt good. This would be a very calculated transition. In business, as in golf, I would stay aggressive and keep attacking. Now was not yet time to judge me, however. No sir. Judgment Day for Greg Norman would come in the year 2000.

The first phase of my plan was to take stock of what I had accomplished in business to date. I had structured successful partnerships with Cobra and Reebok, creating something that went beyond endorsement-only ventures. I had refined and controlled the shark logo, which I knew was a major step in building brand equity. I had started my golf course design business in a safe and measured way. Still, there was more to do, much more.

I wanted to continue generating merchandising and endorsement deals, because these produced significant cash in the short term and thus enhanced my income statement. At the same time, my strategy was to create more long-term profitable businesses that, on a year-to-year basis, might not generate a lot of cash but would add to the balance sheet. With time, the fulcrum would slide from the merchandising and endorsement deals to the longer-term business enterprises, which would ultimately have much greater profit potential. Over the years, I would continually monitor the positioning of the fulcrum as a means of gauging the evolution of my overall game plan.

As a next step, I was going to have to separate from IMG. It was apparent that they were not going to get me where I wanted to go. In walking away from IMG, I knew I'd be leaving the safety and security of a large and influential company.

Up to this point, I had studied, reflected, and then prepared a plan for my business future. Now it was time to take action. Nearly everybody reads, thinks, and comes up with plans and dreams. Few people, however, actually *do something* to achieve them. They're too mired in the daily routine of their lives. They get busy with something else. Or they're simply afraid to change. It takes tremendous will and energy to pull off a major transformation in your life. The only way you can turn your dreams into reality is by turning inertia into action. And that's exactly what I did.

Setting up my own operation turned out to be a daunting task in many ways. There was a major learning curve involved. So here I was, setting off on another journey. I had to hire employees I could empower and trust, who would represent my best interests and my values, and see my vision for Great White Shark Enterprises. Then I had to get involved in choosing pensions, health care programs, and other benefits—all of which I had no previous experience with. Then there was the office setup: capital expenditures, information technology, finance and accounting. The entire experience, I found, was like a process of osmosis. I filtered out what I didn't need and then acquired what was left over.

Identifying a marketing niche and filling it was going to take a little bit of time, and I knew it. Obviously, I had a good head start on that with Greg Norman Collection, taking a product that was closely identified with me to the golfing public. Over time, other products and services would follow. As opportunities came, I planned to evaluate each on its individual merit.

In April 1993, my agreement with IMG expired. I notified IMG that I would not re-sign but that we would continue to explore opportunities of mutual interest on a case-by-case basis. In my mind, this would be an easier transition, and I could then make a more formal break near the end of the year. While I was now free to operate independently, several matters convinced me I was on the right track in gaining independence from IMG.

While Cobra was not in the golf ball business, it was always understood that one day they might enter the fray. Therefore, my Cobra agreement was written in such a way that they had the first right of refusal in that category, and that if I elected to play another ball, Cobra would receive half the income from that contract. IMG was involved with the negotiation of this agreement, and as such were aware of it when they consummated an agreement for me to play the Maxfli golf ball. The result, of course, was that IMG claimed a full commission on my Maxfli agreement (not the net difference), knowing full well I had to give 50 percent of my retainer to Cobra. After taxes, that left me with something on the order of 10 percent of the contract, which was totally unacceptable. During this same period, IMG presented me with an instructional video arrangement. It sounded good on the surface. I would receive a set fee against a percentage of the net profits (not gross, as is typically the case with licensing agreements). As I probed, I learned that TWI, an IMG company, handled both the production and distribution of the series. Understandably, I felt there was a conflict of interest. Who was policing the production and distribution costs? After all, IMG received 20 cents of every dollar for my retainer but 100 cents of every dollar for their production and distribution costs.

For a period of time, my association with IMG was symbiotic, what I consider to be a win-win in many respects. But I had simply outgrown them, and knowing that I might have gotten the short end of one or two deals, I felt comfortable with my decision to move on.

That brings me to the third phase of my plan, which may have been the toughest part of all. I had to recruit an executive who was patient, diligent, and understanding enough to see where I wanted to go over the next seven years—and who would be willing to take the journey with me. Once I had the right person to run the day-to-day operations at Great White Shark Enterprises, we'd really be able to fuel our growth. But who was it going to be? Given my early experience with James Marshall, I knew I had to find someone I could empower and trust. After careful deliberation, I found that man in Frank Williams, whom I had known since 1977. Frank was a founding partner in the Australian Masters golf tournament (which I won six times), which he successfully sold to IMG and then managed their Melbourne operations. Even though he was an IMG employee, Frank was still his own man, more entrepreneurial. I also liked Frank because he presented himself well. A tall, handsome, articulate Englishman who usually wore a double-breasted suit, he had a formidable presence. In addition, Frank had expertise in his field combined with guts. He wasn't afraid to mix it up with industry heavyweights. So, over the course of a couple of months, the two of us had numerous conversations, and Frank agreed to come on board once I parted from IMG, which I did in November 1993.

In the intervening time frame, I continued to seek the advice of other successful businesspeople, just as I had done at the beginning of my golfing career. I was never afraid to speak with Jack Nicklaus or other established pros. I learned that if I sought the opinion of successful people, then I too could become successful. And that was a philosophy I carried into business.

One of the benefits of my various endorsements was that I met quite a few corporate leaders. As a matter of fact, I found business to be a small world. There may only be three degrees of separation among the top hundred industry leaders. Once you operate in that circle, you have a great entrée to almost any person or group. In addition to Kerry Packer and Nelson Peltz, I developed relationships with Jack Welch of General Electric, Lewis Campbell of Textron, Roger Penske, and Bryan Moss of Gulfstream. It got to the point where I would speak with these gentlemen on a fairly regular basis and ask questions. "Hey, here's what's going on," I'd say. "What do you think?" Having this access provided a huge boost to my confidence. I found that, with time, I was often introducing these gentlemen to one another. As a golfer, I was seen as being quite neutral. As such, I brought people together who otherwise might not have connected. And with each good deed, my standing in the business world was enhanced. All I really had to do in order to gain that credibility was to put my ego on the back burner, admit to myself that I didn't know everything, and have the courage to ask for help. By the way, I learned something very interesting when I did that. I learned that most successful people are very willing to share their time to help others become successful. Making some close, lifelong friends in this process was a dividend that I had not really expected.

As 1993 wound to a close, I purchased a home on Jupiter Island at the recommendation of Jack and Barbara Nicklaus and opened my new office in nearby Tequesta. At year's end, I claimed my third Vardon Trophy (for lowest-scoring average on the U.S. PGA Tour), and recaptured the number one spot in the world rankings.

In early 1994, Steve Elkington picked me up at the airport when I arrived to play the Houston Open. On the tarmac was a new Chevrolet Suburban. "Hey, Elky," I said, "what are you doing picking me up in this redneck truck?"

"Bite your tongue, Tiburon," quipped Steve, using the Spanish word for "shark." "You're going to fall in love with this vehicle. It's right up your alley." It was Steve who first coined the nickname Tiburon, which in later years has become a bit of a "diffusion brand" for me. Anyway, Steve was right. I quickly learned to appreciate that vehicle, and when I returned to Florida I bought one for myself. Some months later, Frank and I flew to Detroit and met with several Chevrolet executives. We asked if they were interested in having me represent Chevy Trucks. They could see that I was already passionate about their product. They loved the idea, and shortly thereafter we formalized what would become a long-standing relationship.

Over the years, Chevy Trucks and I worked very closely together. They certainly supported my endeavors, sponsoring the Shark Shootout for more than fifteen years and giving me a number of great opportunities, including the chance to drive the Indy 500 pace car at the Indianapolis Motor Speedway. Equally, I'd like to think I went beyond being just a paid spokesperson, taking the initiative to secure several national accounts and helping build the legacy of their brand. In 2003 I introduced Chevrolet to the elders of the Apache tribe in New Mexico. As an Australian, I took great pride in connecting an iconic automotive company with one of the most recognizable Native American tribes. I thought it was a great fit.

Over the next couple of years, I aligned myself with a number of companies similar to Chevrolet. These companies might not have been the most expensive in their categories, but they were very much best of breed. I realized that such a program helped me reach a broader base of more relevant consumers. In later years I would take this positioning into some of my own consumer product strategies, including apparel and wine. Slowly, I was crafting my own niche.

This time also served as my introduction into golf course design in the United States. Given my six years of experience in Australia and Asia, I knew I was ready. While I had been presented with a number of opportunities, I knew it would be critical for my first project in the States to be world-class. And knowing that I would want to spend a considerable amount of time on site, it was important that it be located in close proximity to my home.

So in 1994, I partnered with two local developers, Bob Whitley and Tucker Fredrickson (who played running back for the New York Giants), to develop what would become the Medalist Golf Club in Hobe Sound, Florida (Hobe Sound is part of Martin County, among the strictest of Florida's 99 counties in terms of environmental restrictions). We selected a site that was both aesthetically pleasing and environmentally challenging. The total site encompassed 1,200 acres of wetlands, upland scrub brush, slash, and sand pines. Of that, we utilized only 120 acres for the golf course and only 60 acres for turfgrass. Several years later we sold 880 acres to the South Florida Water Management District as a preserve. The model for funding this project was based on the premise that Palm Beach County had many courses that were part of larger real estate–driven communities but relatively few courses that were pure golf. We wanted to handpick a membership of serious golfers and create a golf club, not a country club—no pools, tennis courts, or other amenities. This would be purely "by the golfers and for the golfers."

We also brought in Buddy Antonopoulos to serve as head professional. With his respect for pure golf and the traditions of the game, Buddy is the perfect person to have at the helm. Over the years, many people have complimented me on the quality of the staff and the culture we created at Medalist, and that is largely because of Buddy's manner. He and I have traveled the world together, and he occasionally served as my caddie for events in Australia and the Middle East. We have formed a very close, personal relationship.

While I had an excellent team in Australia, clearly I could not transfer their talents to Florida, so I felt it best that I collaborate with another designer for this project. I was very fortunate to be introduced to Pete Dye. Together, we would have the opportunity to create a modern masterpiece.

It didn't take long for Pete to further my education in golf course design, specifically in how to manage the huge amount of sheet-flow drainage in South Florida and other technical concerns that were part of this project.

The more time I spent with Pete, the more I realized that he was much more than a golf course architect. He was part artist, part engineer. I mean, Pete Dye is brilliant. Let me give you just one example of what he did at the Medalist.

County officials came in and told us that we would not be allowed to have any water runoff into the wetlands surrounding the course. "Well, how the hell are we going to avoid that?" I asked. "We're surrounded by protected wetlands."

"That's your problem," came the response from South Florida Water Management.

"Don't worry," said Pete. "We'll figure something out."

"But Pete," I said, "the fairways out here will have a one- or two-percent grade—at most!"

"That's all right. We don't need five- or six-percent grades to channel water," he replied. "Besides, those small grades may make it easier for us to harvest both the rain and irrigation water."

"What do we do with it once we've captured it?" I remember thinking to myself.

Well, Pete devised a system that simply blew me away. On every hole, we built concrete vaults to hold the surface runoff and irrigation water. The water is then pumped into a reservoir lined with a membrane fabric to prevent leaching onto the wetlands. From there, the water is used on the driving range, which we placed at the highest elevation of the site. The water then percolates through the sand and, by a process of natural filtration, goes back into the water table. It is truly brilliant.

As a result, we were eventually able to demonstrate—not only to the authorities but to the golf community as a whole—that the Medalist Golf Club was a model for what an environmentally sensitive golf course in South Florida should be. Both the county and the Audubon Society conducted studies that conclusively demonstrated that we have created a wetlands environment that was a marked improvement over what existed previously. The site now has more sandhill cranes, tortoises, alligators, snakes, and other wildlife than ever before.

While I was working on the Medalist, I became good friends with one of Pete's top associates, Jason McCoy. Impressed with Jason's skill, style, and professional demeanor, I probed for an understanding of his future goals and aspirations. I thought he could be the right "first employee" for my U.S. design group. When it was clear that we not only shared the same golf course design personality but also the same goals and values, I immediately went to Pete and asked for permission to offer Jason a job. Pete was fully supportive of the idea, which again is a measure of the man. Knowing the importance of communication to this business, I structured the U.S. golf course design office so that Jason would report directly to me, just as Frank Williams did for the rest of Great White Shark Enterprises.

The following year, I was commissioned to design the Sugarloaf Golf Club in Duluth, Georgia, for Crescent Resources, a division of Duke Energy. This would be a traditional golf course with a great deal of topography and heavily wooded, but unlike Medalist, Sugarloaf would be developed as part of a larger master-planned community. Not long after we started building the course, Crescent entered into an agreement with the PGA Tour for Sugarloaf to be a TPC course and, more important, become the host venue for the BellSouth Classic. I felt very fortunate that my second major project in the U.S. would be showcased on national television the week before the Masters each year.

While working there, Jason and I struck up a relationship with Chris Campbell, a young man who was just as impressive as he was hardworking. At the time, Chris worked as a construction manager for the project. What impressed me about Chris was his ability to understand and interpret what I wanted to achieve with the final contouring of the golf course. In a very short period of time, we developed a comfort level where Jason and I could leave the golf course and have every confidence that my vision for the final product was being carried out. I could tell Chris that I wanted a half-percent grade on a green, with the water going off the back left side, and if need be he would get on a 'dozer and craft that surface himself. I admired the fact that while he was the project manager he would do whatever was necessary to get the job done.

Knowing we were in the midst of building our team for the U.S. business, Jason came to me and said, "Hey, Greg, this guy is really good. He has the ability to go far beyond what he's doing right now. We should consider hiring him."

The next day I brought Chris on board.

We had a small team, but I liked the idea of running a lean operation. Because everybody had to multitask, I took a personal involvement in helping develop Chris's skills as a designer. On our next project, we were all standing on a tee trying to decide exactly what to do when I turned to Chris. "Okay, mate, what would you do here?"

"Me?" he asked.

"Yeah, you. Build this hole for me."

I put Chris on the spot because I wanted to see how he would handle it. I also wanted to hear a different point of view. He gave me his ideas; I listened carefully, didn't agree, and said, "Fade to black,

Chris. Let me tell you what I think. Let me tell you what my strategy would be for a hole like this."

I enjoyed the process of educating Chris on my design philosophies, which in turn gave me a sense of reassurance that I had absorbed quite a bit of information over the previous eight years.

With time I discovered that it's not just one person who designs a golf course or builds a business. With the right guidance, a collective approach often gives the best results.

Over the next several years, as our golf course design company continued to expand, my ideas and philosophies continued to evolve in many different settings. We were always looking to create uniqueness, an approach that other designers might not adopt. For instance, we left a cave in the middle of a fairway at a course in Mexico, and we kept a Civil War–era cabin next to a green at a course in Virginia. We would also become known for going to the trouble of doing the little things—like moving a tee box in Colorado thirty feet so that golfers would not have to look at an electrical tower off in the distance. We also furthered our reputation for environmental stewardship. Our TPC in San Antonio, for example, is capped with two feet of clay to protect the Edwards Aquifer. Water from that particular formation serves as a primary source of water for the city.

As I continued to gain experience in the business, I developed three additional principles in my golf course design philosophy.

GOLF COURSE DESIGN PRINCIPLE #4:
EMBRACE THE ENVIRONMENTALISTS

I think everybody would agree that we should try to improve the quality of the environment for future generations. Fortunately, there are groups and activists who work hard to protect the environment. While some are overzealous, most have a balanced approach to how they go about their job. I have found that when you work hand in glove with environmentalists, the result of a collaborative effort can be outstanding. Whenever I go out on a site visit, I encourage the environmentalists to come along and walk the course with me. On nearly every project I've been fortunate enough

to foster relationships and attain a mutual respect with the environmentalists. Along the way, I have advocated that golf courses, if
properly designed, built, and maintained, can become viable community assets. Not only can they elevate property values, create
jobs, and provide tax revenues, they can provide green spaces, filter
air, purify water, and enhance wildlife.

Rather than cause harm, we can coexist with and enhance the
environment. We have embraced this philosophy, and the end result
has proved beneficial to both the environment and the golf course.

At Doonbeg Golf Club, a magnificent course on the southwest
coast of Ireland, early in the design process we came to realize that
the site was home to an endangered species of snail, *Vertigo angus-
tior.* One particular environmental agency, led by Evelyn Moorkens,
a prominent scientist in the field, took considerable interest in the
project. As you can imagine, GNGCD was under the microscope, as
were the snails, which, interestingly enough, were not visible to the
human eye. Ten of them could fit on the head of a pin.

This agency insisted that a study be conducted to ascertain the
location and quantity of this species and subsequently how much
of the site would have to be set aside for this snail to thrive. The results of this study would determine how large the special area of
conservation would have to be. This would ultimately dictate the
proximity of the golf course to the ocean and the dunes.

On one of our early site visits, I arranged for a meeting with Dr.
Moorkens. I wanted to understand where she was coming from,
and, of equal importance, I wanted to convey that we were willing to work with her to determine a mutually agreeable solution,
something that would help the snail and also allow us to create
a world-class golf course. We set out to walk the dunes, and while
Dr. Moorkens was teaching me about this species of snail, I was
educating her about the nuances of golf course design. For instance,
I explained to her that we wanted to re-create the dunes to frame
several green complexes and incorporate the native marram grass
into the course. After all, these are inherent features of true links
golf.

The first conservation area Dr. Moorkens suggested would have
eliminated seven oceanfront holes that were the cornerstone of

our original routing. After much deliberation, Dr. Moorkens and her colleagues came to realize that we weren't trying to design anything that would be detrimental to this habitat. The eventual compromise affected very little of our original routing, and we were able to design a golf course that many consider today to be the best links golf course of the last fifty years. This was an exercise in communication, education, and mutual understanding, and I am proud to say that Doonbeg has since garnered numerous environmental awards.

Some years later, I would take the lead in chairing the advisory council for the Environmental Institute for Golf, a philanthropic organization run under the auspices of the Golf Course Superintendents Association of America, whose charter it is to improve the relationship between the game of golf and the environment.

GOLF COURSE DESIGN PRINCIPLE #5: MAKE THE COURSE PLAYABLE FOR EVERYBODY

Alice Dye, Pete's wife, is not only a real sweetheart but a staunch supporter of women's golf. While Pete and I were building the Medalist, she once said to me, "Greg, you never think about the woman golfer who only hits the ball eighty yards! We play those golf courses you design too. Why don't you think about us once in a while?"

"Oh, Alice, come on!" I responded sarcastically. But I did not forget what she said. As a matter of fact, I never again designed a course without thinking about how women golfers could play it. I remember one particular hole we designed on paper that I thought would be absolutely magnificent. It was a par-3 over a deep ravine with a massive rock wall just in front of the green. But when I walked the course, I saw that the tee shot would require a forced carry of 150 yards. So I turned to Bob Harrison and said, "You know, as a pro, I would love to play a beautiful hole like this. And probably 90 percent of golfers would as well. But there's no way ladies could carry the ravine even from the forward tee. We just can't build it."

Many years later, when Grande Lakes Golf Club, a course I designed in Orlando, was rated the seventeenth best course to play for women, I took the article, highlighted it, and sent it to Alice. "You see, Alice?" I wrote. "I *do* listen! Thanks for the tip."

I've often said that it's easy to build the hardest golf course. Anybody can design a 600-yard par-5 that will break the back of even the best golfer. I believe it requires greater talent, and is ultimately a greater challenge, to build golf courses that are fair to all golfers, while at the same time testing even a seasoned professional in competition. Like those of many player-designers, some of my early designs were very challenging. I tended to design courses that would challenge my professional counterparts. At the same time, however, I received criticism that my golf courses did not cater to players of all abilities.

Over time, I'd like to think that I have become more well rounded. A good example is my design at Tiburon Golf Club in Naples, Florida, for WCI Communities. For fifty-one weeks a year, it serves as a great golf course for the Ritz-Carlton resort guests, but the second week of November each year it is the host venue for the Shark Shootout and provides a test of golf for Tour pros.

GOLF COURSE DESIGN PRINCIPLE #6:
TREAT EVERY DOLLAR AS IF IT'S YOUR OWN

Back in the 1980s, when the design business was booming, I witnessed the construction of some very expensive golf courses. The creation of artificial mounds and slopes was dramatic, but, from an ongoing maintenance perspective, extraordinarily labor intensive and quite costly. If you haul something in, it costs you money. If you move a lot of dirt or haul it out, it costs you money. And if you get past a certain point in the construction of a course, making changes can really increase expenditures and could cause you to go over your allotted budget. In fact, that is one of the reasons I make so many site visits: so that I can eliminate unnecessary overruns by giving direction to the contractor on a timely basis. If something has to be changed, it should be done as early as possible in the construction phase.

When clients bring me in to do a job, I will give them a price for my own services and a budget for construction costs. I will also design the course with a great deal of thought directed toward keeping the cost of future maintenance down. One of the things I've wanted to be known for is always coming in at or below budget. Doing so gives me added credibility, which, in turn, serves to enhance my reputation as a golf course designer of choice.

Over the years, I've found that the best way to stay on budget is to make sure that every employee associated with Greg Norman Golf Course Design understands this principle from the moment we start a design to the moment the first golfer tees off on a finished product: Spend each dollar as if it's your own.

My golf course design business has evolved over the last twenty years. Today we have completed more than fifty golf courses and maintain a sufficient backlog of orders. If judged by nothing other than our design fee, we would qualify as one of the most highly sought-after golf course design firms in the world. As a student of golf, I find it interesting to note that the generation of golfers before me—Nicklaus, Palmer, Player—all made a commitment to golf course design, creating a dedicated resource with their own employees and offices. Yet when I look at my contemporaries—Faldo, Couples, Ballesteros—they seem not to have made the same commitment, often preferring to act as consultants, with only limited penetration in overseas markets. Not surprisingly, then, I am very optimistic about the future of Greg Norman Golf Course Design's growth.

PART FIVE
THE WORLD TOUR YEARS

CHAPTER TWENTY-ONE

Iɴ ᴛʜᴇ ᴇᴀʀʟʏ ꜱᴜᴍᴍᴇʀ of 1994 I had a casual conversation over lunch with John Montgomery, a director of the event management firm Executive Sports International and a good friend of mine. John touched on a dream that had been swirling around in my head for more than seven years. But unlike me and the other people I'd discussed it with, John was taking some concrete action to turn his initiative into reality.

"I'd like to form a World Golf Tour," he said, "with the best players playing against each other in a series of tournaments in different countries."

"That is a great idea," I said. "We really have only four major events where the best players all show up [the Masters, the U.S. Open, the British Open, and the PGA], and only one of those is outside the United States."

"Right!" said John. "But I'd like to schedule between eight and twelve tournaments *in addition* to the four majors. I'd like to invite the top thirty or forty players in the world and play at some of the world's great golf courses—not only in the United States but in Scotland, Spain, Canada, Australia, South Africa, wherever the best courses are."

"That sounds great, John," I said. "What can I do to help?"

"I was hoping you'd say that," he replied. "I have some preliminary plans, but I know it could never become a reality without support from the players. So I thought I'd float the idea by you first."

"Well, I'm definitely interested," I said.

The more John and I talked, the more excited I became. It just seemed like an idea whose time had come. After all, it was the era of the international player. Like me, Nick Price, Seve Ballesteros, Curtis Strange, Nick Faldo, Ian Woosnam, José María Olazábal, Colin Montgomerie, Ernie Els, David Frost, and others all traveled the globe on a regular basis. And I was pretty sure they would also support the idea. We all had to participate in a minimum number of sanctioned events on the PGA Tour to maintain our memberships. But we all played in additional tournaments. Personally, I was maintaining a schedule that included twenty to twenty-five tournaments around the world each year. I believed it was fair and reasonable that once I fulfilled my commitments to the PGA Tour, I could play wherever I wanted. In essence, I viewed myself as an independent contractor. And I believed most of the other professionals felt exactly the same way. In soccer, a similar precedent had already been set, whereby the organizers had created the Premier League, which featured the top twelve teams in the UK that would be eligible to play for the FA Cup. Because they had greater marquee value, they had a separate television contract, schedule, et cetera.

As John and I continued our conversation, we discussed the possibility of having an international golf tour interface with the other major tours in the United States, Europe, Japan, and Australia. Such an endeavor might really bring out the best in everybody. And it could really be great for the sport. There was no question in my mind that the game of golf was going global. As it moved into the future, I could be either a leader or a follower. And, given my personality, that was no choice at all.

In the days and weeks that followed our initial meeting, John and I became tied to the hip with the idea. We put all our energies into it. We had numerous discussions, thought long and hard—and then developed a detailed plan and refined it.

We would call our endeavor the World Tour and start it in 1995 with eight to twelve tournaments running from April through November: four in the United States, one in Canada, one in the UK, one in Spain, one in Japan, and one in Australia. There would be no conflicts with the Masters, U.S. Open, British Open, or PGA. However, an event would be scheduled the week before each of those major championships. All tournaments would be held at a first-class golf course. In fact, we would specifically target a number of courses that had fallen out of the rotation for three of the four majors but were classic courses that both players and viewers would enjoy playing and watching. Golf courses such as Merion, Butler National, Ballybunion, and Carnoustie would be considered. The format would be traditional: 72 holes, 18 holes per day, Thursday through Sunday. The top forty players in the world rankings would be invited to participate along with a minimum of ten sponsor-invited golfers. After our first year, we would look into devising a new world ranking system with the participation of the major tours.

Sponsors and television revenues would provide the prize money, just as they did at PGA Tour events. However, we believed that golf's world market was ready to support a significant increase in tournament purses. Our calculations showed that we would be able to offer at least $3 million per event, with $600,000 going to the winner and a minimum of $30,000 for last place. That was a tenfold increase over what the PGA Tour offered, which was an average of $60,000 first-place prize. In addition, each competing player would receive a $5,000 signing bonus and $50,000 per year for travel expenses. So in essence, a player who competed in all eight World Tour events in the first year was guaranteed $295,000. Not bad by comparison with the PGA Tour, where you received nothing if you missed the cut and had to pay your own travel expenses.

This was a point in which I believed very strongly. A few years before, I had suggested that PGA Tour players who played in tournament pro-ams should receive a per diem, just like athletes in other sports. I figured that if we were going to be out there performing media and public relations duties, we should at the very least have our expenses covered. But I was shouted down by the PGA Tour for suggesting such a thing.

In addition to the prize money for each tournament, the World Tour would offer a year-end bonus pool that would pay $1 million to a Player of the Year (determined by a point system). Each player would be required to participate in a minimum of three tournaments per year to be eligible for the year-end bonus pool. However, there would be no limits as to what other tournaments or exhibitions they could play. The players would have the right and the option to play wherever they wished.

But the biggest and most exciting part of our plan, in my opinion, was the fact that this new tour would be owned by the players. This was very much aligned with the original charter of the PGA Tour when it broke away from the PGA of America in 1968, but in the case of the World Tour it would be much more clearly defined. While it would take some time to flesh this out, it was my intention to create a system in which players would receive equity based on their support for the World Tour. Simply put, the more tournaments they played and the better their performance, the more they would have in the way of shares, options, or warrants. In fact, the initial tax advice we received was very advantageous to the players. Thus, they would build an annuity in the very tour that they helped create. Clearly, there would be a greater weighting to the first-generation players, whose commitment it would take to get the World Tour off the ground.

After finalizing our preliminary plans, John and I sat down to develop a strategy to make it all happen. We had a bit of a catch-22 at first, though. While we needed major corporations and a broadcast partner to become involved, we also knew that golf's top players had to go for the idea. How do you get the players involved before the corporations commit? And how do you get the corporations involved without the players? And any corporate sponsor would not even consider the enterprise unless we had television coverage.

I figured the best place to begin was with the players. So while John drew up a business plan, which we would need to attract corporations, I scheduled as many one-on-one personal conversations with my peers as I could.

Nearly all of the players with whom I spoke expressed genuine enthusiasm for the project. I mean, after all, what was not to like? Top-level competition, higher purses, great courses, and a piece of the action. Several of the guys wondered about conflict with the PGA Tour, and I advised everyone to remain on the Tour just like I

THE WAY OF THE SHARK

was planning to do. The general premise was that this was in the game's best interests. After all, television drives so many aspects of the sports industry today, and, as in every sport, viewers want to see the best playing against the best.

After numerous players had committed their support to me, I felt I had the ammunition I needed to attract a television network. But it was unlikely that NBC, ABC, or CBS would embrace this idea because they were the current broadcast partners of the PGA Tour. So I thought: "Okay, Fox!" Fox had recently created the fourth U.S. free-to-air network on the back of their securing joint television rights for the NFL and were aggressively expanding into new markets around the world. They were on the verge of signing the National Hockey League but did not have golf, which was the ultimate corporate sponsorship.

So I called my friend and fellow Australian David Hill, the head of Fox Sports, and set up a meeting. John Montgomery and I flew out to Los Angeles, pitched our idea, and went through our business plan. The Fox executives liked it from the moment we walked in the door. In the weeks following, Rupert Murdoch, chairman and CEO of the Fox Network, expressed his support for the venture, and we entered into advanced negotiations. Our early discussions revolved around starting the inaugural 1995 season with eight tournaments. We wanted players to have the opportunity to easily fulfill their commitments to their respective tours. After 1995 we could think about expanding to ten or twelve events. Fox would have exclusive television rights in the United States, Canada, and Europe, while we—the World Tour—would retain rights in Australia. For each event, and depending on the broadcast window, Fox would pay $2.25 million to $3.25 million on a graduated yearly basis.

In a relatively brief period of time, John and I agreed in principle to a six-year contract with a four-year option with the Fox Network worth a guaranteed $113 million. That was far more than the PGA Tour had in place with all three of the major U.S. networks combined. Everything, of course, hinged on getting players and sponsors signed up.

In the meantime, John left his job with Executive Sports to be-

come executive director of the newly incorporated World Tour, and
he and I both worked diligently on all of the things you have to do
to make a new business succeed. We started working on a mission
statement and a press package and setting up an office. We laid out
plans to inform all the major golf tours and establish working relationships. For financial backing perspective, we approached the
PGA Tour's "shadow" sponsors: If Delta and Coca-Cola were the official sponsors of the PGA Tour, we spoke to American Airlines and
Pepsi. Not surprisingly, we got a very strong and positive reaction
to the concept. We started working on involving some of the great
golf courses around the world. And we began drawing up contracts.
Once the sites were chosen, we'd secure the sponsors—and then the
players would follow.

Or at least that was the plan.

Now, remember that John and I were taking all these steps in
July and August of 1994: talking to players, negotiating with Fox,
speaking with potential sponsors and golf course directors. We
weren't particularly trying to keep anything secret. But we were not
overtly telling everybody what we were up to, either. Not surprisingly, word of our deal with Fox reached people at the highest levels
of the PGA Tour. And their reactions were predictable. "What? A
ten-year, $113 million deal for eight or twelve tournaments! Purses
of $3 million! How did they do that? Why can't we do that?" I mean,
sirens must have sounded at Tour headquarters in Ponte Vedra. If I
had had any idea this was happening, I would immediately have
gone up there to try and ease any fears they might have had. But to
tell you the truth, I didn't know anything about it. John and I were
working hard building our enterprise, and our plan was to speak to
the PGA Tour when we felt the timing was right.

Looking back, we should have considered making an early announcement, even though we didn't have all our ducks in a row.
Because on September 6, 1994, just prior to the start of the Bell Canadian Open, PGA Tour commissioner Tim Finchem gave a speech
in which he noted, among a number of items, that the Tour was taking steps to form "a new international match play event in 1995"
that would invite players from the PGA Tour, the European Tour,
the Japanese Tour, and a combined Australian–South African Tour.

The four winners would then convene for a televised two-day event. Finchem did not say much more than that and noted that detailed information would be completed in a month or two, when sites and dates would be announced. This was one of many items mentioned in a relatively minor speech outside the country. I didn't hear about it at the time, and nobody around me ever mentioned it. So John and I just kept forging ahead with our plans.

A couple of weeks later, at the inaugural Presidents Cup (held at the Robert Trent Jones Golf Club in Manassas, Virginia), Finchem and the heads of the four other major world golf tours (Australasia, Europe, Japan, and South Africa) were reported to have formed a new group (later named the International Federation of PGA Tours) for the purpose of "discussing matters of common interest relating to the internationalization of the game of golf." Once again, this was done rather quietly, without a lot of fanfare from the media. After all, the first Presidents Cup was really the main story.

Within a month's time, however, the PGA Tour had set up a task force to gather information and formally evaluate the World Tour. To head the group, Finchem appointed Ed Moorhouse, executive vice president for legal and international affairs for the PGA Tour. In other words, he was the organization's top attorney (if you didn't count Finchem, who was also a lawyer).

While I was traveling on business and playing golf, John Montgomery began getting calls from the PGA Tour requesting information. So on October 22, 1994, some of our representatives agreed to participate in an informational meeting at Tour headquarters. Our guys gave them the basics of the World Tour as we saw it, discussed our governance with them, made a few proposals, and assured their representatives that we were in no way trying to harm the PGA Tour. Later that day, Moorhouse released a statement pointing out that there were "enormous difficulties in trying to accommodate" the World Tour, that the PGA Tour had "commitments to existing tournaments, sponsors, networks, and charities that we must and will fulfill," and that it seemed "highly unlikely" that anything could be worked out in the short term. A recommendation, Moorhouse wrote, would be prepared for the Tour's Tournament Policy Board to consider.

While the PGA Tour circled its wagons, some strange things started to happen. John Montgomery was contacted by his former employer—whom he had left six weeks earlier—and told that several PGA Tour sponsors had reported being asked to reexamine their contractual relationships with Executive Sports International.

Also, small bits of misinformation began to seep out: "Greg Norman will resign from the PGA Tour." "Fox will own the World Tour." "Executive Sports is running the show." At this point, John and I felt we had no choice but to set the record straight and hold a press conference announcing the details of our enterprise. So we chose Thursday, November 17, 1994—during my golf tournament, the Shark Shootout (at Sherwood Country Club in Thousand Oaks, California). A significant number of media would be in attendance, and it was my "home turf," so to speak. That was sooner than we'd planned to make a formal announcement, but it needed to be done.

On the Tuesday of the Shootout (two days before our scheduled announcement), I was participating in some of my duties as tournament host when one of the pros came up and informed me that there were a number of PGA Tour administrators on the practice tee speaking with players. "They're saying: 'Don't do it. Don't support the World Tour. If you do, you won't be a member of the PGA Tour.'"

Then I received a hand-delivered letter from Finchem. "Dear Greg," it read. "Attached is a copy of a statement that I released this afternoon commenting on the formation of a so-called World Tour. I just became aware of this endeavor over the last forty-eight hours and am attempting to obtain more information. I understand the promoters intend to make an announcement this Thursday."

I have since learned, of course, that Finchem knew about our organization long before the "last forty-eight hours," as he claimed. His letter went on: "I was amazed that the so-called Fox Network World Tour in which you are involved has progressed to [this] point . . . and that the matter had not been previously discussed with me. . . . I considered it essential that I issue a statement clarifying the Tour's position with respect to this matter; a copy is attached."

Obviously, Finchem was trying to lay some sort of legal paper trail because our representatives had, in fact, traveled to PGA Tour headquarters and met with PGA Tour representatives a month earlier. So he was clearly informed, although not personally by John or me.

Finchem closed by stating: "I have had discussions this afternoon with the player directors on the Tournament Policy Board, who are fully supportive of the Tour's position. I urge you to consider your obligations as a PGA Tour member and not become involved in any endeavor which would have an adverse impact on the PGA Tour, its membership, and the numerous charities that rely on us."

To me, that last statement was a veiled threat—and I was angry about it. But that was minor compared to what I read in the attached press statement, in which Finchem had come out hard against the World Tour.

"The PGA Tour has learned today," the statement began, "[that the] Fox Television Network plans to underwrite a series of new professional golf tournaments in 1995 at an annual cost in excess of $25 million. . . . The fields for each event will be limited to 30–40 players and the promoters of these events will seek to include PGA Tour members in their fields."

While I was reading this, I just couldn't fathom why the commissioner of the PGA Tour would issue a statement to the press announcing our World Tour before we had a chance to do it ourselves. Clearly, he was launching a preemptive strike.

"Our policy is to accommodate as many playing opportunities for our members as possible," the statement went on to say. "We are in favor of increased international competition. . . . Over the past few years, the PGA has had discussions with other golf organizations about a series of events that could be scheduled in addition to the various international tour schedules. Any consideration of this project has included three criteria: 1) It must be to the benefit of the game of golf, 2) it must command the support of all golf organizations, and 3) it must be structured in a manner that would have a positive impact on the existing tours and their memberships."

Finchem concluded by stating that, in his view, the World Tour

"fails to meet any of these three criteria," that it "would have a negative impact on existing events," that it would "result in fewer playing opportunities for the great majority of our members," and that
it would lead to "an inevitable reduction in the $24.7 million raised
for charity in the communities where our tournaments were played
this year." Therefore, wrote Finchem, the PGA Tour would "fulfill
its long-term agreements with television networks, title sponsors,
and tournaments by enforcing our television release and conflicting event regulations."

It was very clear to any professional golfer who read this statement that the commissioner would not grant conflicting-event releases, which was tantamount to saying he would suspend and/or
fine any player who participated in the World Tour. A number of the
pros expressed some real concern about Finchem's statement, so I
set up a meeting with them that evening. Although I was clearly on
the defensive (which was the PGA Tour's intention), I spent two
hours with about twenty players explaining the World Tour's format and our true intentions. I told them all that the World Tour
could coexist with the PGA Tour, that each player could still play his
minimum of fifteen events, and that the Tour's threat to not grant
releases or to suspend or fine players was nothing less than an overt
restraint of trade. "Everybody can help each other in this situation,"
I said. "I think the World Tour would bring the best of everything
together, with the best players playing against each other week in
and week out."

The next day (Wednesday, November 16, 1994), Ken Schofield
(executive director of the European Tour) and Jeff Monday (executive director of the American Golf Sponsors) both released statements echoing Finchem's position in regard to the World Tour. They
were concerned, they stated, that it would dilute fields at existing
events and breach PGA Tour contracts with sponsors and networks.
Of course, I knew all too well, as promoter of both a PGA Tour–
sanctioned event and a European Tour event, that the Tour makes
no guarantees to the tournament promoters, sponsors, or networks
with regard to quality of field. It was obvious to me now that the
PGA Tour representatives had prepared ahead of time for the Shark
Shootout. They had spoken with players, sponsors, and directors of

other tours, and put out a consistent message that the World Tour would be bad for the PGA Tour, bad for them, and bad for golf.

That evening a meeting was held in the boardroom of the Sherwood Country Club for all the players who wished to attend. Finchem showed up personally for this meeting. As I sat in the back of the room and listened to the PGA Tour's spiel, I became more and more downhearted. Their message was that the World Tour was a bad idea, a bad concept—and that it was Greg Norman's deal: *about* Greg Norman and *for* Greg Norman.

Just when I didn't think I could feel any worse, Arnold Palmer stood up and gave a long, impassioned plea against both me and the whole idea of the World Tour. By what he said, I felt sure that either Finchem or IMG (which represented Palmer) had spoken with Arnold ahead of time and that his reaction was based on hearing only one side of the story (and perhaps the fact that IMG was feeling a bit upset that they had not come up with the concept). I had never had a conversation with him about any of this prior to his speech. It was one of the most disappointing moments of my life, being dressed down by one of the greats of the game, a man I truly respected, a man who over the years has had his own issues with the PGA Tour. It tore me up, but I just decided to remain silent.

Afterward, a number of players spoke to the press. "I would hate to see anything interfere with the PGA Tour," said one. "It's been the lifeblood of golf and should continue to be the showcase for professional golf. It's not something you rush into without proper concessions. Greg simply moved too fast."

"Having tournaments like the World Tour is probably what everybody in the world wants to see," stated another. "But I think it could be very detrimental to the PGA Tour."

One player did speak up for the concept, however. "If I play the required minimum fifteen events [on the PGA Tour], fair is fair," said Nick Price. "I should be able to play elsewhere. There is room for this World Tour."

After a round of golf the next day (November 17, 1994), John Montgomery and I held our scheduled press conference. We explained the schedule of events and the structure of the World Tour.

We emphasized that charities around the world would be served and that junior clinics with minority involvement would be held in conjunction with tournaments. We stated that there were no plans to expand to full-schedule status, that we intended to work out mutually beneficial relationships with all tours that might be affected, and that I, personally, had no plans to resign from the PGA Tour. I also stated that we intended to be open and honest with everybody—and that I truly believed our tour was going to be good for the game of golf.

But it was really too late. The PGA Tour's efforts had really trumped us. The World Tour had become a negative in the minds of most of the pros, and at this point it would prove almost impossible to reverse those feelings. Still, we weren't going to go down without a fight.

That same day, Fox Sports issued a press release (even though we were still in ongoing negotiations) stating that they had reached an agreement to broadcast World Tour events. I greatly appreciated Fox's continued support.

Finchem, who had been roundly criticized by John Montgomery for stating that Executive Sports International was involved in our venture, then sent a letter to John blaming me for his error. "In a conversation with Greg Norman on Tuesday, he told me that the Montgomerys [meaning John and his son] were involved with a proposed new World Tour being organized by Fox Television Network. I am now aware for the first time that Executive Sports, Inc., is not involved in the proposed new World Tour." Finchem then apologized "for any confusion that may have occurred" but also defended himself by saying that "neither Greg Norman nor your son indicated to me a non-involvement by Executive Sports, Inc."

When I read this, I didn't understand how I would be expected to mention something that wasn't occurring in the first place. It would be like me stating to somebody that neither President Bush nor Santa Claus was involved in the enterprise either.

In his letter, Finchem also made a categorical denial. "I have . . . become aware of a rumor that certain PGA Tour staff had contacted our sponsors asking them to reexamine their contractual relationships with Executive Sports, Inc.," he wrote. "Let me assure you that this is nothing but a rumor. Neither I, nor any other member of the PGA Tour staff, have suggested or will suggest to any sponsor that they not honor any contractual obligations they may have to Executive Sports, Inc."

The next day, American Golf Sponsors executive director Jeff Monday also wrote a letter to John Montgomery clarifying the incorrect statement he had made regarding Executive Sports. But rather than blame me for the error, he blamed an unnamed PGA Tour official. "When initially contacted Tuesday, November 15, I was informed that in conversation with John Montgomery, the Tour had been made aware of an imminent press conference regarding a World Tour," wrote Monday. "It was indicated that Greg Norman had stated he was working with the 'Montgomerys' and, as 'Executive Sports' and the 'Montgomerys' are virtually synonymous . . ."

Clearly, American Golf Sponsors had received false information from the PGA Tour. But we had already suspected that such conversations were taking place behind the scenes.

CHAPTER TWENTY-TWO

AFTER THE SHARK SHOOTOUT, I sat down by myself for several hours to think about everything that had happened. And the more I thought about it, the more dejected I became. PGA Tour executives had reacted emotionally and defensively to our idea for the World Tour. They didn't perform their due diligence and moved too quickly—which is why incorrect statements were made. Moreover, I could tell that a set of "talking points" had been created by the PGA Tour, and that these messages were conveyed in an effective and consistent manner to the players, to the sponsors, to the directors of the other tours, and to the media.

It will harm the PGA Tour.

Tournaments will lose their sponsors.

Sponsors will lose revenues.

It will negatively impact charities.

It will be bad for golf in general.

It is about short-term money gains.

It is about Greg Norman.

Do not bite the hand that feeds you.

Do not turn your back on the PGA Tour.

These points were repeated over and over by different people. For example, several players made virtually identical statements to the press. "You just can't turn your back on the people who supported you all these years," said one. "We can't just turn our backs on the PGA Tour," said another. "Tournaments will lose their sponsors!"

At this point I did not want to give up on the World Tour. I had made commitments, and people were depending on me. I was simply not going to turn my back on my friends or a great idea whose time, I believed, had come. So we attempted to work things out with the PGA Tour.

Along with John Montgomery, I met personally with Finchem and expressed a willingness to be flexible in our planning, and we agreed to have additional discussions. But right after that meeting, the commissioner issued another press statement in which he emphasized that "an accommodation would be extremely difficult." He stated that the PGA Tour didn't have any flexibility at all from January 9 to October 29 because every one of their events is on TV. Then he closed with "Arnold Palmer and the other organizers of the modern PGA Tour set standards for golf and established a structure that has worked well. [Actually, it was Gardner Dickinson who started the PGA Tour.] As we move forward in the world of golf and address inevitable change, we must be vigilant of those standards and structures and make sure that changes better the whole world of golf, not just individual participants."

When I read his statement, not more than two days after what I thought was a productive meeting, it became clear to me that Finchem really didn't want to work anything out with us. And it was also pretty clear to me that he was subtly accusing those of us associated with the World Tour of trying to enrich ourselves individually rather than doing what was best for golf.

On November 22, 1994, a two-and-a-half-hour meeting was held at PGA Tour headquarters, attended by staffs only. The PGA Tour suggested that our events be scheduled during November and December so there would be no conflicts with any of their tournaments. But Fox vetoed that idea because they didn't want golf competing with football. We then offered to stage only six events during the regular season and have the final two after October 29. In addition, we offered a subsidy payment of $300,000 to every PGA tournament for which there was a conflict with a World Tour event. "No, no, you can't do that" was the initial response. "You can't subsidize any event. We won't agree to that." Subsequently, however, the PGA Tour came back with a proposal that we pay them $2 million per event; they claimed to be interested only in the World Tour scheduling tournaments outside the PGA Tour's money season. Obviously, it was completely ludicrous for them to pluck a number like $2 million out of the air and expect anybody to seriously consider it. In truth, I believe it was either a flat-out shakedown or a sign that they never had any intentions of working with us at all.

Over the next week or so, we issued some press releases of our own. Our mission statement described the philosophy and foundation upon which we planned to participate in professional golf. We stated that we were not interested in abandoning any of the present tours around the world; we wanted to coexist and raise the level of competition; and we wanted to preserve the quality and integrity of the game. Another of our communications pointed out that golf was growing at the phenomenal rate of 14 percent per year in the United States—and double that number for the entire world. That growth rate, I believe, was caused by the international players, who were dominating the game on a global basis. The U.S. Tour was basically a domestic tour and was not spreading its wings internationally. The opportunity for a World Tour was ripe in the mid-1990s. Ten years later, however, growth in the game of golf would become stagnant, if not negative.

John Montgomery and I also sent out letters to players and sponsors with hopes of regaining their support. For the players, we attempted to counter the PGA Tour's threat of suspension by offering to provide an exemption into the field of every World Tour event for the duration of the suspension. We also offered players control of their own images outside World Tour events, which was a bone of contention for many golfers.

Meanwhile, the PGA Tour continued to issue press releases of their own and contact players and sponsors. Finchem repeated his intention to enforce the Tour's tournament regulations and stated that a number of sponsors had contacted him "expressing their concern over the new tour and demanding that the Tour honor its contractual commitments." I just didn't buy this last statement, though. It was far more likely that the sponsors were being contacted first by the PGA Tour and asked for their support. I don't believe that any reputable sponsor could possibly suspect that the PGA Tour would not honor its contractual commitments.

On November 29, 1994, immediately after a meeting of the PGA Tour Policy Board, Finchem sent me a letter with an attached press statement. "The Tournament Policy Board has agreed with me," he wrote, "that it is not possible for the PGA Tour to endorse the World Tour since . . . many of its events must occur during our official money season." He informed me that it was a unanimous decision and then urged me to commit myself "to a constructive course of action in realizing our mutual goals."

The attached press release said pretty much the same thing, but it went on to note that the commissioner intended to honor the conflicting event and television release rules. "If a new tour becomes a reality in 1995 or thereafter," stated Finchem, "our members will have to decide whether they want to continue to play on the PGA Tour or play on a new tour." This was a threat that could not be enforced legally because the players had rights. Finchem concluded by stating that he was pleased with the support of the players "and their willingness to put what is best for the game of golf and all of those involved in it ahead of short-term monetary gains."

Two days later, I telephoned Finchem and told him that I was disappointed in his statement, as well as his assertion that this was about my commercial interests and not the game of golf, and that I still wanted to work out a mutually beneficial compromise. It was a cordial conversation, and he thanked me for calling. But later that day, the commissioner issued another formal press release stating that he and I had spoken and that I had indicated I would "not support any venture that would damage the PGA Tour, our tournaments, or their sponsors." He concluded his statement by saying: "I appreciate Greg's reevaluation of this situation."

Well, of course, I hadn't reevaluated anything. Sure enough, the next day, I received a request from a golf writer asking me for a statement because there was now a great deal of confusion as to my position with the World Tour. Was I lessening my commitment to the venture as it now stood, or was I as committed as ever, he asked.

I contacted John Montgomery, and he immediately issued a press release. "I spoke with Greg Norman last night and he reiterated his complete support of the World Tour and we are continuing to move ahead as planned," the statement read. "Greg's position hasn't changed one bit and his commitment is as firm as ever. As we both said in the past, we all share the concern that we don't want to destroy any tour. We feel there is room for both."

From that point forward, the public relations campaign against the World Tour and me personally really ratcheted up. I started receiving negative letters from sponsors and tournament directors from all around the United States. "The World Tour threatens our very existence," read one. "We will lose NBC-TV. Dollars that were raised for youth-oriented charities will be nonexistent. Our city will not have a professional golf tournament. Golf will become a sordid mess. This will destroy the very proving ground that Greg Norman and others used to get where they are now. I ask you to consider what this will do to the Tour as a whole. Money should not be the overriding issue here."

As with the previous player comments, these letters were very consistent in the points made. And I could just imagine someone from the PGA Tour scaring the sponsors and tournament directors to death and then coaching them on what to say.

The media also had a field day. "The Tour War has produced more spin than a Greg Norman wedge shot," wrote one reporter. And that was an understatement. Headlines and subtitles included things like "The World Tour will have immediate ramifications for the PGA Tour and golf around the world" and "It will change the shape and scope of professional competition." And then there were the personal attacks on me. "Greg Norman blindsided the golf world." "Norman is asking golfers to bite the hand that feeds him. He's going to destroy the PGA Tour, a billion-dollar industry." "This World Tour is bad for the game of golf." "Greg Norman is bad for the game of golf." "The only reason Fox is involved is because Rupert Murdoch and Greg Norman are Australian buddies."

Heck, NBC even filed a petition with the Federal Communications Commission asserting that the Fox television network was illegal. They wanted Fox to reduce its level of foreign ownership because more than 99 percent of the corporation's equity was held by Murdoch, who was based in Australia.

The things that bothered me most, however, were the personal attacks on my businesses. We received telephone calls from PGA club professionals all around the country canceling their orders with Greg Norman Collection. They didn't want our business, they said, because Greg Norman was trying to ruin the PGA Tour.

Well, I obtained the phone numbers of every one of the pros who canceled orders and called them personally. "Look, you've heard one side of the story," I said to them. "I'd like you to hear my side of the story, and afterward I'll respect your decision. But I won't respect you if you cancel and don't hear my side of the story."

Each call lasted about five minutes—just long enough for me to get a concise message across to them. And you know what? One hundred percent of the people I spoke to reordered with Greg Norman Collection. I hate to think what would have happened if I had sat still and not fought back. Fortunately, today our clothing line is a strong business and growing at a rapid rate.

I wish I could say the same for the World Tour.

By February 1995, the whole thing was unraveling real fast. Nearly all the players from whom I had received verbal support had changed their minds. "If the PGA Tour is not involved, I won't play," said one. "I like the concept because it's the free enterprise system at work," said another. "But I'm not going to turn my back on the PGA Tour."

And that about sums it up. Without the players, we agreed with Fox to postpone the discussions for several months and reconsider launching the World Tour in 1996. But in all honesty, the damage had been done and we had lost all momentum. Interestingly, that next year, the Fox Network purchased the television rights for NASCAR, which today has the second-largest viewing audience after the NFL. Clearly, Fox had the appetite to televise another mainstream sport, and golf had lost its opportunity to have their support.

CHAPTER TWENTY-THREE

THAT'S BLOODY GREG NORMAN!" the groom shouted. "That's bloody Greg Norman!"

Bart Collins and I were cutting through one of Sydney's back-streets on the way to our hotel when we heard the shouting. "Look! It's a wedding party just coming out of the church," said Bart.

My first reaction was to tap the brakes, then hit the accelerator, then the brakes again. I couldn't make up my mind whether to stop or just wave.

"Awww, okay, okay," I finally said, pulling the car over to the curb. Then I jumped out and went over and shook hands with everybody.

"Could we get some pictures with you, Greg?"

"Absolutely, mate. Let's do it."

I stood for pictures with the bride and groom together, the bride alone, the groom alone, the best man, the matron of honor, most of the guests, and, of course, the minister. Then I shook every-body's hands again, got back in the driver's seat, and started back to our hotel.

"I didn't think you were going to stop," said Bart.

"Aw, how many times does a guy get married?" I replied.

I had pulled Bart out of a tuna tower while we were fishing for black marlin on the Great Barrier Reef. He had been with IMG for twelve years, was Steve Elkington's first agent, and was currently running IMG's Singapore operations. Before he was transferred to Asia, Bart and I had worked together, from 1987 to 1991, when he was my IMG representative in Australia. As a matter of fact, he was the guy who worked with me to form and manage my partnership with IMG for golf course design.

I had invited him down for some fishing and diving, and I began telling him about my long-term business strategy. Bart immediately understood what I was talking about. Then he began speaking about GWSE, about establishing a brand, and about business in general. He was bright, dedicated, and focused—three things that I always look for in people. So I asked him if he would consider returning to Australia to head up my operations there.

"How will it work with Frank Williams?" Bart asked.

"Frank runs the show in the U.S. You'll run the show here. Both of you will report directly to me. And in a few years, the two of you might switch jobs if you like. Frank spent thirty years in Australia and wants to come back."

Bart and I talked for quite a while about details, terms, and the intricacies of working together. When he indicated he wanted an employment contract, I smiled and said, "I'm sorry, Bart, but I don't do employment contracts. This is all about good faith. You just have to jump in with both feet."

After an extended pause, he looked at me and asked an interesting question: "I notice that you're right-handed, but you wear your watch on your right wrist. Why do you do that?"

"Well, when I was a kid and got my first watch, I looked around and saw that everybody else wore their watches on their left wrists. I just wanted to be different."

"Tell you what," Bart responded. "I'd be happy to come work for you under the terms we've just discussed, and as a show of good faith, I'll wear my watch on my right wrist as well. It will symbolize our agreement—my loyalty." I'm pleased to say that, ten years later, Bart is still wearing his watch on his right wrist.

Several years later, Bart would switch jobs with Frank and move to Florida. And when Frank eventually retired, Bart became president of the company. Meanwhile he ran all aspects of GWSE in Australia and Asia as we began to expand our business portfolio.

When Bart first got rolling with my company, I could tell he was a brilliant marketer. He had all the smarts, all the talent, all the energy, the trust, the loyalty—everything was there. But due to his time with IMG, he had more of a tactical approach than a strategic one. So I focused on teaching him to be more in tune with my long-term vision. I wanted him to think fifteen years ahead. Eventually, Bart became an integral part of the success of GWSE. And now I listen to his opinions and confidently delegate authority to him.

Not long after I set up the Australian base of our operations, I bought out IMG's interests in my golf course design business. It wasn't a major transaction, as it was a service-oriented business that relied on my personal interaction. With that buyout, my legal ties to IMG were now completely severed.

Back in the United States, I created an opportunity off the back of my golf course design business. Given my experience playing and designing golf courses around the world, I came to realize that architects had only a few choices when it came to selecting turf grass for their golf courses in the United States. In the Sunbelt, there were really only two hybrid Bermuda grasses. Because the use of these grasses was so extensive, it was often difficult to get quality stock of a pure strain. The result, unfortunately, was that the grasses would often mutate into less consistent turf grasses after one or two years. Jason McCoy, who'd graduated from Lakeland College's School of Agronomics, and I reflected on this quite a bit. We felt that if we could identify a pure strain of hybrid Bermuda grass, we could give designers and developers a better alternative.

The answer, interestingly enough, came out of Perth, in Western Australia. There we identified a pure strain of hybrid Bermuda grass that we had used on golf courses in Australia. It was just being introduced into the U.S. and was midway through FDA registration. We approached Hugh Whiting, who owned the patent—literally the DNA fingerprint—and bought the master license for the grass in the U.S., which we then branded as GN-1. We hired David Barnes and opened a turf farm in Avon Park, Florida, that would maintain the foundation stock for GN-1 as well as other test plots. The foundation stock would then be accessed for the

Jamie Hutton, sporting the winner's plaid jacket, was an inspirational force during the 1988 MCI Heritage.

This was just after I chipped in for birdie to win the 1995 World Series of Golf.

Gregory helps me read a putt at St. Andrews during the 2005 British Open.

Traffic came to a stop on Sydney Harbour Bridge when I ran
with the torch prior to the Opening Ceremonies for the 2000
Summer Olympics.

Helping promote the Australian Tourist Commission with their commercial
shoot in Sydney Harbour.

A 2003 shot of *Aussie Rules* during a stopover in Bora Bora on its maiden voyage from Australia to the United States.

Reviewing a herd of Greg Norman Australian Prime cattle at Ganoo Station in Queensland.

Golf Digest took this photo during the 2001 PGA Merchandise Show. That's my Bell helicopter in the background.

In Australia's Yarra Valley with Greg Norman Estates manager Hugh Cuthbertson (1998).

Posing with my daughter, Morgan, for a Greg Norman Estates Father's Day promotion.

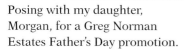

At a Medallist Developments board meeting. Seated across from me (second from right) is Bill Moss of Macquarie Bank.

Billboard in Times Square for Greg Norman Collection (1995).

Reviewing one of our early routings for Tuscany Reserve with Pete Dye (left) and Jason McCoy.

Staring at Doughmore Bay and the majestic Irish coastline on one of my early site visits to Doonbeg.

Reviewing the Ellerston golf course during construction with Kerry Packer (left) and Bob Harrison (center).

An unorthodox golf course design visit to Cornerstone in Ouray County, Colorado. Jason McCoy and Chris Campbell are seated on the right.

My induction ceremony into the World Golf Hall of Fame in November 2001.

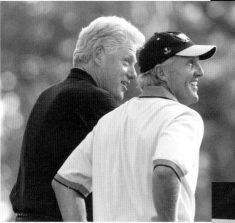

With President Clinton during the 1998 Presidents Cup at Royal Melbourne.

My good friend Paul Fireman, founder and former chairman of Reebok.

Sharing a laugh with President George H. W. Bush during Three Friends: One Goal, a fundraiser for tsunami relief.

With good friends Nelson Peltz (left) and Kerry Packer before a round of golf at Shadow Creek in Las Vegas.

Exchanging jabs with The Greatest, Muhammad Ali, before the 2004 American Australian Association's annual benefit dinner.

Being awarded an honorary doctorate at Griffith University in Queensland, Australia, in 1998.

A camel train walks across what will soon be the eighth fairway at Jumeirah Golf Estates in the United Arab Emirates.

On the helipad at the Burj-Al-Arab in Dubai with Sultan Ahmed bin Sulayem, chairman of Nakheel. *The Palm* is visible in the background.

My office for 600-plus hours a year, a Gulfstream G550.

establishment of other turf farms, golf courses, et cetera. We began specifying the grass for our own golf courses, which immediately gained a very strong reputation for quality, durability, a quick recovery rate, and a distinct emerald-green color. Our next step was to expand the business by licensing to other growers across the Sunbelt of the United States. To do that, we needed to market the product aggressively in order to create a high demand. In just three years, GN-1 was used for two Super Bowls and a World Series and was the grass of choice for the 2000 Summer Olympic Games at Sydney Olympic Stadium.

Greg Norman Turf Company (GNTC) is a classic example of capitalizing on an adjacent-space opportunity. Within only a few years, GWSE had several top-quality turf producers throughout the United States—including those in Florida, Georgia, North Carolina, Oklahoma, Texas, New Mexico, Arizona, and California—that were licensed growers of our sod. This new business turned out to be a good profit center for us, and it also provided a good and timely source of grass for our golf course design business.

With the turf business, however, I made several mistakes from which I would learn. First of all, I learned something in terms of how *not* to brand. We called our first two varieties of turf grass GN-1 and GN-Z, the latter being a strain of zoysia. In hindsight, those were probably not great names. Why? Because other golf course designers, especially those who were former professional golfers, were not likely to specify a grass that contained the imprint of another designer. In fact, it was my experience that they would go out of their way *not* to specify our grasses, even though they were two of the best products available. With time, we dropped the Norman imprint and developed other products, including another strain of hybrid Bermuda grass, which we named Aussie Green.

Another mistake I made was in deviating from the original plan by opening the business in Florida rather than appointing a licensee. We believed we could reap a higher profit if we operated Florida ourselves. So we purchased additional land and developed sales, marketing, delivery, and transportation capabilities. Handling all those operations in-house was a stretch. But we corrected that mistake by selling our turf farm and restructuring our company under a licensing model, whereby we had low overheads and earned our income through royalties.

All the time we were building golf courses and entering the turf business, I was playing a full schedule of golf. In 1995, I finished third in the Masters, was runner-up again in the U.S. Open, 15th in the British Open, and 20th in the PGA Championship. We played the 1995 U.S. Open at Shinnecock Hills on Long Island, but, unlike in 1986 when they had armed guards patrolling the galleries because of death threats I'd received, the galleries this time were pulling for me. What a difference nine years can make!

I started Sunday's final round tied for the lead with Tom Lehman, with whom I played in the final group. On the very first hole, though, there was an ominous sign that it might not be my day. I blasted a beautiful long drive down the center of the fairway and had only a short wedge for my approach shot. I just knew I was going to get it close and have a good chance at birdie, but my ball hit the flagstick and kicked off the green. That's the way my entire round seemed to go. Meanwhile, Corey Pavin, playing one group ahead, was having a great round. And when he came to the 18th hole, he was clinging to a one-shot lead over me. When I was told that Corey had a 229-yard approach shot to the green, I figured I might have a chance to catch him if I could birdie one of the final two holes. But then I heard a tremendous roar in the distance. It turned out that Corey hit one of the great shots in U.S. Open history. He used a 4-wood to knock his ball pin high and only five feet from the hole. His animated run up the fairway to get a glimpse of where his ball had come to rest is still remembered by golf fans. With that shot, Corey Pavin won the U.S. Open and forever shed that dreaded moniker, "best player never to have won a major."

I felt I could have done better toward the end of that particular tournament. I played the last two rounds 7 over par and actually went 32 consecutive holes without a birdie. But as I told the media afterward, I wasn't going to lose any sleep over finishing second. The 1995 U.S. Open was the seventh time I'd finished second in a major golf tournament.

I did manage, however, to win four golf tournaments in 1995 (the Memorial, the Greater Hartford Open, the World Series of Golf, and the Australian Open). In all, I played in sixteen tournaments on the PGA Tour and was in contention virtually every week. I finished in the Top 25 fourteen times and had nine Top 10 finishes. It was only my withdrawal from the MCI Classic after two rounds (due to a back injury) that prevented me from winning the Vardon Trophy for best scoring average. That honor went to my buddy Steve Elkington, and I was glad for him. I was fortunate to lead the PGA Tour money list that year, with a single-season record of $1,654,959. And that total moved me ahead of Tom Kite as the all-time money leader, with $9,592,828.

When people speak to me about 1995, however, they usually bring up my victory at Firestone Country Club in the World Series of Golf, because it occurred amid controversy. I began the final round 6 strokes behind the leader, Vijay Singh. But after firing a 67, I ended regulation in a tie with Nick Price and Billy Mayfair, so the three of us proceeded to sudden death. On the first playoff hole, while Nick and Billy were eyeing birdie putts for victory, I ended up chipping in with a 7-iron from sixty feet off the green. And when they missed their putts, I was the one who had finally snatched victory from the jaws of defeat.

The controversy in this tournament occurred during Thursday's first round, after which I almost withdrew. I was on the 7th green when I saw my playing partner, Mark McCumber, repair a spike mark on the line of his putt. Now, that was a blatant violation of the rules, and it should have resulted in a 2-stroke penalty.

I've always had a strong-driving internal force: When on the golf course, you had to do the right thing. I don't manufacture things. I don't start rumors. I don't imagine things. I deal only in facts. And when I saw what McCumber did, I just had to say something. So I immediately called him on it, but he said it was only a pebble. Not satisfied with his response, I informed a PGA Tour official about the infraction. What disappointed me most, however, was the fact that McCumber's story changed with time. One minute it was a pebble, the next minute it was a twig. Then it was a leaf. And then a bug.

At the end of the day, we were separated in the scorer's hut. They cleared everybody out—players, volunteers, everybody. One official took me aside to hear my story. Another official got McCumber's version. The officials finally ruled that there was inconclusive evidence because it was essentially one person's word against another's. But then McCumber pulled me aside. "Well, if this is going to create an international incident," he said, "then I'll take the penalty."

After all of his denials, and after putting us through that entire charade, I must admit that I just lost it. I was so angry I could have bench-pressed five hundred pounds. "You know what?" I said. "For you to make that comment at this juncture is ridiculous. I've had enough of this. I'm withdrawing from the tournament. I'm out of here."

I refused to sign McCumber's scorecard, and I went straight to the locker room and packed my bag. Then I hurried to the parking lot, got in my car, and drove off. I picked up my mobile phone and called Laura. "I'll be home tonight," I said.

After I explained to her what had happened, she tried to talk me out of leaving. But I was hearing none of it at that point. The next call I made was to my pilot, Guy Maira, telling him to get the plane ready.

Then it was my phone that started to ring. Tony Navarro, my caddie, was beside himself. He tried to talk me into staying. Then Slugger White, a Tour official and good friend of mine, called and tried to talk me into staying. "Come on back, Greg," he said. "You don't want to cut off your nose to spite your face. Going out there and winning this golf tournament is the best thing you can do right now."

And then I got a call, believe it or not, from Tim Finchem, who also tried to talk me out of leaving. "Too bad!" I snapped back. "I'm out of here."

My phone rang off the hook all the way back to the hotel. By that time, however, I had begun to cool down, eventually bringing myself to the conclusion that it would be better to play the tournament and try to win.

This particular episode made a lot of headlines. Some people said, "Bravo, Norman." Others said I had violated an unwritten rule of golf by calling another player on breaking the rules. But in one of my very first tournaments, I was called on something by Bruce Crampton. That's the way professional golf is. There has to be a code of honor out there, and we cannot simply turn our heads when we see what we believe is an infraction. I saw what I saw and I stepped out for the game of golf.

Another reason I reacted so strongly is that I have always had a very deep sense of right versus wrong. I place the highest priority on my integrity and ethics in life, in business, in golf—in everything I do. I am not the kind of person who sits back and says, "Well, let someone else handle it." I wasn't picking on McCumber for any particular reason. I'd done it before to other golfers.

On one occasion I called out Jumbo Ozaki—in his home country of Japan—but I felt I was absolutely justified. Jumbo had a habit of hitting a tee shot and then strolling down the fairway with his driver still in his hand. That's all well and good, but occasionally he would use the driver to tap down the grass behind his ball, thus improving his lie.

I had seen Jumbo break the rules before—a couple of times, in fact. The first incident occurred during an Australia-versus-Japan team competition. Jumbo flipped the coin he was using to mark his ball several inches closer to the hole before a critical putt. This happened very early in my professional career, and I decided not to say anything about it.

The second incident happened on the 72nd hole of a tournament when we were both in contention. It had rained all week, so the fairways were extremely soft, yet we were still playing the ball down. The finishing hole was a par-5, and Jumbo tapped down the soggy grass behind his ball, which had the effect, essentially, of setting his ball on a tee. He knocked his second shot on the green, 2-putted for birdie, and won the tournament by a shot. I approached several players and tournament officials in the locker room after that round and explained what had happened, but nobody was willing to do anything about it.

In the third instance, I was paired with Jumbo in the Chunichi Crowns, a prominent event on the Japanese Tour. On the second hole of the final round, Jumbo hit his tee shot into the right rough. I was on the left side of the fairway and watching him every step of the way. Sure enough, as he reached his ball he began tapping down the grass behind his ball with his driver. I turned to Tony Navarro, my caddie, and said, "Did you see that?" "Yes, I did," he replied. "Well, enough is enough," I thought to myself. I walked right across the fairway, asked an official to join us, and then explained to Jumbo that he was not allowed to do that. Well, naturally, Jumbo denied any wrongdoing. The official could see this was going to get heated, so he pulled the two of us into the middle of the fairway, away from the gallery. Again I explained what I had seen, and again Jumbo denied tapping the grass. But the official refused to do anything. At the time, Jumbo was to golf in Japan what Arnold was to golf in the United States in the 1950s. He proceeded to par that hole and eventually beat me by a single shot. To say the rest of the round was played with a chill in the air is an understatement. In the end, Jumbo prevailed, but the incident continued after the round with more discussions with tournament officials in the clubhouse. In the end, no penalty or reprimand was levied, and I left the country saddened because the game of golf had been tarnished.

There's an old expression in Australia, "What you miss on the merry-go-round, you pick up on the roundabout." In that sense, I am not immune to rules infractions. The difference, of course, is how one handles them. In 1989, while playing the Palm Meadows Cup in Australia, a tournament I had won the previous year, and at a golf resort for which I was the touring professional, I was tied for the lead midway through the third round. On the 14th hole, my drive landed very close to a water hazard. I addressed the ball, hit my second shot, made par, and moved on. After I signed my card, I was informed that on the 14th hole I had grounded my club while standing in the hazard. Understandably, the tournament promoters, the television broadcast partner, and the resort owner were panicked that I would be disqualified and brought pressure to bear with the PGA Tour of Australia to let me continue playing with only a 2-shot penalty. But because I had already signed my scorecard I was disqualified, so I spent Sunday in the broadcast booth and chalked it up to a lesson learned.

A more bizarre incident occurred during the 1996 Greater Hartford Open. After my second round, I was informed that the ball I was playing, the Maxfli Revolution, was deemed nonconforming. The ball itself had passed USGA testing, but the markings on my ball were different from those on the ball that was tested. So as a result of some misprinting on the assembly line at the Maxfli plant, I was disqualified.

The rules of golf, while at times difficult to swallow, are there to protect the game, and it's the responsibility of everyone who plays to understand and abide by them. But that's one of the things I love about the game of golf. It instills ethics and a strong sense of morality because we police ourselves. There isn't an official walking with every group explaining what's right and what's wrong. It's the responsibility of the player to know the rules of golf and follow them. And I have carried those same values into everything I do.

CHAPTER TWENTY-FOUR

A LOT OF PEOPLE thought I was wrong to support the World Tour and, at the same time, challenge the PGA Tour. Interestingly enough, there was one other entity also willing to take on the Tour: the Federal Trade Commission. But in the end, they too failed.

It turns out that the U.S. government had been conducting a four-year, nonpublic investigation into the legality of the two rules that the PGA Tour used to shut down the World Tour: (1) Golfers could not play in non–PGA Tour events without the commissioner's permission; and (2) the commissioner could veto a golfer's participation in televised golf-related programs that, in turn, could result in forcing the sponsor to pay high appearance fees to the Tour. The FTC's investigation revolved around whether or not these rules violated the Sherman Antitrust Act. That investigation came to a head at the same time John Montgomery and I were trying to form the World Tour.

In September 1994, the FTC issued a consent order to the PGA Tour that would have allowed players to appear in non-Tour events without the commissioner's approval. In response, the PGA Tour refused to agree and informed the FTC that the players had rejected the order. Well, Greg Norman was a player on the PGA Tour and I was never even informed about the matter. So I wrote a letter to Finchem challenging his response to the FTC. Now, no one should misunderstand that I had my reasons. Obviously, if the Federal Trade Commission found the PGA Tour's rules in violation of anti-trust laws, professional golfers would be free to join the World Tour.

We exchanged several letters, and when it was all said and done, it seemed to me that the PGA Tour may have given lawyers for the FTC the impression that the players had voted on this issue. In fact, they had not. The consent order had been reviewed and rejected by the Tournament Policy Board, and the membership had been informed of the decision *afterward* at a general players' meeting. I was not aware of PGA Tour players being informed (or asked their opinions) of the consent order prior to the decision being made.

At their request, I sent the Federal Trade Commission copies of my correspondence with Finchem, and in December 1994 the government antitrust lawyers recommended that the FTC file a formal legal complaint against the PGA Tour to nullify the two rules in question. Before that could be done, however, the PGA Tour launched a comprehensive public relations and political campaign to save their controversial rules.

Consultants helped the Tour develop and deliver a series of nationwide press releases and media interviews. A massive letter-writing campaign to the FTC was undertaken, led by the Tour's charities and tournament sponsors. NBC donated $750,000 worth of free airtime during major sports events to run pro–PGA Tour commercials. In February 1995, the Tour also sent out a petition to all the players in support of the two controversial rules. Once signed, it would be sent to the FTC. "We are in favor of the rules because they insure the support of sponsors and broadcasters for PGA Tour events," the petition read. "If the sponsors and broadcasters discontinue their support of PGA Tour events, it would result in fewer tournaments with smaller fields, lower prize money, and less tournament golf on television. We would also be unable to continue to raise millions of dollars for charity in the communities where our tournaments are held. We urge the federal government not to take any action that would eliminate these rules and do serious harm to the quantity and quality of professional golf."

I was amused to find that I had received my copy of the petition three to four days after most of the other players. So I immediately sat down and penned a letter to the commissioner, telling him I thought the petition was misleading. "I am sure my fellow professionals are not aware of the ramifications regarding the Conflicting Events and TV Release Regulations, and I believe it is unfair for you to send a form to them that takes advantage of that lack of knowledge," I wrote. "Tim, I think a reporter in Australia best sums up the situation when he stated that if it was not for competition and the stimulation that it brings, we would all still be driving black Ford motor vehicles."

The PGA Tour's lobbyists also put Finchem in personal contact with all the FTC commissioners and key members of Congress. Senate Majority Leader Bob Dole (running for president at the time) and Florida's two senators led the charge on behalf of the Tour. Dozens of letters and phone calls from both Republicans and Democrats descended on FTC headquarters, urging that the PGA Tour rules investigation be dropped. Dole even brought the subject up on the floor of the U.S. Senate. "I question whether the public interest would be served by eliminating the foundation for the success of the Tour," he said.

One member of the House who chaired an FTC oversight committee (and regularly played for free in an exclusive golfing event associated with the Kemper Open) pressured FTC commissioners to "disregard the staff's recommendations to file a complaint against the PGA Tour." And to top it all off, the PGA Tour investigation by the FTC came at the same time as the Senate approved legislation threatening to slash the FTC's yearly $100 million budget by a staggering 20 percent.

The political pressure must have been too much for the Federal Trade Commission—even though the agency is supposed to be an independent regulatory and law enforcement body. By a vote of 4–0 (taken on September 1, 1995), FTC commissioners rejected the antitrust lawyers' recommendation to take legal action against the PGA Tour. The decision was announced on the Friday before Labor Day weekend and garnered almost no media coverage. Soon thereafter, the Senate's proposed budget appropriation for the FTC was restored to its full amount.

Of course, that was the last gasp for the World Tour. We still had a chance if the FTC declared the PGA Tour's restrictive rules in violation of federal antitrust laws, but that was highly unlikely. And I must admit, you've got to hand it to Finchem. He really pulled it off. His direction, commitment, and energy really made the difference. I believe the fact he had just taken over the top spot for the PGA Tour also played a role. Finchem became the Tour's third commissioner on June 1, 1994, succeeding Deane Beman. Prior to that, he had served for seven years as both staff vice president of business affairs and chief operating officer. And when he was elevated to commissioner, I'm sure he wanted to protect and make his own mark on the organization.

The PGA Tour was formed in 1968 by Gardner Dickinson and a handful of other professionals who wanted to break away from the PGA of America. Previously, the Tour was run as a division of the PGA of America, which is a membership organization for club professionals, but there were no longer any synergies between club pros and touring pros, so in 1968 Dickinson and his colleagues formed a new corporation. Originally formed as the Tournament Players Division, the new body would allow touring professionals to self-govern and essentially control their own destiny.

Today, the PGA Tour's governance is murky. The Tour is governed by the PGA Policy Board, which is made up of four PGA Tour Player directors, four independent directors, and one representative of the PGA of America. Under that, there is a 25-member Player Advisory Council (PAC), made up of playing members that serve three-year terms.

Following the World Tour, I believed I could institute greater change from within. So I inquired what it would take for me to be a player representative on the Policy Board but was informed that I would first have to serve a three-year term on the Player Advisory Council. By the time I would be eligible to sit on the Policy Board, I would be playing on the senior tour. But then I would only be eligible to serve on the Policy Board for the senior tour.

The following year (2004), I resigned my membership from the Tour and then asked what it would take for me to be appointed to the Player Advisory Council as an independent director. Surely I had sufficient business experience: I had sat on numerous boards in the past, and I understood the business of golf. Quite frankly, I also thought it was a way to tilt the balance of power, effectively breaking the parity of the board, which had equal numbers of independent members and players. Unfortunately, I was told that, as a former player, I did not qualify as an independent director. I still haven't found that language in the player handbook.

To be perfectly honest, I've asked a lot of questions over the years. How are the independent directors selected? Why aren't they captains of industry? Do they make independent decisions? Or are they yes-men for the executive staff? How does the commissioner get selected? Who is on the compensation committee for executive salaries? Are players represented on that committee? What are the salary structures? Are there bonuses involved? Does the compensation encourage executives and board members to make equitable decisions for the player members?

I've never really received adequate answers to these questions, even though I'm a member of the PGA Tour and, as such, believe I have a right to know anything and everything about my organization. As a matter of fact, as a member of the PGA Tour, I have requested copies of board meeting minutes (and been denied) and have asked for an independent external audit to be conducted of the Tour's financial statements (also denied). In April 2006, I took the unfortunate but necessary step of retaining legal counsel to represent me in a bid to review the records of the organization of which I am a member. On that same note, I found it interesting that starting sometime around 2003, the Tour began referring to players as independent contractors. By using this term, the Tour not only acknowledges player rights but also creates the impression that the Tour is somehow segregated from its members.

Well, what are we? Are we independent contractors or are we members of an association? I think we're both. We are independent contractors as long as we abide by the rules, regulations, and by-laws of the PGA Tour, which state that if we play a minimum of fifteen events, we are members. It's that simple.

In my opinion, the PGA Tour's original charter states that it is to be a membership organization by the players and for the players. And that's a point I try to teach young golfers who have just joined the organization. The commissioner, the executive staff, and the board members do not own the PGA Tour. We the players do. They work for us. We don't work for them.

The players do have a retirement plan, but it is not a pension plan. Rather, it is a deferred income plan, and as such, it is an asset of the PGA Tour and vulnerable to any legal action taken against the PGA Tour. When Karsten Manufacturing Corporation, creator of Ping golf equipment, filed a lawsuit against the Tour, an out-of-court settlement was eventually reached. Had that not happened, it could have seriously impacted the players' retirement plan. Fortunately for the PGA Tour, company founder Karsten Solheim had a kind heart. But will the next plaintiff be so benevolent? In fact, the newly formed FedEx Cup is partially subsidized by the Tour's retirement plan.

Another thing most young players do not realize is that they are required to give up the rights to their names and likenesses for non–PGA Tour events. For instance, when I played in an exhibition match with Nick Faldo back in 1994, I had to obtain permission from the commissioner to participate. I received $200,000 for winning. Nick received $50,000 as the other competitor. But the PGA Tour received $250,000 from the promoter for our names and likenesses to be shown on American television. The Tour also pulls in millions of dollars in corporate advertising in which the players do not share. No other tour in the world takes advantage of its members in such a manner.

In my opinion, part of the problem with the PGA Tour is that it is very much a closed shop. I just don't think there are enough independently minded businesspeople involved at the highest levels. Rather, professional administrators wield too much power over the membership. As an example, look at the 1951 charter of the LPGA Tour. It clearly states that the players are shareholders of the organization and that they determine the direction of the tour and its events. The PGA Tour charter's wording regarding 501(c)6 status and corporate governance is a sea of molasses compared to that of the LPGA charter. As a membership organization, the Tour caters to the lowest common denominator. There's no problem with one man, one vote, but Tour members should recognize that the television rights, licensing, and other merchandising fees that the Tour so successfully leverages come off the backs of the game's current stars. It's no wonder, then, that Finchem and the PGA Tour executives felt so threatened by John Montgomery's original idea for a World Tour.

I have since come to realize that the PGA Tour executives reacted in a perfectly predictable manner. They were defensive. They became emotional. To them, it was a matter of self-preservation. That's why Finchem drew a line in the sand and threatened the players with suspension. That's why I was attacked personally. And that's why the PGA Tour rebuffed all of our conciliatory offers. It was human nature. It was resistance to any kind of change that they did not create themselves.

Less than three months after the final FTC decision was announced, *Golfweek* published an article revealing that the professional tours in Europe, South Africa, Japan, and Australasia were working with the PGA Tour on what Finchem described as a "specially designated series of events with an international context." The date of the article (November 18, 1995) was almost exactly one year after the formal announcement of the World Tour at the Shark Shootout. Then, approximately five months later, a formal "federation" was created among the five tours with the intent, according to Finchem, to combine their efforts and bring professional golf into line with the world marketplace. Right around this time, the commissioner approached me at a tournament and asked if I would attend some of the meetings on the subject. "Sure," I said. "I'd be happy to attend some of the meetings." But that was the last I ever heard about it. I viewed that as another one of those "Finchemisms" where he throws out an olive branch, but the olive branch is not attached to anything.

Fast-forward to the Presidents Cup held at the Robert Trent Jones Golf Club in Manassas, Virginia. There, on Friday evening, September 14, 1996, I was informed that Finchem intended to hold a press conference on Sunday night to announce the official formation of the International Federation of PGA Tours. The leaders of the participating five tours would all be on hand for the event, including Brian Allan (PGA Tour of Australasia), Shoichi Asami (PGA Tour of Japan), Brent Chalmers (PGA Tour of South Africa), Ken Schofield (European PGA Tour, via telephone), and, of course, Finchem, who would be the spokesperson.

Together, they would also announce, I was told, a conceptual agreement involving the joint sanctioning of competitions for golf's top players. Plans included at least three world championship events beginning in 1999. These three events would include team competition, stroke play, and match play. A new structure would also be devised for a worldwide ranking system.

Gee, what an original idea!

The next day, I was invited to participate in the press conference, but I declined. In fact, I couldn't bear to even attend the conference. I was really pained about the whole thing.

So on Sunday, September 16, 1996, Finchem made his announcement in front of a packed house filled with members of the media. From written accounts of the conference, I found a number of things he had to say very interesting. For example, he referred back to the inaugural Presidents Cup in 1994 and stated that this new endeavor was simply a continuation of what he had termed the World Forum of PGA Tours. "The World Forum has continued to meet and discuss a manner in which increased competition among the world's best players could be accomplished in a manner that would: 1) be beneficial to the game of golf and positively impact the image of the sport and its players, 2) command the support of the world of golf and the major golf organizations, and 3) be compatible with the world golf structure that has worked so well, and be consistent with the existing competitive playing opportunities sponsored by the existing tours and their memberships."

Finchem implied that these three principles had been agreed upon in September 1994—which, of course, would predate the World Tour's November 1994 announcement. But I don't think that is the case. They were first mentioned publicly at the 1994 Shark Shootout, when the commissioner initially came out against the World Tour. It "fails to meet any of these three criteria," he stated.

I may be incorrect, but I believe the September 6, 1994, announcement about the "World Forum of PGA Tours" was simply a part of the PGA Tour's "get the jump on Norman" pattern. The idea was to get a statement on paper and mention it publicly before I could. That way the Tour could claim it was their idea first and actually did this in a number of incidences: The Tour got the jump on the FTC before it could file formal legal action. The Tour got the jump on us at the Shark Shootout before we made our scheduled public announcement. And I believe the September 6 announcement simply fit into that pattern.

Consider also that Finchem closed his Presidents Cup announcement by stating: "Over the next several months, the International Federation of PGA Tours will develop a plan. . . . No schedule has been set and discussions with players and sponsors will continue on a variety of topics related to the new events." Well, this is almost exactly how he closed out his brief September 6, 1994, announcement. And consider this: "Several months" later, in November 1994, Finchem was declaring war on the World Tour. There never were any additional discussions set with players and sponsors because there never was any real talk among the five world tours—except, of course, about what John Montgomery and I were doing.

At the 1996 Presidents Cup, the media, those who had a good memory, were fairly astute about what was going on. After Finchem's announcement, one magazine headline read: "PGA Tour Announces International Events to Shark's Chagrin." Another pointed out that the whole thing "was the same concept for which Greg Norman was roundly criticized and vilified two years ago."

A little more than a year later, on October 29, 1997, more details were released about what was now being called the "World Golf Championships." The purse for each event would be approximately $4 million, and the tournaments would be broadcast by either ABC or CBS. It is also interesting to note that this time, Finchem mentioned both the World Tour and me personally. "Over the last three years, as we've looked at these competitions," he said, "we have done so . . . in the aftermath of the proposal that was advanced in 1994 for a 'World Tour' and endorsed at that time by Greg Norman. At the time . . . we took issue with it from a timing standpoint. We certainly weren't able to accommodate it. We had some differences of opinion on structure."

The commissioner went on to try to give me some credit. "Conceptually, Greg Norman's commitment to the internationalization of the game has played a role in the development of the new marketplace as we've tried to match new competitions to the marketplace," he said. "I want to congratulate him for his continued effort and his continued commitment and articulation of the need for more internationalization to the overall structure of the PGA Tour. I think he's had a positive influence. We have had a positive—I want to underline *positive*—communication and discussion over the last two and a half, three years on issues related to this. I want to thank Greg for his continued involvement and commitment."

In my mind, by giving me credit he also neutralized any potential counterattack, so Finchem was being the consummate politician. Clearly, as an adviser to Walter Mondale, he was well versed in the Washington, D.C., spin game.

Right after the 1996 Presidents Cup announcement, I was sitting in the players' locker room when Bart Collins came in to tell me the details of what they had said. He had in his hand a memento that the PGA Tour had given everyone. It was a little squishy ball with a map of the world on it, inscribed: "World Golf Championships." Bart gave it to me, smiled, and shook his head.

"I'll tell you what they can do with this," I said.

Then I stood up, threw that little squishy ball against the wall as hard as I could, and shouted: "Fuck 'em!"

At the time, I had my reservations about the legitimacy of the World Golf Championships. From the outset, the Tour promoted a number of different formats as part of these events—stroke play, match play, the World Cup—with different qualifying criteria for each. What I was trying to create with the World Tour was consistency of format, participation, qualifying criteria: eight events, the top 30, 72 holes, stroke play. I think the PGA Tour was very calculated in ensuring there was not a consistent format that could potentially undermine mainstream PGA Tour events. After all, they wanted the more than forty PGA Tour events to be the "Premier League." It's also interesting to note that ten years on, there are no more World Golf Championship events than when the series was first created. And that of the four "world" events, three are played in the United States.

I don't believe this series, if you can call it that, has improved the internationalization of the game, and I would suspect that if the opinion of the original members of the International Federation of PGA Tours was sought, they wouldn't see any parity in the game today. In fact, most of the other tours are ailing by comparison to the PGA Tour. I do not believe the PGA Tour has done much to create unity among the various tours. In fact, I distinctly remember thinking at the time—and still feel this way today—that the PGA Tour's creation of the International Federation of PGA Tours and the World Golf Championships was a defensive move so that no other group could rally support from the other tours and pose a threat to the PGA Tour. I don't believe the Tour ever had a genuine interest in developing such a series. It was a rearguard action at best.

Independent of the success or failure of the World Golf Championships, it may appear on the surface that the PGA Tour has done a good job of shoring up the U.S. circuit. But by virtually any key performance indicator (KPI), the sport of golf, and golf as a mainstream television property, is challenged. Participation levels, especially among entry-level golfers—the game's future constituency—is down.

Moreover, with a new television agreement set for 2007, the PGA Tour will have one fewer network in the fray as ABC/ESPN pulls out. So what is the Tour doing to increase participation and increase its relevance to the television viewer? They have created the much-vaunted FedEx Cup, which is akin to NASCAR's Nextel Cup. Clearly, the Tour is trying to make golf more exciting by drawing attention to the Top 30 players. Will it work? I hope so. But I often ask myself the question: What would golf look like today if, beginning in 1995, there had been eight World Tour events held each year featuring the Top 30 players? I suspect that, after the majors, those events would have been among the highest rated on television. Equally, there might have been a greater balance of power in the international arena.

Fortunately, the PGA Tour is now attempting to create something that might make the game of golf more exciting for everyone around the world. And *that* is a very positive step indeed.

ONE OF THE TOUGHEST THINGS for me to swallow in the wake of the World Tour was losing the friendship and camaraderie of other professional golfers. There were definitely breakdowns of relationships with certain players whom I had long considered good friends. At first I didn't understand how it all happened. So I spent a lot of time thinking about it. I really needed to understand what had happened, why it had happened, and how I felt about it all.

What happened was, in my mind, a fairly simple question to answer. I had tried to create something that I believed would be good for the game of golf and for the players. It would also have provided power to the players. But instead of saying, "Greg, you have a great idea, let's work together on this thing," executives of the PGA Tour unleashed a propaganda machine that did a masterful job of painting me as somebody I'm not. "Greg Norman is ruining the game of golf." "The World Tour is just a money-making scheme that will benefit Greg Norman." "Greg Norman is bad for the game of golf." Despite all the negative branding, in the end, the World Tour was an idea that the PGA Tour did itself.

Why this all happened was a little more tricky to answer. I believe that Tour executives felt threatened that a World Tour would infringe on their domain, dilute the prominence and money-making abilities of their organization, and hurt their professional status. In short, I think it was all about self-preservation.

The professional golfers, I believe, were biased by the Tour's propaganda campaign. They became concerned about change, about losing their security blanket. If you think about it long enough, it really makes sense. The guys were playing for millions of dollars in prize money each week. They received free cars, free food, free dry cleaning, discounts on airlines. Everything was given to them, they liked it, and they didn't want to see it disrupted. Somehow they got the message that it would all be threatened by the World Tour. And that brings me to another reason it all happened, a reason that revolves around the inner workings of human nature.

People tend to believe what they hear. Rather than try to find out whether it's true or not, they formulate an opinion that is tough to change. Propagandists for the PGA Tour took advantage of this. The hard truth is that once people have a set opinion, they would rather talk behind your back than speak directly to you. It has to do with a general avoidance of confrontation. It's the nature of the game.

I also believe that what I went through involves the nature of change itself. All the great change in the world was accomplished by a few daring people who weren't afraid to challenge the status quo. And they were *always* attacked because of it. In the case of the World Tour, I was the point guy. I took the bullets. As a matter of fact, I remember saying to the media a number of times that all the attacks on me were just about "slaying the dreamer."

There are leaders and there are followers. I can't think of anything in the way of progress that has been created without going against the grain. To this day, I continue to ask tough questions of the PGA Tour. Last year, I put in a request for copies of the minutes from all PGA Tour board meetings, and I asked for an independent audit of the PGA Tour books. Of course, both requests were denied. Regarding the minutes, the Tour responded by saying, "Why don't you send us your questions and we'll pull the excerpts of the board meetings that we deem necessary for you to see?"

When I called my attorney to explain the situation, he responded by saying that the PGA Tour had no right to make that stipulation. As a member of the PGA Tour, I have a right to receive copies of the minutes. I've therefore undertaken formal legal action to obtain that information.

What am I looking for in all of this? Well, first of all, I want to see whether there were transparency and consistency in how corporate governance was conducted over the past thirty years. And the only way I'm going to know that is by reading the minutes of board meetings. If that consistency is not there, then I believe it will be apparent. That, in turn, will lead me down another path. Second, I want to give the PGA Tour back to the players, to whom it rightfully belongs. Today it is run by administrators who represent their own individual interests, not the best interests of the members.

On March 6, 2006, so there would be no room for misunderstanding, I sent an e-mail to members of the PGA Tour explaining my reasons for taking action. I also invited players to contact me if they wanted more information. To this date, I've received responses from only two players.

Over the years, I have spent a lot of time reflecting on the World Tour years. Once I had completely thought through *what* had happened and *why* it had all taken place, I had to understand *how* I really felt about it all. And the answer to that question turned out to be pretty painful to admit. The whole ordeal dented me up pretty bad. I was hurt—and I was angry, very angry. That emotion, in turn, siphoned away much of my energy. I no longer had the desire to go out and play golf. And when I did, I found myself asking the question "What the hell am I doing out here?" I just didn't want to support the PGA Tour anymore. I now viewed myself as nothing more than a pass-through entity, and I no longer felt like doing anything to promote the PGA Tour. "What's the use?" I remember thinking.

I was down, and I turned to several self-help books, in particular *Way of the Peaceful Warrior,* by Dan Millman. I read a couple of books on Zen. I spoke to a sports psychologist. And I studied other leaders in history who had gone through similar negative experiences.

Tennis legend Billie Jean King is a great example of someone who not only tried to enact change but was successful in doing so. Back in the early 1970s, when she was the number-one-ranked player in the world, female tennis players played for purses that were a fraction of what their male counterparts earned. Four times a year, tennis, unlike golf, features two-week events with both male and female tennis players, and it was Billie Jean King who forged the prospect of parity with tournament purses, which then led to the formation of the Women's Tennis Association (WTA). Billie Jean was followed by several others, including Rosie Casals and Chris Evert. Each made her mark on the sport.

I also recalled a powerful encounter I had with Nelson Mandela at the 1995 Alfred Dunhill Challenge. Here is a man who spent thirty years in prison. "How can a guy go through what he went through and not have hatred in his heart?" I wondered. "How could he not have the desire to get some kind of retribution or vindication?" Well, I asked Nelson Mandela that very question. And I can still see the sincerity in his eyes when he responded. "Greg, I don't have any ill feelings toward anyone," he said. "I just want to make sure it never happens to anybody else." That was a very powerful moment in my life. If he could put it all behind him, then certainly I could as well.

During this time, I was at an ebb and sensed that it might be a good time for me to reconnect with, and possibly move back to, Australia. After all, I had been on the treadmill for nearly twenty years, and the thought of settling down in Australia was very appealing to me.

I reasoned that this was a point in time when our kids could be moved without a great deal of negative impact. Gregory was not quite a teenager, and Morgan was about to enter high school. So the four of us sat down to dinner one night and discussed it. I explained how I felt about things, but I said this had to be a unanimous family decision. "If one of us doesn't want to move to Australia," I said, "then we all have to support that one person." After a long conversation, Morgan voted yes, Laura voted yes, and I voted yes. But Gregory sat back and said, "Oh, I'm not too sure."

"Why aren't you sure?" I asked.

"I have to think about this a bit," he replied. "My friends, my school, I really like it here."

And I said, "Gregory, I'm very proud of you for saying that. I'll tell you what, I want you to think about it. We'll have another family discussion on Friday night."

Well, it was obvious that Gregory had done a lot of thinking about the entire matter, because when we got back together again two nights later, he stepped forward and said that he just didn't want to go. "Dad, I like it here too much," he said. "My friends mean a lot to me. I don't want to move to Australia. I want to stay in Florida."

"You know what, bud?" I said. "We made a deal with you. If one person doesn't want to move, then all four of us will stay. And that's what we're going to do. We're going to stay."

More than anything else, I was moved by Gregory's strength of character. At the time he showed wisdom and faculties well beyond his years. With the innocence of youth, my son told me exactly how he felt and what he wanted to do. And that jolted me back to reality. It helped me remember what was really important in life: that it wasn't all about me, that I had other important people in my life to think about, and that my family came first. Based on that, I regroomed my whole philosophy. I got my head on straight again. "Sure, I miss Australia," I said to myself. "But I go back six times a year. I can go down there to the Great Barrier Reef and dive or fish or do whatever I want to do during those visits. We don't have to move the kids just because I'm feeling bad about life right now."

During this time, I committed myself to open communication with my family. Whenever possible, we would have dinner together, and when we did we took the time to have some deep, insightful conversations. With time, it turned out to be a great forum for the kids to express themselves and for Laura and me to impart some life lessons. We would get into some important discussions about drugs, sex, and peer pressure. Morgan and Gregory would ask questions and we'd answer them. We tried always to be open and frank and leave all emotion out of it. Some of my friends expressed dismay that Laura and I were so open about so many subjects. But I explained to them that I thought it was best for our children to hear about these things from us rather than from other kids at school. Interestingly enough, many of Morgan's and Gregory's friends wanted to come over to dinner and be part of those conversations.

More than anything, I think what I did best was to treat our children as young adults. In this day and age, children grow up quickly, and I've found that you run the risk of losing the connection if you speak down to them rather than communicate with them on the same level you would any other adult.

I think one reason I took this approach with my children is that I didn't have the opportunity to communicate with my father in that same fashion. Dad was simply a product of his generation, when men tended not to speak openly about such sensitive subjects.

Today I have a very close relationship and an extremely tight bond with both my son and my daughter. And that means the world to me.

CHAPTER TWENTY-FIVE

O N JANUARY 24, 1996, Cobra was bought by Fortune Brands, Inc., the parent company to Acushnet, which itself is a holding company for Titleist, FootJoy, and Pinnacle. It was one of the biggest golf industry transactions in history. Tom Crow and Gary Biszantz both made small fortunes, and my share of the deal brought the sum total of my earnout to something just over $40 million. Not bad for an initial investment of $1.8 million (for 12 percent ownership in the company). The exit strategy that Tom, Gary, and I originally planned had, indeed, come to fruition—and it had taken only five years.

Two years before, after building Cobra up to $220 million in sales, we had taken the company public. In listing Cobra, however, we took a few unusual steps. Historically, club professionals around the world sold most of our products. But in the mid-1990s, there was a significant growth in off-course retail outlets like Edwin Watts, Golf Galaxy, and Golfsmith. As a result, the club professionals were losing some of their momentum with respect to sales of hard goods.

Because Tom Crow and I had both been club pros, we maintained a very high respect and a deep-seated loyalty toward them. Accordingly, before we listed the company, we reserved a percentage of our shares for the club pros who did business with us, and we offered it to them at a discount price per share. Tom and I both agreed that this move rewarded the professionals who stayed with us. It also encouraged them to continue to promote and sell our products because they now owned a piece of the action. It all made sense. If Cobra did well, the club pros too would profit.

At the time, our investment bankers advised us not to pursue this course of action. It was simply too unconventional, but Tom Crow, Gary Biszantz, and I wouldn't have it any other way. And in the end, we were proved right. The club professionals stayed loyal to Cobra, and our company continued to grow at a rapid rate over the next few years. As an interesting footnote, at the time Cobra listed, IMG attempted to collect a commission on the value of my shareholding, which I rebuffed given that they had advised me against the transaction. I had purchased my interest in Cobra. It was not bequeathed to me as part of my endorsement arrangement.

Our rapid growth had attracted Acushnet to take a hard look at acquiring Cobra. Acushnet was looking to expand its golf holdings. It already had two iconic brands in Titleist (golf balls) and FootJoy (golf shoes). Clearly they wanted to add a thriving golf equipment company to the portfolio.

At first Wally Uihlein, Acushnet's CEO, endorsed the acquisition, but he wanted to keep the purchase price reasonable—perhaps in the neighborhood of $30 per share. However, several members of the board of directors of Fortune Brands became heavily involved in the acquisition and chased the share price up to more than $36—for a total purchase price of approximately $700 million. At that point I was no different from any other shareholder and, as such, sold my remaining shares.

The sale was finalized in January 1996, so I entered the golf season with a new sense of security and self-confidence. I won three tournaments that year (Doral Ryder Open, South Australian Open, and Australian Open). But the biggest story of 1996 for me by far was what happened at the Masters.

On Wednesday morning, the day before the tournament began, I woke up with terrible back pain. On the driving range, I could hardly take the club back, so I canceled my practice round.

I was very frustrated. "Why now?" I asked myself. "Why now, of all times?"

Later that morning there was a knock at my door. Fred Couples, whom I'd seen on the practice range, had sent over his back therapist to help me. And help me he did, because the next morning I felt great. As a matter of fact, I made 9 birdies on my way to a course-record 63 later that day. That was good enough for a first-round, 4-stroke lead over Nick Faldo (6 over Phil Mickelson and David Frost). After shooting 69 and 71 on Friday and Saturday, respectively, I took a 6-stroke lead into Sunday's final round. Faldo remained in second place, 2 ahead of Mickelson and Frost.

I recall waking up on Sunday morning feeling hopeful and relaxed. My back was still in good shape, so I knew I had an opportunity to fulfill one of my career dreams. I love everything about the Masters—the golf course, the way the tournament is run, everything—and being able to win it at least once meant a great deal to me.

Unfortunately, I sensed early in my round that things weren't quite right. My hands didn't feel comfortable. My distance was a bit off. And my accuracy on the first few holes left a lot to be desired. "Boy, it's going to be a tough day," I said to my caddie, Tony Navarro. I just could not feel what I had felt over the previous three days. And the more I tried to get that feeling back, the more it went away.

Overall, I was hanging in there until I hit my approach shot to the 9th green. When my wedge came up three feet short and the ball rolled back down the hill, I knew I was going to have a big problem, because you have to be very precise with your shots on the back 9 at Augusta. And on that day, for whatever reason, my precision just wasn't there.

By the time Nick Faldo and I walked to the 10th tee, I had squandered 4 strokes, so that meant my lead was now down to 2. And then *everything* started to cave in. And I do mean *everything*. I couldn't hit a good shot to save my life. At the same time, Nick played extremely well. To make a long story short, by firing a 67 to my 78, Nick Faldo won the Masters that year. Many people think I

finished second, but that distinction went to Davis Love III. My performance dropped me to third place, 5 strokes off the pace. The
story might end there except for something out of the ordinary that
happened on the 18th green.

Over the previous four hours, Nick and I had barely made eye
contact with each other, let alone get into a conversation. But when
he holed his final putt, rather than celebrate victory, Nick came directly over to me. "I don't know what to say," he said. "I just want to
give you a hug."

And for that brief moment, the two of us embraced like brothers. Then, just before we parted, Nick leaned in and said, sincerely
and succinctly, "Don't let the bastards get you down."

He didn't have to point to the media center. I knew exactly what
he was talking about. He was genuinely concerned about how I
would handle what happened that day, and how others would handle it. That gesture on the 18th green by Nick Faldo was pure class.

As devastated as I felt at the time, it was important for me to
live up to my responsibilities by going to the media center and enduring the bullets that were going to be fired at me. I think I surprised some people, however, by not offering any excuses and by
candidly admitting that I had played poorly. "I screwed up today," I
said. "My thought pattern was good, but my rhythm was off. My
good shots weren't good enough and my bad shots were pitiful. And
that's pretty much it. I just didn't have it today. I place all the blame
on myself."

When I was asked about any lingering effects this loss might
have on me, I responded as honestly as I could. "I'm not going to
fall off the face of the earth because of what happened here," I said.
"It's not the end of the world for me. It's really not. I have a pretty
good life and I have things I can look forward to. A few minutes
ago, my son told me that I'm still his hero."

I stayed until the last question had been answered. Then I got
up, walked away, and said to myself that it was over and done with.
Upon arriving at the airport, I was touched that a number of fans
showed up to offer some words of encouragement. And when I
got on my plane, I hugged all my friends and family, who were
clearly concerned about me. "I'm sorry I let you all down today,"

I said. "I love you." Then I sat down, had a beer, and tried to cheer up everybody else.

In the immediate aftermath of the tournament, I was surprised by the reactions of most of the mainstream press. Many writers praised my sportsmanship after losing the tournament. And one normally cynical, hard-nosed sportscaster described my reactions as the "classiest, most noble response to defeat" he'd ever witnessed. After everything that I'd been through over the past few years, that was particularly nice to hear. But I must admit that I was totally unprepared for all the good wishes that flowed into the offices of Great White Shark Enterprises.

Jack Nicklaus, Raymond Floyd, Fred Couples, and many other players telephoned. When Nick Price called, he told me that I'd earned more respect and more friends by handling myself the way I had. Notes arrived from President George Bush, Byron Nelson, former Australian prime minister Bob Hawke, and countless friends and acquaintances. I received thousands of faxes from all over the world, including several written in other languages that had to be translated. And then there were the words of goodwill sent by so many people I had never even met. "Keep your chin up, Greg." "You're still my hero, Mr. Norman." "Thanks for being such a great example of good sportsmanship, sir." I was particularly moved by a note from a young man who wrote, "Be happy and know that there are a million kids like me who love and respect you."

That first week back home, I went to my son, Gregory's soccer game, and at halftime, one of the other parents came up to me. "You know, Greg," he said, "I want you to know that how you handled that loss did more for me than anything you could have done if you'd *won* the Masters. The embrace with Faldo, the way you stepped up to the microphone afterward and took every question. It really impacted me. My attitude about life has changed because of you."

As painful as it was to fly up to Hilton Head for the Heritage Classic forty-eight hours later, I knew it was what I had to do to get on with my life and put the Masters experience behind me. When I arrived, a number of my fellow professionals, including several who did not agree with my stance on the World Tour, made a point of coming up to express their sympathy and extend their best wishes. I was not only surprised by all this, I was truly moved and gratified. I really didn't realize how they all felt. Perhaps something good did come from the entire experience.

I never would have thought that I could reach out and touch people by *losing* a golf tournament. It was extraordinary. At a time when I might have been driven to a low point in my life, I was uplifted by the warmth of thousands of people, most of whom I didn't even know. All of the good wishes, the kind words, the hugs, the renewed friendships—it was all like a shining light coming out of the darkness. And that light caused me to see life in a different way. It made me realize that there is goodness in all people.

A month later, I took off on a golf course design trip with Jason McCoy and Chris Campbell. I was feeling a lot better about life now. The depression I'd felt after the World Tour had dissipated. You might even say my loss at the Masters had helped give me a greater perspective on life. I love going on these design trips because it helps me relax, escape from the public eye, and get back to business.

On this particular trip, one of our stops was in Houston, Texas, at a course called Meadowbrook Farms, where we were conducting one of our early site inspections. My plane landed just after dawn at a small airport in Sugarland. From there we went immediately to the course. And what a day we had. It was hot, humid, and rainy. We trudged through creeks, thick brush, barbed-wire fences, and thorny bushes. By the time we got back to the airport, all of us were dirty, sweaty, and strung out. There was only a small terminal building at this airport. It had only one small bathroom, into which we all went to wash up and change.

I finished up first, and when I walked back into the lobby, about fifteen six- or seven-year-old kids had just walked in with their teachers. "How are you kids doing?" I said. "Shouldn't you all be in school?"

Meanwhile, I heard the two teachers whispering, "That's Greg Norman." But the kids were too young. They didn't know who I was.

"We're on a field trip," said one of the youngsters.

"Oh, I'll bet you've come out here to learn about airplanes," I said.

"Yes, sir, we have," replied one of the teachers. "We were hoping to get an up-close look at a Piper Cub."

"Well, I've got a friend who can take you through an airplane," I said. "Follow me." I took all the kids and their teachers out to my Gulfstream jet. "How about giving the kids a tour," I said to my pilot, Guy Maira. So the kids got on the plane. It was a lot of fun to see them jumping around, with their heads bobbing up and down through the windows. Guy showed them everything: the cockpit, the galley, the bathroom, the baggage compartment. And he explained how airplanes operate in quite a bit of detail. After about twenty or thirty minutes, all the kids came back into the terminal, where I gave each of them and their teachers one of my lapel pins with a shark logo. "Okay, kids, I'm happy that you're all in school," I said to them before leaving.

Before the end of the year I would win three other tournaments, including the South Australian Open, which was important to me from the standpoint of getting back into the winner's circle. Winning in Australia was particularly important, as I wanted my country to see me as a champion.

Toward the back half of 1996 I also had to renegotiate my relationship with Acushnet. I was no longer part owner in Cobra, yet I was still their distributor in Australia. Clearly, there was going to be some integration going on over the next twelve months, as virtually every market had two distributors, one for Titleist and another for Cobra. It would stand to reason that in most instances the Titleist distributorship would win out over the Cobra distributor. As such, I felt it important to meet with Wally Uihlein and retool my affiliation.

Right off the bat, Uihlein took the position that he did not want me aligned with Cobra from an endorsement perspective. Rather, he wanted me to play Titleist products exclusively. I didn't necessarily agree with his logic, given that my name was virtually synonymous with Cobra. Titleist's strategy was to have virtually every player on the Tour using their ball so they could win the Darrell Survey (the weekly ball and club count). But that strategy would put me into a pool of talent that, in my mind, didn't play to my strengths.

At the time, I thought it best to give Uihlein what he wanted, as a concession for a creative approach that would both pay me quite well to play Titleist and secure distribution rights for the full portfolio of Acushnet products. As part of this arrangement, Uihlein and I executed a side letter, which essentially stated that in addition to my being a distributor for Acushnet in Australia, I would have the first option to become distributor of Acushnet products throughout Asia (not including Japan or Taiwan). In other words, if we consistently hit our numbers, we would be rewarded with contracts to distribute Acushnet products to a third of the world's population.

My long-term plan was to effectively use Australia as a base of operations for Southeast Asia, just as I had done successfully with my golf course design business. I had learned that the supply lines to Asia were shorter, and that we could be more responsive to our customers by operating in virtually the same time zone. As a bonus, we were also able to recruit quality people from Australia to manage our businesses.

Now loaded with a full complement of Acushnet products, I purchased the remaining 50 percent interest in Cobra Golf Australia, rebranded the company as International Brands, and ramped up our staff from twenty to eighty-plus employees. In doing so, I established a new board of directors, with my father serving as chairman. Because I couldn't attend all of the board meetings, Bart Collins, who also sat on the board, served as my proxy. Often he would comment that my father and I have a lot in common. "Your father's mannerisms, his points of view, his analytical approach— they're all very similar to yours," Bart told me. "It's a bit scary."

At the end of the day, my father helped us run a very successful business. He was instrumental in seeing that International Brands became the leading distributor of golf equipment in all of Australia. We had become something of a conglomerate distributorship with Cobra, Titleist, and FootJoy. At the same time, we became the distributor for Reebok golf shoes and Greg Norman Collection. So as to touch every part of the consumer pyramid, we created our own private label, Shark and Tiburon clubs and accessories. Overall, sales of International Brands surpassed $25 million annually—equivalent to one-third of the entire golf soft- and hard-goods market in Australia and New Zealand.

I felt that my association with Acushnet fit well into my seven-year plan. On one hand, I was getting paid to play Titleist clubs. On the other hand, I created the enterprise value of the distributorship that in theory would pass the mortality test. In other words, people would be buying Acushnet products long after I stopped playing golf. Overall, as I had planned, with time, the fulcrum would slide more toward the long-term enterprise value of International Brands.

Unfortunately, in the world of international business, things don't always work out as you would hope. Starting in the year 2000, Cobra's domestic sales went into a free fall—eventually falling from a high of $220 million to somewhere around $46 million. It was rumored that Uihlein, who hadn't supported the Cobra acquisition for more than $30 a share, was running down Cobra so that he could write off Acushnet's business and reduce the debt. In 2004, Acushnet made a one-time write-off of $517 million. International Brands, however, never fell into a slump. As a matter of fact, during the same period we increased sales for Cobra, Titleist, and FootJoy. And our accessories business for the Cobra brand matched that of U.S. sales of accessories.

During our quarterly meetings our staff would question Uihlein and his executives on Cobra's poor performance. Remember, I was one of the former owners of Cobra; I sat on the board and could not understand why their sales were plummeting. "What gives?" we asked. "Something is not right!"

We never really did get adequate answers to our questions. Overall, I sensed that Acushnet viewed the success of International Brands as an embarrassment. Essentially, it made the rest of the company look quite weak.

In the intervening years, we not only hit our numbers, we exceeded them. Based on my side letter with Uihlein, I was anticipating a tremendous expansion of our business. But in 2004 Acushnet started a paper trail claiming that International Brands was not a good custodian of their brand and that we did not achieve our min-

imum sales, essentially citing a technical breach. In short, they
stated that our sales of noncurrent Cobra equipment did not qualify
against our minimum sales requirements. To me, this was utterly
ridiculous. With respect to the minimums, we purchased all of our
products from Acushnet, and they banked every royalty check. Yet
when it came to renewing the agreement, they counted only those
clubs that were in the current catalog.

At this point I had a decision to make: I could either fight a pro-
tracted battle in court or I could sell Acushnet the assets of the business and negotiate other concessions. After consulting with my
lawyers, I decided not to fight Acushnet. It was better to just bow
out gracefully. After all, why should more than eighty employees
and their families have to suffer? Because of that decision, I'm
proud to say, all but three of the International Brands employees
kept their jobs.

My experience with Acushnet taught me a valuable lesson. I
thought that in dealing with a major corporation personalities
would not come into play and that our performance would pre-
vail. I came to believe that personalities were the primary driver. I
think Acushnet didn't like the management team we put into place,
nor did they like the fact that we challenged their performance and
agenda in running the Cobra business.

Six months after my relationship with Acushnet ended, I was
quoted in a newspaper article as saying I had reservations about
golf ball technology and what it was doing to professional golf—like
making some classic golf courses obsolete. I commented that the
PGA Tour should enforce a technical specification that would limit
how far the ball could fly. I also went as far as to say the golf ball
should be "wound back" to technology that existed in the late 1980s.
In fact, I made an analogy with Major League Baseball, comparing
professionals using wood bats versus college and recreational
players using aluminum. I believe Uihlein took some exception to
my comments and put one of his staff players up to writing an
editorial that labeled me a hypocrite. At the time I had switched
to MacGregor equipment and appeared in their television campaign endorsing technology as good for the game of golf. I've always said that we need to let technology develop for amateurs but

dial it back for professionals. Uihlein seemed to miss that distinction.

So to clear the air, I put in a call to Acushnet's corporate headquarters in Fairhaven, Massachusetts, and tried to speak to Uihlein man-to-man. "Mr. Uihlein is not available right now," came the response. "But I'll certainly give him your message, Mr. Norman."

A couple of days went by and Uihlein had not returned my call. So I tried to call him again but received the same response. "He's not available right now, Mr. Norman."

That's when I sat down with my assistant. "I want you to place a call to Wally Uihlein at Acushnet every day for the next fifty business days and leave a message that I would like to speak with him."

To this day, Wally Uihlein has not returned my calls.

PART SIX

GOING GLOBAL

CHAPTER TWENTY-SIX

W‌E ONLY TAKE ON a limited number of high-quality projects."

This statement is one of the great fairy tales in the golf course design business. It's like "Your check is in the mail." Everybody says it because it makes their clients feel good about buying into something exclusive. But the truth is that most golf course designers will take whatever they can get.

Not me, however. I can't afford to. If I want to play professional golf, look after my other business interests, *and* stay involved in golf course design, I really must take on only a limited number of high-quality projects. But if I'm not going to ramp up the number of projects I take on, then how can I extract more profit from fewer projects?

The golf course design business is very profitable, but it is essentially a service-oriented business and as such doesn't pass the mortality test. In other words, the day I don't want to participate is the day this business ends and the income derived from it stops. I love golf course design, but I also want to build a sustainable business.

At first blush, the obvious answer was that we should have an equity stake in some or all of the projects we undertook. Clearly, my brand as a signature designer elevates the value of a developer's real estate and helps them accelerate sales, but the real money is in real estate development.

So I challenged my team to develop some options for my consideration. "If we really believe in the equity of our brand," I said, "then we should have a deeper involvement than just that of golf course design."

Of course, this was not a new idea. Others had done it—including me a few years earlier, at Medalist Golf Club in Florida. But when we began our due diligence, we realized that development is typically a very localized business. You need relationships with local builders, state and county officials, and the community. As a result, developers in one state rarely venture outside that state. Lyle Anderson, the king of real estate development in Scottsdale, for instance, has developed only a select few projects outside Arizona. There are national *home builders*, such as Toll Brothers, Centex, and Pulte, but very few national *developers*. Our conclusion was that creating a national—or international—development company would be challenging. But the prospect of a uniform brand that cut across numerous regions held great promise.

Before I formulated a plan, I once again looked at the generation of golfers ahead of me. Jack Nicklaus had pioneered many different avenues in business, and in the early 1980s he had partnered with a reputable developer, but in doing so he had apparently signed some personal guarantees on one or two projects that didn't pan out. In the end, that part of Jack's business enterprise didn't fare too well. Clearly, I wanted to learn from that and not put my own capital at risk.

From that story and others like it, I started kicking around the idea of partnering with an institutional investor, such as a bank. I wanted somebody with a strong balance sheet, not only to ride out the inevitable real estate cycles but to give the company a halo effect for securing debt. Typically, investment banks provide funding to established developers that have a solid track record, management team, and fund profile. At this point in time, however, I merely had a concept. I had not built a management team, nor did I have a track record or a pipeline of potential projects. So I reasoned that I would need a financial institution that was entrepreneurial, one that was willing to work with me to create enterprise value. But who would it be? In the wake of the United States savings and loan crash in the 1980s, that avenue had largely been sealed off by federal regulators.

As I was pondering these questions, I received a call from my Sydney office about a creative opportunity that would ultimately lead to the creation of my development company. Three golf courses in close proximity to Sydney—the Lakes Golf Club, East Lake, and Bonnie Dune—were situated on land that was controlled by the Sydney Water Board. The golf clubs had been paying peppercorn rent, and now, after half a century, the leases were up for renewal. My Sydney office suggested that we organize a consortium to bid for the lease and restructure the membership in such a way that one of the three golf courses could be repositioned as a high-end, private club. As we assembled our bid, my team met with the consulting division of Macquarie Bank, which was representing the Sydney Water Board. In the end, we abandoned our bid because the prospect of recasting the membership would have been too complicated and too litigious. However, Macquarie Bank and Great White Shark Enterprises had begun a relationship. As it turned out, we liked each other, we had good chemistry, and we had similar interests and like-minded values.

The banking laws in Australia permit financial institutions to be more flexible. The banking and property group within Macquarie, led by Bill Moss, had a strong reputation for its entrepreneurialism, often achieving extraordinary success in taking a position on businesses or projects in challenging times. As an investment bank, Macquarie formed numerous property trusts that held a variety of assets in which Macquarie earned management and incentive-based fees. They just seemed like a natural fit for us. As an Australian banking icon, they brought to the table a twenty-year history in property development and financing, 7,000 employees operating in twenty-three countries around the world, and more than $20 billion in property under management. GWSE brought golf course design, golf expertise, and brand know-how. In my mind, Macquarie was potentially the ideal partner for us.

Once again, the key was to identify a niche, and to that end, I understood all too well that Australia was light-years behind the

United States in developing golf course–driven real estate communities. In the late 1990s, Australia had one or two good examples, but these were in resort destinations. Nobody had created the type of product that is so plentiful in the United States for primary residential real estate. As our business negotiations progressed, Bill and I discussed the idea of creating a development company that would operate as a joint venture. We would work to refine our business in Australia before moving to other markets, but in the back of my mind, I knew that if we were able to be successful in Australia, Macquarie would see it as an ideal vehicle for other markets.

From the outset, I understood that this new company would have to deliver a value proposition for the consumer. If someone was going to buy an expensive house in a golf course community, they were not going to do so simply because a celebrity's name was on the marquee. We were going to have to deliver a better product, it was going to have to be better planned, and there would have to be a better sense of community than in other developments.

The basics of GWSE's partnership with Macquarie were straightforward, and for the most part, we had no trouble agreeing on terms. The bank would provide equity and expertise in raising third-party capital as well as other management and financial engineering services. We would bring in our expertise as golf course designers, the Greg Norman branding, and our know-how regarding community development. Macquarie would receive a 70 percent interest in the venture, and GWSE would receive 30 percent free-carried interest. Separate from the shareholding, it was important to me that this venture pay GNGCD its standard design fee for work completed. Early in the process of our negotiations, Macquarie requested that I contribute my design services gratis. I balked at that suggestion, because I have a general rule that each division of GWSE should "wash its own face." In general, I didn't want to have a situation where GNGCD subsidized my participation in a development company, nor did I want the development company to get a free ride from design. Overall, I try to have each of my businesses operate independently, so there is no confusion with respect to individual profitability.

While structuring the joint venture was relatively uncomplicated, finding a suitable name proved to be a bit more challenging. Macquarie wanted to call the enterprise the Greg Norman Development Company. I didn't. Rather, I made a conscious decision early on that this company would be more suitable as a related brand. I wanted it to be more like the Cobra deal. The fact that my name was not in the title of the company would give me a clean exit. In that case, the only name left hanging over the front door was Cobra. What I was really trying to do here was think ahead. I was "beginning with the end in mind," and I was already planning a suitable exit strategy. At some point in time, this new company was going to have a capital event, and I did not want to go through any legacy issues. In the end, Macquarie agreed to create equity in a related brand.

When Macquarie Bank and GWSE first incorporated our new development company, we did so under the name Turnberry Resort Developments. The idea was simple. I had won my first British Open at Turnberry. The name resonated with our audience and it was connected to me—but not too closely connected. Unfortunately, we encountered some trademark opposition from Starwood Capital Group, which owned the Turnberry Resort in Scotland. So we chose Medallist Developments, which came from my golf club in Florida (Medalist Golf Club). I knew we wouldn't have any trademark problems with this, but in order to create some more separation, we added an additional "l," which also reflected a more traditional, Commonwealth, Queen's English spelling.

Along these same lines, each project would enter into a project branding agreement, which stipulated that after all homesites were sold, the project would be entitled to use the Medallist branding but would no longer have access to my name outside of my involvement as a golf course designer. Ultimately, this protected Medallist's interests so that it could undertake another project in the same area at a later date with no saturation or overlap of the Norman branding.

In establishing a board of directors for Medallist Developments, we agreed it would be best to have six members, with Bill Moss serving as chairman and having the deciding vote in the event of a deadlock. I wanted to make certain that we chose people who did not all think alike. Rather, I wanted directors who complemented one another's skills, abilities, and personalities but would offer constructive and sometimes opposing points of view. In the end, we were able to balance Bill's entrepreneurial genius with the calculating wisdom and experience of Richard Sheppard, deputy managing director of Macquarie Bank, and Tony Fehon, from Macquarie's leisure group, who would also serve as CEO of Medallist (a position later to be handed off to Neil Gamble). Bart Collins and Bob Harrison also served on the board, along with me. Overall, we had the strength of diversity on our team. We also built some strong interpersonal relationships, as we enjoyed one another's company.

Medallist's first development happened to be in my old backyard—just north of Brisbane in the town of Caloundra. This project was a 2,000-acre tract of land owned by the Henzle family, who had engaged GNGCD to do an initial routing for the golf course in hopes of attracting a reputable development company. As we were just forming Medallist, we applied more of a banking approach to this first endeavor. Essentially, we formed a special-purpose vehicle, with the Henzles contributing their land and Medallist matching the value in equity. From there, we financed the remainder of the project. As we had not yet built up our resources, we appointed the Henzle group as project managers and real estate agents. From the outset, I felt that GWSE was able to offer quite a bit of value to the process, as we refined the routing of the golf course to unlock considerable value in the property by creating more golf course frontage. Already, I was challenged to think as a golf course designer intent on getting the best possible result for the golf experience, while at the same time balancing the commercial aspects of being a property developer.

As a testament to the success of the project, my parents took the ninety-minute drive up from Brisbane, built a house, and became residents of Pelican Waters. I say "testament," because my father is a very discerning buyer and, given the nature of my interest in the development, I was able to offer only a small discount on the sale. Over the last five years, my parents have enjoyed their experience at Pelican Waters. In fact, my mother has claimed the women's club championship on two occasions. In 2005 we sold the golf course and the remainder of our real estate at Pelican Waters, and I'm pleased to say the project turned over a very respectable 27 percent internal rate of return (IRR), which netted $20 million for Medallist.

Over the first few years Medallist went through some growing pains. After all, we were combining an entrepreneur with a major bank. Our objectives were aligned, but our methodologies were sometimes different. At GWSE, we were go-getters. When we identified a golf site, we'd say, "Hey, this development is perfect. Let's bring in Medallist."

But while we were ready to roll the dice and play, the bank was much more conservative and cautious. The entire process was rigorous and disciplined, and it often took three or four months to complete. In certain instances, the laborious nature of the bank's due diligence caused us to lose projects—and that frustrated me. Bill Moss, however, always counseled me to be patient and think more long-term. "Greg, I've been in this business for a long time," he'd say. "Ninety percent of the real estate deals I've looked at have been good deals. But ninety percent of the developers I've worked with have gone broke. One bad deal can put you out of business. Never rush into a deal. We may have lost this one particular project, but others will come along. Be patient!"

Over time, we streamlined the evaluation process and I learned to be a bit more patient. To be frank, however, I think working with GWSE reminded the bank of its roots, which were entrepreneurial. The organization was actually established back in 1969 by only three people. Initially starting out as a subsidiary of an English merchant bank, Hill Samuel, it had spun off into Macquarie in 1985 and, within two decades, had grown to one of the top twenty companies on the Australian stock exchange. Actually, if you rank it on a consolidated capitalization, Macquarie is one of the top 150 companies in the world.

The development business, as I quickly found out, is not just an easy street to make money. You really have to understand the industry. And indeed, there was a lot of learning to do on my part. Before I was introduced to Macquarie, I knew very little about running an integrated development company. I'd had success with a number of property transactions, but operating an eighty-person organization that would ultimately be creating real estate communities on three continents was an entirely different exercise. Macquarie helped me understand the development business, which gave me perspective for not only our development company but also my design business. Ultimately, that knowledge changed my perspective of macroeconomics and the cyclical nature of the development business.

Additionally, Bill and Richard gave me some direction on how to manage a large organization. Formally, they called their leadership style "Freedom Within Boundaries." Informally, it was referred to as "Loose-Tight." Everyone had to adhere to specific and very "tight" boundaries. Beyond that, outlying offices could operate under a "loose" set of guidelines. The resulting effect was to encourage innovation, create a sense of ownership among employees in their various businesses, and provide the benefits of an entrepreneurial approach. That particular leadership style would really come in handy for GWSE as we expanded our business interests in later years.

As Medallist took on more projects, we began to evolve into a more integrated business. We developed skills that would enable us to control more aspects of a project, which enabled us to accelerate our rate of sales and build more value in that project. For example, in 1998 we had to make a determination as to whether we were going to manage the golf operations of the courses we built or outsource this function. In making that decision, I recalled what the European hotelier Lord Forte had advised many years before when I was the club professional for one of his resorts. "Talk to the janitors, the maids, and the front desk personnel before you go in to see the general manager," said Lord Forte. "That way, when you ask a question, you'll know whether or not the answer you receive is the truth." Because Australia was not long on sophisticated, Western-style golf management companies, we decided to import that talent by forming a joint venture with Scottsdale, Arizona–based Troon Golf. We considered partnering with others, but from my first meeting with Dana Garmany, Troon's founder and CEO, I knew we were singing off the same hymnal sheet. In addition to being a great operator, Dana shared my view of the golf course experience from a player's perspective. He spoke in great detail and with great passion about the strategy of Alister MacKenzie's design at Royal Melbourne. Unlike many of his American counterparts, Dana understood that golf course maintenance need not be about wall-to-wall turf grass. It was about the player's experience. And as a management company, it was about quality and service. So at my suggestion, Medallist formed a joint venture with Troon in Australia and Asia. With time, this initiative became an important part of Medallist's skill set.

Today Medallist controls project management, real estate marketing and sales, brand management, database management, and funds management for our projects. As such, we have evolved into an integrated development company. This has enhanced the company's overall performance, and I learned to adopt the same principles in my other businesses, golf course design in particular. Just as I had created an adjacent-space opportunity some years earlier with my turf grass company, I worked with my golf course design team to create a construction management capability that was akin to what we were doing with Medallist as project managers. By adding a construction management service to our portfolio, the developer could now choose to have us manage the construction of the golf course (for an additional fee). At this point, like Medallist, my other businesses were growing tentacles and providing a more comprehensive range of services.

Today I stay very involved with Medallist Developments. Not only do I participate as an active member of the board, but I work hard to make sure my business values are practiced at Medallist, as they are in the other arms of Great White Shark Enterprises. We maintain steadfast ethical standards, treat our clients' construction dollars as though they were our own—which, in the case of Medallist, they are—and have expanded our commitment to environmental stewardship as one of our guiding principles. We combine information collected from local and regional environmental organizations with our own expertise and knowledge of different geographical terrains. We pay great attention to detail and local design influence. As a result, we're able to build more than just simple housing communities. We're able to create coastal sanctuaries and other innovative concepts.

It didn't take long for Medallist Developments to expand beyond Australia. Within two years, we opened an office in the United States and set our sights on expanding throughout the United States, Mexico, and South Africa. This expansion turned out to be a great opportunity for Macquarie Bank. As a powerhouse in a small market, it gave them an opportunity to enter a big market in a specific niche. In recent years, Australia has had a voracious appetite for investing in real estate overseas. In part, this desire stems from the nation's superannuation system, which is akin to the U.S. Social Security system. In 1992, the government legislated that employers must match 9 percent of workers' salary. That reserve now totals $750 billion and is expected to reach $1.5 trillion by 2015. Because Australia's markets are too small to accommodate this level of investment, the government has been forced to look abroad, and it stipulated that only certain types of stable investments would be allowed. Property in the form of listed trusts—equivalent to a real estate investment trust (REIT) in the U.S.—is one such acceptable investment instrument. Macquarie Bank was one of the nation's leaders in leveraging their short-term balance sheet into long-term equity participation in overseas markets. As a matter of fact, by 2006, Australia was the second largest investor (after Germany) in property in the United States—and Macquarie represented an astounding 80 percent of that investment. That fact, in part, is how Macquarie Bank became one of the largest and most envied investment banks in the world. Today Macquarie is one of the world's largest infrastructure financiers, owning and operating a wide array of monopolistic assets, ranging from airports to toll roads.

In making the move to the United States, we acknowledged that Medallist couldn't have the sort of penetration we were accustomed to in Australia, where there are only three major markets (Brisbane, Sydney, and Melbourne). As much as I wanted to see Medallist dominate, the reality was that we could really balance only three or four projects at a time. In and of itself, that would make Medallist a sizable golf course community developer. At the same time, though, Greg Norman Golf Course Design (GNGCD) could still take on fifteen or more projects a year in the U.S. So in order to avoid conflicts and create prospective opportunities, I had to make certain that there was always good communication between Medallist and our design business.

Specific to the United States, we created a unique product, Norman Estates, which would prove to be a major asset to both Medallist and GNGCD. We realized early on that GNGCD was the perfect conduit to create a number of smaller and more immediate development opportunities. By following GNGCD's coattails into projects, Medallist could work with a major developer that had already spent millions of dollars and considerable time securing land and entitlements. Norman Estates is, essentially, a gated community within a gated community, developed under the auspices of Medallist. Ultimately it became the forerunner to Medallist developing a new product in the United States. It also proved to be a good sales tool for our golf course design business by promoting the idea of me (through Medallist) making a direct investment into the project. For Medallist, it provided immediate success in a variety of markets. More important, however, it helped smooth out earnings when layered across the inevitable peaks and troughs of projects in which Medallist was the principal developer. Our first such project in the U.S. was done in partnership with WCI at the Ritz-Carlton in Naples, Florida; the second was in La Quinta, California, at the Norman Course located at PGA West.

Overall, Medallist is an embodiment of my long-term business model. Residential golf course communities have a gestation period of between seven and ten years. As there is no quick turnaround on capital, it only makes sense to structure things for the long haul. There are a number of possible long-term strategies for Medallist, including a capital event of some description. While we could structure the company as an IPO, it's often difficult to run a development company in the public forum because earnings are typically unpredictable given the cyclical nature of the business. More likely for us is the prospect of selling down a portion of our business or operating it under a dividend distribution policy. I find it interesting to note that, as the business has grown, so too has my role within the company: In the early years, I was limited to golf course design.

Today we continue to build on our brand, even moving into lifestyle-themed, non-golf initiatives. And as the business evolves, I find myself excited about the challenge of contributing in other ways. Most recently I have spent time in New York and the Middle East raising capital. With the right support structure, I feel very comfortable and thoroughly enjoy the challenges in this new environment. It seems that every day an opportunity to enter another country presents itself. But it takes discipline to turn down opportunities that could stretch our resources too thin. In all cases, however, we stay with our call. All of this growth occurs quietly. Unlike my pro golfing career, it has fallen beneath the radar screens of the media and out of range of their television cameras.

CHAPTER TWENTY-SEVEN

IN MARCH 1997, I learned a valuable lesson in my never-ending quest to stay out of the headlines: Don't allow the sitting president of the United States to bust up his knee on your front porch.

It was a freak accident, I admit, when Bill Clinton's knee buckled and he collapsed into my arms. Nonetheless, it was an alarming moment for everyone involved. The president had come to Florida at my invitation to play golf in a member-guest tournament at Medalist Golf Club. I had first met him during a round of golf in November 1996. And that is an interesting story in and of itself.

The White House called my office in May 1996 and asked if I would be able to play golf with the president during the week in November when he would be in Australia. I responded by saying, "Well, let me take a look at my schedule. I know that's the week of the Australian Open. I'm not sure whether I'm going to have time. Let me get back to you."

At that time, I was not a Clinton fan. I wasn't a fan of his policies or his politics, and I didn't like a lot of the things I heard on the news about him. So I called up my friend former president George H. W. Bush to ask for advice. "Mr. President," I said, "I have this request from the White House to play golf with President Clinton when he's in Australia in November. I'm not sure I want to play with him, so how should I handle it?"

"I'm just going to give you one piece of advice, Greg," Bush responded. "You must always respect the office of President of the United States. You should play with him."

"If you think I should play with him, then I will," I replied. So I made a few phone calls and worked everything out so I could play golf with President Clinton on Thursday afternoon, after my morning round in the Australian Open.

When November rolled around, we arranged for the New South Wales Golf Club, of which I'm a member, to close the entire golf course while the president and I were playing. As we began our round, I learned that President Clinton was not only an avid golf fan but was good enough to break 80.

We were enjoying our round of golf together when, in the middle of the 16th fairway, we stopped for a break and started stretching. Then we sat on the ground and engaged in a lengthy conversation. It was just President Clinton, myself, and Tony Navarro, my caddie. We were isolated from everything. (There were a few Secret Service agents in the vicinity, but that was it.) President Clinton asked me about my workout routine. And after a little while, he brought up the 1996 Masters and its aftermath. The president said he admired the way I'd conducted myself. But he also surprised me by saying that he too had learned from my experience. Throughout the 1996 presidential campaign, he was miles ahead in the polls. People were taking it for granted that he was going to win handily. "Whenever anybody on my campaign staff pointed to those leads," he said, "I would respond by saying 'Remember Greg Norman at the Masters.' It doesn't matter how good you are or how big a lead you have. You can still be caught before it's all over."

Through that round of golf, President Clinton and I developed a strong bond, one that would ultimately lead to a close friendship. We stayed in touch by phone over the next several months. At one point President Clinton indicated that he wanted to play another round with me, so I invited him down to Florida for our local tournament. The plan was for him to stay overnight in the carriage house on our property, play golf the next day, and then have dinner with us that evening. Between golf and dinner, President Clinton had also made arrangements to visit Lighthouse Elementary School in Jupiter to speak with students and their teachers.

He arrived about midnight but wanted to talk for a while before going to bed. So we went into the main house and sat down. The president had a sandwich and a soda while I had a beer. We talked about our kids, about golf, about Australia and other international affairs. And then I took the opportunity to ask him a few questions about the U.S. Constitution, which I had read several times over the years. Finally, at around one-thirty in the morning, President Clinton looked at his watch and pointed out that we were both going to have to be on the golf course in a few hours, so we'd better get some sleep. "Okay, let me walk you over to the guesthouse," I said.

On the way out the door, we were still chatting amiably, when we started down the front dark-wood steps that lead to a stone landing. President Clinton apparently misjudged the final step, because he caught his right heel on the step's edge and, in trying not to lose his balance, instinctively lurched backward. But his knee buckled, there was a loud pop, and he fell back into me, writhing in pain. Thankfully I managed to catch him before his head hit the ground, but his weight caught me off guard. I managed to place my leg under him while cradling his head in my arms, and a Secret Service agent immediately called for help. All of a sudden more than a dozen people showed up. Secret Service agents, paramedics, police officers, and a deputy sheriff all came running out of the garage. "Oh my God!" I thought. "What's going on?" I didn't know at the time that the "pop" we heard was the tendon tearing loose from his right kneecap. Meanwhile, I was supporting his body weight with my left leg. After a short time, the paramedics pulled the president off me and checked his vital signs. "It's my knee, my knee!" he said. "There's something wrong! I can't straighten it!" They quickly put ice and a splint on his leg, lifted him onto a stretcher, and whisked him off in an ambulance. For obvious reasons, there were no sirens.

In a flash, everybody was gone. One moment I had been talking to the president of the United States, and a moment later I was standing on my front porch by myself. The only thing I could think of doing at that moment was to go back in the house to tell Laura. "Laura, you're not going to believe what just happened."

She sat up in bed and said, "What?"

"The president fell on the steps outside and they've taken him to the hospital."

"What? The president fell?"

A counterassault team accompanied Clinton to the hospital, but another group stayed on the property. Approximately thirty minutes later, I received a phone call informing me that he was going to come back to the house. So everybody scrambled into motion. As the president could no longer negotiate stairs, we decided to put him in our son's room on the first floor. We had everything ready for his arrival, but at four o'clock we received another call and were informed that the president would not be coming back to our house after all. Rather, he was going to be taken directly to Air Force One and would be flown back to Bethesda Naval Hospital in Washington for surgery. President Clinton, however, asked us to come over to the airport because he wanted to spend a little time with my family.

When Laura, Morgan, Gregory, and I showed up on Air Force One at six o'clock, the president was in the front of the aircraft, lying down with his leg strapped in a splint. We could tell he was in pain, but he would not take a strong painkiller. Under law, if the president of the United States takes a narcotic, he has to hand over power to the vice president while he's on that drug. Attempting to mask the pain with only aspirin, he smiled, chatted, and posed for pictures with all of us. He joked with me that his golf handicap was going up by the minute. And before we departed, he apologized to us because he knew there would be a media firestorm. In all, we were aboard Air Force One for thirty minutes, and President Clinton could not have been more accommodating.

While flying back to Washington, President Clinton explained to some members of the media (via telephone) that what had happened was "just an accident," and that "accidents happen to people." Another measure of the man is that the president even spent ten minutes on the phone with the kids and teachers of Lighthouse Elementary School. "I'm so disappointed," he said. "Please give me a rain check and forgive me for not being there as promised. I'll come back, though. And next time, it will be without incident."

Back at Bethesda, President Clinton underwent successful surgery. He had torn 90 percent of the quadriceps tendon, which connects the upper thigh to the kneecap. The surgeons cut a four- to five-inch incision down the outside of his right leg and drilled holes into his kneecap to reconnect the tendon. He was in a cast or brace for more than eight weeks, then had to undergo months of rehabilitation. I found it amazing that, just one week after the incident, President Clinton traveled to Helsinki, Finland, for a summit with Russian president Boris Yeltsin.

President Clinton was 100 percent correct that the media would pounce. Countless radio and television talk shows tried to get me to comment on the situation. "Come on, Greg, what really happened?" You can imagine some of the rumors that circulated. Through it all, though, I declined every interview. The only comment I made was to set the record straight: The president had not been drinking before he fell. President Clinton did come back to visit Lighthouse Elementary School, and he invited my family to the White House later that summer.

I must admit that prior to meeting President Clinton, I had drawn an erroneous conclusion about him. I had let the media influence my view. And you would think that I, of all people, would know better. President Clinton is a tremendous person. He's also one of the most connecting individuals I have ever met. I have a great deal of admiration for him, and we maintain a strong bond to this day.

That entire escapade was unfortunate, and it was somewhat symbolic of how my game fared over the next two years. In 1997, I missed the cut in the Masters and U.S. Open and finished tied for 36th in the British Open and 13th in the PGA. There were a couple of bright spots, though. At the St. Jude Classic in Memphis, Tennessee, I pulled out a putter I'd had since I was sixteen. It was the first time since 1989 that I used it, but my putting had been so poor in recent months I figured it couldn't hurt.

Saturday's third round was nearly canceled because of inclement weather, so I had to play 15 holes Sunday morning and then go out and play the final round. I began that last 18 by parring every hole on the front 9. Frustrated and stuck in the pack with only a few holes left, I began my charge on the 16th, blasting a bunker shot to within two inches for a tap-in birdie. On 17, I hit a 4-iron within four feet of the flag and made the birdie putt to tie for the lead. And then on 18, I hit a 6-iron from 190 yards and made a 30-foot birdie putt. That was enough to win by one stroke. In the media center afterward, I was informed that with this victory I became the first PGA Tour player to surpass $11 million in career earnings. It also extended my streak of consecutive years with a victory on the PGA Tour to six.

This victory still wasn't enough to quash the media naysayers. In fact, a headline in *Golf World* read "Big Fish in a Little Pond," a reference to the quality of the field in Memphis. The negative slant continued when I missed the cut in the U.S. Open. "Greg Norman is too old to win another major," people proclaimed. "He can no longer take the pressure." To tell you the truth, I laughed when I read that statement. Even at forty-two, I still went out there to win every single week, no matter if I was playing in a major championship, a regular PGA Tour event, a charity tournament, or the Medalist member-guest. To me the game of golf was still a challenge. I enjoyed the competitive atmosphere, and whatever the event, I was always trying to make the shot.

Ten days after the U.S. Open, I teamed up with Brad Faxon to win the Fred Meyer Challenge in Oregon. It was only a two-day event, but man, did we sizzle. We shot a tournament record 11-under-par 60 in the first round and followed it up with a 63 in the second round. I personally carded thirteen birdies and an eagle over that two-day span—all with my old putter. And when you combine that with Faxon's stellar play, we sailed to a third consecutive victory in this event.

Two weeks later, I picked up my 20th PGA Tour victory at the NEC World Series of Golf in Akron, Ohio. The Firestone Country Club that year was pelted with heavy rains, and once again my putter was hot. I don't know what it was about playing in the rain that year, but I seemed to swim to the top of the leaderboard each time. I managed to make three birdies in a four-hole stretch on the back 9 to edge out defending champion Phil Mickelson. I appreciated Phil's comment afterward. "I don't feel like I lost today," he said. "I just didn't go out and win it—but Greg did. He deserves the trophy."

That victory earned me a ten-year exemption on the PGA Tour, but I still was not satisfied with my overall performance in 1997. When I was asked how I rated the year, I responded by saying "Poor plus." I have always set extremely high goals, and I believe that drives me to work even harder.

I began the 1998 season in February by finally winning the tournament I owned and operated in Australia, the Greg Norman Holden International at the Australian Golf Club, the course where I played my first Australian Open twenty-two years earlier. It was even more special because it fell on the week of my forty-third birthday. After shooting 68 and 73 in the first two rounds, I trailed Spain's José María Olazábal by 7 shots. I came from behind to beat him by a single shot with closing rounds of 64 (a course record) and 67. But the real drama occurred on the very last hole of the tournament, the par-5 18th.

Olazábal was trailing me by 2 shots when he pulled his drive into the trees on the left side of the fairway. I drove my ball right down the center and was talking to my caddie about laying up with a 9-iron and then hitting a safe wedge to the middle of the green. After all, Olazábal was 230 yards from the green and his approach shot was blocked by trees. I figured a conservative par would give me the victory. Olazábal, however, pulled off one of the best recovery shots I've ever seen.

Using a 3-wood and standing under a tree with his ball buried in the rough, Olazábal kept his shot low until it cleared the overhanging branches. Then the ball rose majestically, faded toward the green, which was guarded by both water and sand, and came to rest only 30 feet from the flag. Now he had a putt for eagle to tie me. It was a tremendous shot! My mind flashed back to the 1987 Masters, when Larry Mize holed his miracle shot, and I remembered to always expect the unexpected. Rather than being shaken, I calmly put my 9-iron back in my bag and pulled out a 3-iron. I knew I had to go for the green in two, and I was well aware that if I miss-hit this shot and landed in the water, I'd be handing Olazábal the tournament. "The hell with it," I thought. "I'm going to win this thing right now." And sure enough, I put my ball on the green. We both 2-putted, and I walked away with the trophy.

At that point I was really looking forward to the upcoming season, especially the major tournaments. Unfortunately, I began experiencing some discomfort in my left shoulder and missed the cut in the Masters. Then, while preparing for the Players Championship, the shoulder became so aggravated that I scheduled two appointments with orthopedic specialists. "It's a posterior injury," they both said. "This type of injury was caused by your golf swing and your practice regimen over the years. If you want to make a complete recovery, you'll have to undergo surgery. And the sooner the better."

As a result, I withdrew from all my scheduled PGA Tour events and had shoulder surgery in late April. I was away from golf for seven long months. Finally, in November, I goaded my doctors into clearing me so that I could play in the Shark Shootout.

Before we hit our first drives, I turned to my partner, Steve Elkington. "Okay, mate," I said, "I'm wearing steel spikes so that I can ride your back for the entire tournament."

"No worries, Greg," Elkie replied with a big grin.

Surprisingly, we finished regulation in a tie with Peter Jacobsen and John Cook. That forced the first playoff in the history of the tournament. On the third sudden-death hole, Elkington landed his approach within two feet of the pin. I sank the putt and finally won my own tournament after a decade of trying.

Overall, my shoulder felt pretty good—and I especially enjoyed the pressure shots and the camaraderie of the event. At the press conference afterward, Elkington actually had the nerve to throw a zinger my way.

"Did you enjoy playing with Greg?" someone asked.

"Yeah, it was good to see the old man playing again," Elkie responded.

Despite my seven-month layoff, I stayed very active. I used the downtime to concentrate on, even accelerate, my seven-year plan. For example, I contacted a company that had been making a lot of headlines in the sports marketing world. SFX was to entertainment what IMG was to sports. It owned or operated many outdoor amphitheaters and promoted nearly all of the major summer concert tours across the United States, from Madonna to the Eagles. During the past three years, SFX had been aggressively expanding into sports management and had spent over $300 million buying some of the major sports agencies in the business. These included FAME, David Falk's agency that handled such celebrity athletes and agents as Michael Jordan, ProServ, the Hendrick brothers out of Houston, and Arn Tellem, to name a few. In very short order, they became a dominant force in athlete representation, but they could not penetrate golf, where IMG held a monopoly.

As I was making note of SFX's growth-by-acquisition strategy, I reflected on what relationship, if any, could exist between our two groups. Eventually, I came to realize that while I had done a good job of building businesses around myself and while it was not critically important to have more endorsements, it would probably serve me well to have two or three well-placed endorsements that would help maintain my profile as I played in fewer golf tournaments. It made sense, I felt, to explore the notion of subcontracting to SFX the task of finding those best-of-breed endorsements. Knowing that SFX would gain a great deal of credibility by signing me (because I was formerly represented by IMG), and believing that an integrated sports management group would be well positioned to execute on this strategy, we entered into discussions with SFX. What began as a fairly straightforward arrangement turned into a complex, 300-page agreement covering myriad business-to-business activities and the sale of my event management company in Australia.

Specific to Australia, SFX wanted to penetrate this market as both an entertainment and sports marketing company. While they controlled the summer concert tours in the U.S., they weren't effectively leveraging those acts into overseas markets. Thus, the prospect of creating an entertainment company in Australia held great promise. Given my standing in Australia, we agreed to sell to SFX my events company, which operated the Greg Norman Holden International and the Australian PGA Championship. We then brokered an arrangement whereby SFX would purchase the Heineken Classic, giving them three tournaments—in Sydney, Melbourne, and Brisbane. For this I would receive a mid-seven-figure payment for the sale, a 15 percent participation in SFX's sports business in

Australia, and a 10 percent participation in their Australian entertainment business in perpetuity.

While I had successfully run my events business for a number
of years and while it was quite profitable, I had the general sense
that, in the wake of the Olympics, the sponsorship market in golf
was becoming quite soft. But at the same time, the consolidation of
the premier events on the Australian Tour made eminently good
sense. In the U.S. there were two components to GWSE's arrangement with SFX. The first centered on my becoming a merchandising client; and while I was confident SFX had the wherewithal to
secure two or three major merchandising relationships, we negotiated a mid-seven-figure guarantee that was paid as an advance. As
SFX secured the endorsements, they would receive a dispropor-
tionately high commission to offset their advance. But in the event
they were not successful, I would retain the advance.

The fifth component of our agreement included adding me to
their client roster. For this I would be granted a 15 percent interest
in their golf division. The theory was that I would validate their capabilities and, in so doing, attract other players to come aboard.
This was not unlike Arnold Palmer maintaining a small percentage
ownership in IMG.

In 1999, Bob Sillerman and Mike Farrel sold SFX to Clear Channel Communications, the owner and operator of 2,000 radio stations and significant holdings in outdoor advertising. Quite frankly,
I was surprised that the acquisition received FTC approval, because
now Clear Channel had effectively cornered the market through
their radio, venue, and promotion business. As much as the entertainment business made sense to Clear Channel, there were some
serious challenges with integrating the new sports agenda. Aside
from having few or no synergies with radio, I thought the growth-
by-acquisition strategy SFX had employed was flawed. Why would
an agent such as David Falk operate as a salaried employee after his
business had been bought out for $100 million? And why would he
stay with the SFX program after the expiration of his employment
contract? It just didn't make sense to me, and, predictably, there
was quite a bit of infighting. In the end, SFX Sports Group became

a series of independent agencies whose only common thread was their ownership structure.

So where did GWSE come out in the equation? Well, we didn't get the long dollar by virtue of our participation in three of their business units, but in April 2006 we negotiated a buyout of my participation in those businesses, which, together with the merchandising advance and the sale of my events group, made for a reasonable windfall.

When I take a moment to reflect on the sports marketing aspect of my career, I realize I've run the full gamut. I had the experience of being taken advantage of by an impresario (James Marshall). I enjoyed a good relationship with IMG, but I learned that, ultimately, that firm was more tactical and less strategic. And I've managed my own businesses and formed ventures with large sports and entertainment companies. Throughout the entire process, I've been vigilant in representing my own rights, and I believe I've come through it all in fairly good shape.

CHAPTER TWENTY-EIGHT

I HAVE ALWAYS BEEN PROUD of my relationship with Qantas Airways, the eighty-six-year-old carrier and perhaps the most recognizable Australian brand in the world. As part of my effort to be a global ambassador for golf and Australia, I signed a formal deal with the airline—one of my earliest endorsements—in 1976, and I am exceedingly proud to have featured its logo on my bag for thirty years. Given that I have owned my own aircraft for the past fifteen years, you might think that my Qantas relationship would have dissolved. But the company continues to utilize me, more as a spokesperson for Australia as a destination than for the airline. I have also been a spokesperson for the Australian Tourist Commission (ATC) on two different occasions, the first targeting the U.S. market through a clever television campaign and the second targeting Asia.

Through my interaction with Qantas and the ATC, I have learned that, according to consumer research, Australia was the number one destination that Americans most wanted to visit. Sadly, though, very few Americans make the journey because of the distance and the time required. Of course, this statistic confirmed what I had always believed: that there is a great affinity between Australia and the United States. We have the same values, and we place priorities on the same things, although my fellow countrymen are a bit more socially inclined. I'm also proud to say that since World War I, Australia is the only country that has stood shoulder to shoulder with the United States in every war and major conflict, and reciprocally, the U.S. has always looked out for its little brother down under.

Because so few Americans make the trip, I've found that, to a certain extent, America's image of Australia is often trivialized by advertising campaigns for various products and services. In some small measure, I find it frustrating that many of the products have no connection to Australia whatsoever. As much as I enjoy my relationship with Chris Sullivan, of Outback Steakhouse, you won't find anyone in Australia that has the vaguest idea what a "bloomin' onion" is. Mind you, we do it to ourselves. One of the more famous television campaigns for Australian tourism revolved around Paul Hogan throwing a "shrimp on the barbie." Even though we refer to shrimp as prawns, the spin doctors clearly didn't think throwing a "prawn on the barbie" would resonate with the U.S. consumer. The point here is that the U.S. consumer feels a connection with Australia, but there are very few authentic Australian products that have been brought to the U.S.

In the early days of Greg Norman Collection, we sent our designers to Australia to draw inspiration from some of the aboriginal artwork, as well as styles and sourcing. It was important for me to have some connection with Australia for my apparel group. While I was proud to make that connection, I hadn't really succeeded in bringing an Australian product to the U.S. Rather, I had only drawn inspiration from Australia.

I knew I wanted to take the next step and truly validate an Australian product in the United States. So I set up a workshop with my Sydney office to flesh out what brands or products we could take to the U.S. Australia at the time had only two brands with international recognition—Qantas and Foster's—but there were others that could potentially be unlocked and brought to the U.S. Examples include Crown Lager, R. M. Williams, Country Road, and Vegemite. These brands were iconic in Australia, but after our full consideration, we recognized they did not play to our strengths. After all, we did not have expertise in consumer product marketing and distribution. Therefore, we turned our attention to a different strategy, one that would align my brand with a product category that already had some form of distribution into the U.S. It wasn't long before we identified wine as the ideal product.

From the time I drove up to the Sonoma Valley with my friend George Kelley on my first trip to America back in 1976, to my travels while on the European Tour, until now, wine is something I've always been passionate about. As I tried wines from various regions, my palate naturally led me to compare everything to the wines made in Australia. And naturally, wherever I went, I engaged in conversations where I continually sang the praises of my home country's wines. After some initial research, we recognized that Australian wines were somewhat in vogue in the U.S., but the consumer could not differentiate among the brands, the varietals, or the regions. Clearly, the U.S. consumer needed some leadership with regard to Australian wines—and that was the genesis of our creating a brand of premium Australian wines.

So we put together a business brief and shopped it to Australia's three largest producers. We began with Mildara Blass, owned by Foster's. Over the years, I had built a solid friendship with Ted Kunkel, CEO of the Foster's Group. He used to head up Molsen in Canada, and at that time we played a lot of golf together. Over the years, Foster's sponsored my golf tournaments, in both Australia and the U.S., but we were never able to find a strategic fit. Part of the problem rested with U.S. federal regulations that prohibited an active athlete from advertising alcohol. In the United States, for instance, I could never be used in a Foster's television campaign. And with a 60 percent market share at home, Foster's didn't need me to bolster sales in Australia.

My Sydney team approached Ray King, the CEO of Mildara Blass, and his executive team, and were met with a lukewarm reaction, in part because they did not have a good understanding of the U.S. market. At the time, Mildara Blass had achieved good penetration in Canada with Wolf Blass but not much depth in the United States.

We then approached Southcorp, Australia's largest winemaker, who produced some of the best wines in the world, including the famous Penfolds Grange, voted the best wine in the world by *Wine Spectator* on several occasions. As a highbrow producer, Southcorp scoffed at the idea of creating a wine in partnership with a golfer.

Finally we pitched our idea to BRL Hardy in Adelaide and found an enthusiastic executive in the form of the company's chief strategist, Chris Day. "I like it," said Chris. Over the next few months, we worked with BRL Hardy to refine the business plan, on the pretense that we were still shopping the deal.

After some refinement, we took the plan back to Foster's. On this occasion, however, we went directly to Ted Kunkel and told him that there was a qualified party very interested in consummating a deal. To Ted's credit, he agreed to intervene personally and placed a call to Chris Sullivan, owner of Outback Steakhouse. Over the years, Outback had poured a lot of Foster's beer at their more than 800 restaurants. "Chris, I'm in discussions with Greg regarding a partnership on a wine venture. Can I rely on you to purchase one case each month for each of your restaurants?"

Sullivan agreed, and Ted then put in a call to Ray King. "Ray, I've just talked to Chris Sullivan at Outback. He's agreed to buy an amount of Greg Norman Estates wine equal to half of the sales minimum in the first year. I would strongly suggest we consider moving forward on this opportunity." With that call, and after reading our revised and more detailed business plan, Ray King agreed to proceed.

Now it was time to iron out a business agreement with Mildara Blass. When working with partners, my philosophy has always been that it has to be beneficial for everyone involved in order for it to be beneficial to anyone. Mildara Blass wanted to improve their standing in the United States, and GWSE wanted to get into the wine industry. Based on those two mutual needs, we structured what we now term a "brand joint venture."

Together, we created an unincorporated joint venture called GN Wines. Foster's would have a 70 percent interest, and GWSE a 30 percent free-carried interest. GN Wines then entered into a licensing agreement with me for my name and likeness and the shark logo. The licensing agreement also incorporated my personal services, and under the terms of the licensing agreement I would receive a 6 percent royalty set against a minimum guarantee of sales.

This brand joint venture structure is unique in that I have an equity stake in the business, and as such it goes far beyond a one-dimensional licensing agreement. Having a shareholding stake also provides me with an exit strategy in the event we spin off the company or have some other form of a capital event (such as a secondary listing). In this instance, I also applied a lesson learned from the Akubra deal. In the event that sales exceeded the minimum as set out in the licensing agreement, the higher sales figure would set a new benchmark for my minimum royalty. We also put in some language to the effect that if my royalty did not earn the equivalent of 80 percent of sales from the previous two years (on an average-weighted basis), then we had the option to terminate the agreement.

As part of the same negotiation, we structured an endorsement arrangement between Foster's beer and myself. While we would market Greg Norman Estates to the consumer, I would also work with Foster's "below the line" for business development and client retention activities. So at long last, I had finally created the opportunity I'd always wanted with Foster's. It was part business partnership and part endorsement with one of Australia's most recognizable brands.

In building our new business, the first thing we had to do was identify a niche. And while that seemed easy enough, we had to be very astute in how we approached the subject. While Outback Steakhouse helped kick-start things, we also wanted to create a premium brand. My bottom-line proposition to the team was to over-deliver on quality at our price point.

With the advice of professionals at Mildara Blass, we made the strategic decision to position ourselves on the low end of the premium range. By closely studying California wines, we concluded that their average prices ($16 to $18 per bottle) could be undercut by a dollar or possibly two dollars a bottle. What's more, given Australia's relatively low cost of goods, we could deliver an exceptional wine and healthy margins at this price point.

This wine deal didn't materialize because I'm a connoisseur. Rather, it came about because I had built up credibility in my brand. I firmly believe that the only way you can establish long-term value in a brand is *by being that brand.* You have to ensure that whatever endeavor you undertake, the highest possible quality will be achieved and maintained. In this case, I knew the brand would protect the wine. But we had to make sure the wine would protect the brand. I recognized that the appeal of my brand might motivate a consumer to try the wine, but whether or not he or she was a repeat customer would depend entirely on the value proposition and the quality of the product.

Given the importance of this project, I spent a week in Australia meeting with our executive team and visiting five of the finest wine-growing regions in Australia. The Limestone Coast has a mild climate like that of the Bordeaux region in France. It encompasses the regions of Coonawarra, Padthaway, and Wrattonbully. The Yarra Valley is in the heartland of Victoria's southeast. The Adelaide Hills is known for its Chardonnay and Pinot Noir. It is characterized by steep peaks and valleys, and its climate is typically Mediterranean. Langhorne Creek vineyards are planted on the alluvial wash of the Mount Lofty ranges. And McLaren Vale is defined by the Gulf of St. Vincent to the west and the Mount Lofty ranges to the north. The gulf's onshore breezes provide the region with a cool marine climate.

I immediately struck up a good relationship with Foster's chief winemaker, Chris Hatcher. Because I could have my choice of people to work with, I asked Chris who the up-and-coming individuals in winemaking were. He immediately pointed me to Andrew Hale, whom he considered one of the rising stars in red wines. For white wines, he recommended Matt Steel. I then went directly to both Andrew and Matt. Just as I hired my own staff, I wanted to meet and get to know these two men personally. After all, if they were going to create a product that had my name on it, I wanted to make sure they had the proper pedigree. And reciprocally, I wanted them to understand who I was. Only then could we create some fantastic wines together.

Moreover, I wanted to know that Chris, Andrew, and Matt would be in this venture for the long term and that they would always be thinking about the high quality of my brand. I also wanted to strike up a friendship with both of them so that we could engage in straightforward and honest dialogues. They didn't need to throw their professionalism around to squash my novice ideas, and conversely, I didn't need to make them think I knew more than I really did.

Over the next several months, I learned a great deal about wine. One of the first things we had to ask ourselves was what, exactly, the American palate was looking for. That's when I was told that the per capita consumption of wine in the United States was only 2.8 gallons per year. Compare that to France, where the per capita consumption is 20 gallons per year. On the other hand, Americans drink more than 40 gallons of soft drinks per capita per year. That was the mentality and the kind of market with which we were dealing. Another useful statistic I picked up revolved around the fact that at cocktail or dinner parties, 70 percent of people drink wine. With all this information, we arrived at a collective decision that Greg Norman Estates would be true to its Australian heritage and reflect active leisure and accessible luxury.

On a second visit to South Australia, I spent time learning more of the winemaking process. I walked through the vineyards and watched as the grapes were pruned. I observed the crush and how they barrel it. All of this was fascinating to me. Most consumers take it for granted that we can buy a bottle of wine, pull the cork out, and drink it. We don't take into consideration the years of preparation that go into every single varietal. It reminded me of the reactions I often received as a professional golfer. People never seemed to understand that it took years of preparation to get to a level where I could actually play on the professional tour.

After my two trips to Australia and my meetings with Chris, Matt, and Andrew, they set about the process of creating our first offering. Collectively, we decided to produce five varietals: Yarra Valley Chardonnay; Limestone Coast Cabernet Merlot; Limestone Coast Shiraz; Coonawarra Reserve Shiraz; and South East Australia Sparkling Chardonnay/Pinot Noir. We felt these represented what Australia was best known for. After some months, Bart Collins came across from Australia with some of our samples. Before leaving the office one night, he left a bottle of our Cabernet Merlot on my desk with a note.

That night I was having dinner with Ian Merideth, a friend and fellow Aussie. I realized it was a great opportunity to experiment with my wines. Before dinner we pulled the cork, allowed the wine to breathe, and then served it with our entrée. Before I sampled my wine, I allowed Ian to partake and with great pride asked for his opinion. After some deliberation, Ian looked me straight in the eye and said, "Greg, this stuff is bloody awful. I think it's the worst wine I've ever tasted." After I sampled it myself, I agreed with him. Feeling more than a bit embarrassed, I opened a bottle of Penfolds Grange and served it with dinner. When I got into the office the next day, I lit Bart up on our little venture with Foster's. "What the hell is going on?" I said. "I took a lot of my time and energy to educate Chris and the team on what I wanted. I thought we had a great connection." Bart burst into laughter and responded by saying, "Greg, that was merely a sample for the label. I have no idea what junk they put in that bottle. The barrel samples have been taken to your cellar."

When the first bottles of our Reserve Shiraz came out, I took a case to my friend Paul Fireman and went through the intricacies of the entire arrangement we had with Foster's. "Let me tell you something, my friend," Paul said. "Greg Norman Estates is the best example of extending a brand into the lifestyle arena that I've ever seen. It's perfect—a classic case study."

Sure enough, when Greg Norman Estates hit the shelves in the United States, consumers realized that we were offering high-quality, good-value wine. We were very fortunate early on to have a very capable brand manager in Hugh Cuthbertson working on the business. Hugh championed many of our early successes in launching Greg Norman Estates into the United States. Hugh also coined the phrase "you need to feed the monster," in reference to keeping up with the demand for our product. The response was so overwhelmingly positive after our initial launch, and our ratings were so strong in publications such as *Wine Spectator,* that the business skyrocketed.

One school of thought was to sell through our initial allocation and hold the line to create demand for future vintages. But it was Hugh who championed the notion of doing whatever it took to increase our production in order to keep up with demand in the first eighteen to twenty-four months. His theory, rightfully so, was that once a wine label has plateaued at a certain volume, it tends to stay at that level. By doing everything in our power to "feed the monster" in that first twenty-four-month period, we peaked at 120,000 cases, then had more measured growth over the next five years to take us to 220,000 cases per year. Had we not adopted this approach, Greg Norman Estates could potentially have plateaued at 60,000 cases, and we would have had a much longer gestation period in becoming a major brand.

Greg Norman Estates was clearly a success. And I truly believe that the long-term planning, the team aspect of our joint venture, and the hard work really made the difference. The enormous amount of energy, knowledge, and thought that we all put into this deal was the reason for the success. And at the end of the day, it was the wine's quality—not the name on the label—that kept wine lovers coming back for more. Within two years after consummating our deal, Foster's purchased Beringer, the iconic California winery that sells in excess of 8 million cases a year. And a few years later, Foster's also purchased Southcorp, the organization that originally declined to pursue this venture. Thankfully, the current management team has little or no ties to the group to whom we originally presented. So now we not only had built-in distribution outlets in the United States, but GWSE was in bed with one of the largest wine producers in the entire world—with more than 150 labels and shipping 20 million cases of wine a year.

By the close of 2003, GNE was selling in excess of 230,000 cases annually. Our Nielsen rating, the measurement that shows our penetration in the grocery and retail channels, indicated that we had an astounding 60 percent market share in the Australian premium category. "Premium" is defined as wines having a retail price of $10 and above. We also continued to receive the highest possible ratings and accolades by *Wine Spectator*.

While the potential existed to continue to grow the on-premise distribution, we came to the realization that we owned a very large slice of a very small market. Wanting to go to the next level, we considered our options, which revolved around opening new markets—such as Asia and Europe—or creating a diffusion brand, which would allow us to reach into more of a mass-market channel. I preferred not to pursue a diffusion brand, because I felt it might have a knock-on effect on some of my other products, Greg Norman Collection in particular. As for new markets, we would pursue them, but over time.

Eventually, we turned our attention to creating Greg Norman Estates California. In our corner, we had a 600-pound gorilla in the form of Beringer. And the California segment was 20 times that of Australia. If we could successfully launch a California brand, we might double or triple our volume. However, I was told that no winery or brand had ever transcended the region from which it originated. In other words, California wineries never went to France, South African wines never went to Spain, and so on. The only example that was remotely close to what we were contemplating was Moët & Chandon, which was bottled in a number of different countries under the same label. In reality, what we were contemplating was cutting edge, and potentially risky.

As a first step, we spent quite a lot of time, energy, and money on consumer research. We needed to know if the consumer would buy into the proposition of GNE California. Our consumer research taught us some very interesting lessons. In particular, the consumer did not identify Greg Norman Estates as Australian wines, but quite simply as high-quality wines. And in fact, we were losing some sales because the consumer was looking on the wrong shelves of the wine section. But what was the story? What point of difference could we bring to the consumer in a credible way? Was it that Greg Norman was bringing Australian winemaking to California? No, we didn't think that was the right approach. Rather, the right approach would be to feature wines that were classic California vintages. Just as we focused on the best of Australia, we would do the same with California—and perhaps other regions in the future. In doing so, we would also avoid cannibalizing our varietals.

Our California range would include Cabernet Sauvignon, Pinot Noir, Zinfandel, Petite Sirah, and Chardonnay. We were comfort-

able with the Chardonnay overlapping with our Australian Chardonnay, because it would show the consumer the different styles of
Australia and California.

Having identified what varietals we wanted to produce, I again
took a very proactive stance in selecting my winemaking partner
and immediately had a very good connection with Ron Shrieve, an
opera singer turned winemaker—truly a Renaissance man.

Together, we determined that we wanted to break the norm with
some of our varietals. Specific to the Pinot Noir, we chose to move
out of the Napa Valley and down to Santa Barbara. Ron and I both
had a personal affinity for this region, so in 2004 we chose to make
a Santa Barbara County Pinot Noir. Little did we know that six
months later, the movie *Sideways* would come out and the wine
world would go crazy for Santa Barbara County Pinot Noirs. Unlike our launch in 1998, we couldn't feed the monster, because we
had only so much product to work with. Otherwise, I think we could
have sold 30,000 cases of our Pinot Noir as opposed to the 10,000
cases we move each year.

In the midst of our exhaustive due diligence, I remembered a
lesson from my experience with Wally Uihlein and Titleist. Just after Acushnet bought Cobra, they became very serious about developing Titleist golf clubs (in order to position the Titleist equipment
for the better player and Cobra as more of a game-improvement
club). I remember Uihlein telling me that they spent tens of thousands of dollars in due diligence to determine the viability of Titleist golf clubs. But in the end, the decision to go or not to go came
down to one simple question: "By launching Titleist golf clubs, are
we going to harm the Titleist golf ball franchise?" That same question swirled through my mind in launching Greg Norman Estates
California. The due diligence was stacking up, but would it harm
my core business?

Now that Greg Norman Estates had successfully added California to our wine portfolio, we had a solid model that would help us
go into new markets in the future. For instance, we could do the
same thing in South Africa, Italy, or even France and produce wines
for which those countries are best known. Ultimately, I'd like to

think that Greg Norman Estates is well positioned to create best-of-class wines anywhere in the world.

That potential was validated, I might add, in 2005, when *Wine Spectator* voted our 1999 Reserve Shiraz one of the Top 10 wines in the world at the New York Wine Experience. I remember being at the Marriott Marquis in Times Square sitting next to Eric von Rothschild Lafitte XV in a ballroom with more than a thousand people. To them, this award was like winning the British Open. For me, it was an honor, and it gave me pause to reflect on the fact that this recognition was really an amazing accomplishment for a golfer who, a decade earlier, had never even considered being in the wine business.

CHAPTER TWENTY-NINE

WHEN OUR WINE VENTURE took off, a lot of people began taking notice of Great White Shark Enterprises. I received numerous requests for interviews and speaking engagements. Almost everybody recognized that we were involved in a variety of businesses—golf equipment, apparel, golf course design, real estate development, restaurants, and wine—and they seemed both intrigued and perplexed by it. "What's next, Greg?" they would ask.

"Well, we're always looking for something new," I would respond. "We'll see what comes along." But that didn't seem to be a satisfactory answer. They wanted to know some specifics about how I conducted business.

"What exactly *is* your business philosophy?" they would ask. "Do you have a set business plan? What structures do you use? Do you set limits? Or does anything go?"

These are not easy questions to answer, because I think of myself as an entrepreneur. The truth is that every deal is different. Accordingly, we attempt to be flexible so that the best possible arrangement can be worked out for each venture.

While the principles, guidelines, and deal structures are critically important, a lot of people underestimate the importance of how best to structure an entrepreneurial company. A good friend and business associate of mine, Jay Margolis, who was head of Liz Claiborne and Reebok before he became president of Boston Beer/ Limited Brands, indoctrinated me concerning a fashion term, "the house." Fashion brands such as Claiborne, Versace, and Armani built their businesses through strategic partnerships and licensees, maintaining all the while a very tight group that managed the core business and the brand, or "the house." Inherently, I knew that I wanted to have a lean team and, from there, manage a series of relationships that would help take me where I wanted to go. There are, however, several bottom-line principles that GWSE adheres to: select ventures that have a high probability of profitability; partner only with corporations and individuals who are high value, high integrity, and best of breed; and have an end strategy.

Of course, there are numerous ways to structure a contract that meets these criteria. Currently, GWSE employs four different structures:

(1) *Merchandising,* in which I get paid a fee to endorse someone's product. I've been doing this since I signed a contract with Qantas in 1976. While most athletes view such endorsements purely on the basis of immediate financial gain, I place equal value on my partners' ability to further the reach and build the equity of my brand. My relationship with Land Rover is a good example. Equally, if I'm not going to manufacture a particular product, whether a $90,000 SUV or a $40 million corporate jet, then I'm better served endorsing best of breed in those categories.

(2) *Licensing,* where we license my name or logo. My clothing arrangement (Greg Norman Collection) with Reebok is a good example. Clearly, this is a strategy that takes a great deal of patience and a long-term view on building equity in one's brand. Off the back of our success with the shark icon, we developed a number of different diffusion brands, including the typeset shark logo and Tiburon. These reach different consumers at various price points.

(3) *Wholly owned business,* such as golf course design or our turf grass business. Whether these are service- or

product-oriented, one has to develop a competency that is as good as or better than whatever else is available in the market. The strength of one's brand cannot overcome any deficiencies in providing products or services.

(4) *Brand joint venture,* of which Medallist Developments and Greg Norman Estates are prime examples. This is a fairly unique concept, and one that I take pride in having pioneered. In bifurcating my participation as a shareholder from my role as the brand, I have a greater degree of control over the operation of the venture, better cash flow, and a cleaner exit.

After establishing our mainstream businesses, we created opportunities for other associated ventures in what we call "lateral" or "adjacent" space. I often use the phrase "concentric circles" to illustrate this concept. Greg Norman Turf Company and Medallist Developments are good examples. We formed them on the periphery of golf course design. Another example might involve our venture with Troon or the development of the real estate product Norman Estates in association with Medallist. In fact, we are reviewing the possibility of forming a real estate sales and marketing organization that would manage the marketing, sales, and database management activities for Medallist Developments. Why should we pay third parties a commission on $3 billion in property sales? In general, we find it is much easier to create businesses that are adjacent to our mainstream businesses than it would be to create a new business from scratch in another industry. However, as with every business we pursue, we make certain that each adjacent-space opportunity is viable in its own right. The internal phrase we use to address this issue is that "each business must wash its own face." In other words, we do not want to create a real estate company on the back of Medallist if that company isn't as good as or better than what we could outsource.

By building adjacent-space opportunities, I'm able to better compartmentalize my time, and by focusing on the mainstream businesses and ensuring that they are well managed, I find that I don't have to commit as much of my own time and resources to the peripheral ventures. This allows me to have a fairly flat reporting structure within GWSE, while each of the individual businesses is vertically integrated. While I find that this works quite well, I must admit that I could potentially be better served by having fewer direct reports. I currently have as many as fifteen to twenty direct reports, which is not only reflective of my management style but also a function of the business. After all, most of the time, I am the widget! As much as I want to build long-standing businesses that pass the mortality test, it still takes a great deal of my personal involvement to seed those businesses and build them up to the point where they are self-sustaining. As fortunate as I have been to interact with captains of industry, I've often felt that a group such as McKinsey & Company or Booz Allen would have a great deal of difficulty trying to understand my business and make significant recommendations to improve its efficiencies. It's difficult for somebody else to understand what it takes to hit the right shot under pressure—or, in this instance, manage a $300 million business around one person.

Overall, it's really a matter of setting priorities, which have to be reviewed on a regular basis as business ebbs and flows. At GWSE, our priority businesses are pretty obvious:

(1) *Greg Norman Golf Course Design* is a service business. It gives me substantial cash flow. I love it, and it will be my legacy in terms of leaving my imprint on the environment. As an operating company, I will continue to manage the business for many years to come on a dividend-distribution basis. Given that it is at the epicenter of so many adjacent-space opportunities, GNGCD is of strategic importance to the long-term prospects of GWSE.

(2) *Greg Norman Collection*, an already successful golf lifestyle brand, is poised to become a dominant sports luxury brand. Like René Lacoste, the French tennis player who in the 1930s developed the Lacoste crocodile brand, Greg Norman Collection will be my legacy and afford me the opportunity to continue to license or operate the business for years to come.

(3) *Medallist Developments*, a great partnership with Macquarie Bank, affords me the opportunity to drive significant development income through our worldwide activities. As a property development company, Medallist can operate virtually without boundaries.

(4) *Greg Norman Estates*, a non–golf lifestyle consumer brand, will generate opportunities for other branded consumer products. Essentially, it is my calling card to the hospitality industry.

With these core businesses in place, Great White Shark Enterprises has continued to build myriad other ventures—all adhering to our three bottom-line principles, and all falling, more or less, into one of our four types of deals. In merchandising, we've added MacGregor and Merrill Lynch. In licensing, we've developed golf equipment under the Shark and Tiburon brands. We also created the Greg Norman Production Company, a wholly owned events-management business, and refined our restaurant concept, Greg Norman's Australian Grille.

A number of people have asked me how we pick and choose, how we find the right mix for our company. My consistent answer is that I look at it very much like an investor would build a balanced stock portfolio. We want to manage both conservative investments and higher-return investments. We want short-term gain and long-term equity appreciation.

As a system of checks and balances, I'll constantly review the three Ss: *Strategy, Structure,* and *Staff. Strategy* is nothing more than having a blueprint and beginning with the end in mind; but as businesses evolve, so too should the strategy. *Structure* involves not only how the relative parties interact with one another but the capital structure and resources that are required to execute the plan. *Staff,* of course, is the people in our organization who have the ability to execute. For every venture, we must have expertise, we must be diverse, and we must work as an effective team.

I also believe that whatever the structure of your venture, whether it's an endorsement, a licensing agreement, or a joint venture, you need to be a good partner—not only from the standpoint of integrity and fairness, but you need to respect your partners' skills and talents. With Medallist Developments, rarely do I impose myself on our capital strategy. Macquarie Bank does this better than I ever will, just as I have certain skills that they respect me for as the authority. With wine I try not to direct operations of production or distribution. As a friend once said to me, "There's no sense in having a dog and barking yourself." If I'm not going to listen to my bankers or my partners in winemaking and apparel, then I'm selling myself short—and, more important, I'm eroding the goodwill and integrity of the very relationships I'm trying to build.

I never went to college, but I like to think I'm a quick learner. Over the years, I have been able to seek guidance from a good many people. Whether it's Bill Moss and Richard Sheppard of Macquarie Bank educating me on the loose-tight management structure for maintaining entrepreneurialism within a large organization, Kerry Packer's advice about identifying and exploiting a particular niche, or Nelson Peltz's guidance on capital structure and risk management, I have received a lot of advice and have done what I believe to be a good job of filtering out that which I did not view as being particularly relevant, and I have adapted and adhered to that which I felt was of value.

It all sounds simple, but it's not easy to do. And it brings us back to the one thing that separates successful people from unsuccessful people: the ability to turn strategy into action. Remember, nearly everybody comes up with plans and dreams. But few actually *do something* about them.

When I was just starting out in business and was all by myself, it was easy for me to take action. That's the way I'm built. I have tremendous energy, and I knew I could pull it off if I could just learn to focus and apply myself. But there comes a point in time when even the most energetic executive realizes he can't do it all. The more a business grows, the more crucial it becomes to tap into the energy, expertise, and enthusiasm of your employees. Of course, the only way to do that is to have in place solid leadership and management practices.

For Great White Shark Enterprises, all that (and more) came together on the other side of the world, in a place called Dubai.

CHAPTER THIRTY

$\mathbf{D}$ATING BACK to the late 1980s and early 1990s, when we expanded our design operations throughout Southeast Asia, I've always enjoyed the prospect of developing businesses in emerging markets. Such a practice allowed us to accelerate our growth beyond what would normally be attainable in a mature market like the United States. While we had the ability to design golf courses and distribute our products around the world, there were certain markets that were unique and deserving of committing more time and resources and forging long-term relationships. But choosing exactly which ones to take on involved substantial thought. After all, there was a lot to consider: language, relationships, size, and manageability, to name just a few. And because Great White Shark Enterprises is a small, entrepreneurial company, we had to be careful not to spread ourselves too thin. So we took our time thinking about such places as China, Eastern Europe, the Middle East, and South Africa. In the end we selected the United Arab Emirates (UAE) as a market deserving of our commitment. It was anything but a spur-of-the-moment decision. Rather, it was a lengthy process that began when we had only one or two arrows in our business quiver.

Throughout my career, I have been paid appearance fees to play various tournaments and exhibitions around the world. It was against the rules on the U.S. PGA Tour (even though it often happened under a different guise), but the other tours have no such restrictions, and many of the best golfers in the world take advantage of the opportunity. It made a lot of sense for tournament operators who would not otherwise have been able to feature marquee players. Appearance fees gave them the talent, which in turn helped them secure greater sponsorship and higher revenues. It really is the free market economy at its best, because tournament promoters are ultimately the sole arbitrators in determining whether or not they get value for their money. It's unlikely that a tournament would pay me a $500,000 appearance fee, for instance, if they couldn't make more money through increased sponsorship, television rights fees, or gate takings. I felt that appearance fees were, ultimately, a great barometer for measuring a player's star power and value in the marketplace.

I first played the Dubai Desert Classic in 1994, which was memorable because I shot four rounds in the 60s and finished second to a young South African, Ernie Els. (A few months later, Ernie would go on to win his first U.S. Open.)

During those years traveling to Dubai, I not only built a number of solid friendships, but I was captivated by the scope, speed, and unbelievable growth in the area. It seemed like every time I came back, there was something grand going on, something brand-new being built. It was fascinating to me, in part because I like to move fast and achieve things quickly. So I began to study the area in depth.

Dubai is part of the UAE, a federation of seven emirates located at the northeastern portion of the Arabian Peninsula. The UAE is bordered by Saudi Arabia to the west and Oman to the south, and it has a coastline on both the Arabian Gulf and the Gulf of Oman. The second largest of the seven emirates, Dubai originally based its livelihood on fishing, pearling, and trading. But it was the influx of money from oil production in the late 1960s that catapulted Dubai to extraordinary wealth and prosperity. However, because the emirate is small—approximately 1,000 square miles—it was readily apparent that its oil and gas reserves would quickly be depleted. The government then came to the conclusion that they would either have to reinvent who they were or do what so many other Arabian oil nations had chosen to do with their revenues, which was to make large strategic investments in Europe and the United States.

Dubai chose an entirely different path, which can be traced directly to their leaders, Sheikh Rashid bin Saeed Al Maktoum (one of the founding fathers of the UAE) and his sons H. H. Sheikh Maktoum bin Rashid Al Maktoum and H. H. Sheikh Mohamed bin Rashid Al Maktoum. In the early 1980s the men came up with a grand vision for the future of their city-state. Given its strategic location, Dubai, they reasoned, could become a destination for international business, tourism, and recreation for people on every continent of the world. It was an ambitious idea. With a huge oil revenue stream at their disposal, and with a determination to turn dreams into reality, the leaders put together a brilliant four-step plan.

First, they created an extraordinary world-class airline as a hub for business and leisure travel. Emirates Airlines, tremendously successful and rapidly expanding, operates a sizable fleet of jets and provides convenience and connections so that Dubai can be a stop-over for anyone traveling from India to New York, London to South Africa, or China to North Africa.

Second, the leaders of Dubai fashioned an open-door policy for foreign investors, where the world's Fortune 100 companies can set up a base of operations (which includes the subcontinent of India and Pakistan, Eastern Europe, North Africa, and, of course, the Arab states). With this zone of commerce, Dubai could generate a catchment for the approximately 2 billion people in the countries surrounding the UAE. With this, Dubai would be to its geographic region what Singapore is to Asia and what Switzerland was to Europe.

Third, Dubai was set up as a tax-free domicile for individuals. For those of us who are either U.S. citizens or tax residents, this doesn't mean a lot, as we pay taxes on our worldwide earnings no matter where we live. But in most countries, if you are not domiciled as a resident, you are not taxed in your home country. So the prospect of living in a tax-free haven such as Dubai is quite attractive.

And in the fourth strategic step, Dubai would be made a haven for tourism and recreation, including water sports, social activities, and golf. In addition to hosting the Dubai Desert Classic, Dubai also boasts the world's richest horse race, the world's richest offshore powerboat race, and many other notable events.

Two decades after this plan was put into place, modern Dubai has reaped the benefits of extensive growth, as has the entire United Arab Emirates. A majority of expatriates are from the surrounding GCC (Gulf Cooperation Council) states—India, Pakistan, Oman, Bahrain, and Qatar. There are also a large number from the Philippines, Egypt, Lebanon, the United Kingdom, Australia, and New Zealand. Moreover, Dubai itself has become not only the UAE's most important port but also one of the world's leading centers of trade and commerce. Skyscrapers and new highways form a modern cosmopolitan city with a variety of shopping venues.

Walking in New York recently, I stopped in midstride as I passed the shop front of the Louis Vuitton store on Fifth Avenue. Like many luxury retailers, Louis Vuitton trumpets their geographic reach, specifically noting that they are in the most desirable, fashion-forward cities. I found it interesting that Dubai was displayed front and center on the main window of the store, flanked by London, Paris, and Milan. In a very short period of time, Dubai had achieved a great deal of respect as a center of fashion and culture. In addition, Dubai's open-door policy has attracted the business of more than 900 international companies, many of which have seen fit to establish regional headquarters in the city.

As I studied Dubai, I came to the conclusion that there couldn't possibly be a better emerging market for Great White Shark Enterprises to enter. All the positive elements were there: (1) We could identify and forge lasting business partnerships. (2) Dubai was a very entrepreneurial and brand-conscious society. (3) It was a gateway to a number of other peripheral markets. (4) We could introduce our partners and products into the market. (5) We could raise capital in Dubai for our other ventures.

As I began building relationships and laying the groundwork to make an entry into this emerging market, the Dubai Desert Classic grew into one of the European Tour's premier events. No longer do players see it as a hardship to play in Dubai. The tournament has now attained the status of one of the preeminent events on the European Tour.

In my research on Dubai, I came to understand that there are three or four "pillars" who have been given a great deal of responsibility and latitude as stewards of the Royal Family. I found it interesting that there were no particular lines of distinction or barriers of entry for these individuals, meaning that they were not relegated to particular industries or segments of the economy but rather had the opportunity to delve into all aspects of the economy. The names that were continually referenced were Mohammed Ali Alabbar, Sultan Ahmed bin Sulayem, and Mohammed Al Gergawi. Often they would compete with one another, a circumstance that seems to make everybody stronger, more aggressive, and hungrier.

Not surprisingly, golf course design was the first activity I embarked upon, as real estate and resort development were very much on the rise. Having played the Dubai Desert Classic on a number of occasions, I came to know Mohammed Ali Alabbar, the chairman of Dubal (the world's second-largest aluminum smelting works), which underwrote the Dubai Desert Classic. Alabbar was also the director of the UAE golf association and ran a very powerful real estate development company, EMAAR. Alabbar and I had a very positive, personal relationship. We would spend time together when I was in Dubai, and he would visit me in Florida or San Diego, where he had a home. His son, Rashid, was a bit younger than my own son, but he had taken a keen passion for golf and I enjoyed watching his progress.

In 2000, EMAAR launched what would be Dubai's first integrated golf course–driven real estate community. Up to this point, Dubai's golf courses were stand-alone entities with little or no real estate incorporated into the land plans. Alabbar's idea was to create a 36-hole development that would feature championship golf courses. Colin Montgomerie and the late Desmond Muirhead were contracted to design the first course, and my design firm was contracted for the second. The plan was to develop the courses sequentially, so as to tie in with the absorption of real estate sales. After we completed some of our initial design work, it was determined that the project would yield better financial results with only 18 holes, and so, unfortunately, the Norman course was never completed. Thus, my efforts to create a business-to-business relationship in Dubai were stalled. While I understood the rationale, I felt some disappointment because I recognized that even though Dubai was growing at a rapid pace, golf course design opportunities were few and far between.

Feeling that I might have missed out on the opportunity to design Dubai's second-generation golf courses, there was still very much the need in Dubai for bringing professional Western-style management to these facilities. As such, I felt that a different tack could be employed by bringing Troon Golf management into Dubai. After all, if I didn't have the opportunity to design, then I should at least pursue the opportunity to manage. With that, Jeff Kuhne, from Medallist, and David Spencer, from Troon, began to pursue Dubai as a new market. (Interestingly, I had worked with David many years earlier when he redeveloped the Grand Golf Club, my first project in Australia, and brokered Medallist's involvement in Pelican Waters.) Troon Golf quickly secured a number of management contracts in Dubai, including the Montgomerie and Arabian Ranches. So by applying some creativity, I gained the opportunity to work with Mohammed Ali Alabbar and EMAAR through my minority shareholding in Troon Golf.

Within a year of our opening the Troon office, information began circulating about a series of huge, imaginative development projects that were to be built along Dubai's coastline jutting into the Arabian Gulf. Just the names of the projects gave us a visual picture of the scope involved: the Palm Jumeirah, Deira and Jebel-Ali, The World, Jumeirah Islands, International City, Lost City, Atlantis Resort, and the Arabian Waterway. Perhaps most amazing of all was the fact that many of these developments were going to be built on reclaimed land in the Gulf, which would extend Dubai's beachfront tenfold. The World alone would consist of a manmade archipelago of 300 islands laid out like a map of the world. Collectively, these projects represented the largest civil works project on the planet.

The company behind these unprecedented projects was named

Nakheel, which in Arabic means "palm." And the man behind Nakheel was Sultan Ahmed bin Sulayem, who, we soon learned, had a desire to create championship golf courses in conjunction with his megadevelopments. As our discussions progressed, he created a division, Nakheel Golf, and hired David Spencer away from Troon Golf to manage the group. I realized that Nakheel and Great White Shark Enterprises were on the same page with a number of important business principles. We shared the same work ethic and ambitions. Like GWSE, Nakheel's aim was always to challenge norms and existing standards and then take those benchmarks to new heights. They had great vision and a solid reputation and were uniquely focused.

In November 2004, GNGCD was commissioned by Nakheel to design four golf courses and a training facility for Nakheel. Three of these golf courses and the training facility would be located within a large, master-planned community, Jumeirah Golf Estates (JGE). The fourth would be connected with a resort development titled Lost City. Already, Nakheel had acquired strategic shareholding in Kerzner International, the publicly held South African–led resort developer that had created such iconic properties as Sun City, One and Only, and Atlantis Resort. Realizing the magnitude of work we were about to embark on, Greg Norman Golf Course Design opened an office in Dubai and staffed it with personnel who would be dedicated to the region. On my first site visit to JGE, I was pleased to receive a call from Mohammed Ali Alabbar of EMAAR, congratulating me on winning the contract with Nakheel. Alabbar knew I was excited to be working in Dubai, and this gesture meant a great deal to me.

Designing golf courses in Dubai provided a number of unique and exciting challenges that I had rarely encountered in other areas of the world. First of all, terrain in nearly the entire emirate consists of rolling sand dunes. Rainfall is rare, and high winds called shamals sometimes create daylong sandstorms that can wreak havoc on the earthworks during construction and on operations after completion. Despite these obstacles, I was determined to maximize all aspects of the natural landscape. In short, I would maintain the same design principles, offering wonderful views from the dramatic natural elevations and incorporating indigenous flora, which in this case included olive, date, fig, and palm trees.

In Dubai, we were also able to take our least-disturbance approach to the next level by formally creating a set of minimum standards that focused on the relationships among developers, designers, construction personnel, and management teams. In doing so, we would refer to the two designs at Jumeirah Golf Estates as Eco-Signature courses. The Eco-Signature concept was developed by Sultan Ahmed bin Sulayem and myself. Soon after entering into a partnership with Nakheel Golf, I invited Sultan to serve on the advisory council of the Environmental Institute for Golf. He accepted the invitation and then encouraged me to put the concept into practice at Jumeirah Golf Estates. Through our collaborative efforts, the term Eco-Signature was born. While the topography of the desert possesses its own unique characteristics and offers ample opportunity for creating a unique design, our Eco-Signature approach took on almost a "brownfields" methodology, meaning that we had to create a lot of the drama and work within a number of very difficult design constraints. To this point, developers in Dubai had tried to emulate American-style golf courses with wall-to-wall turf grass, which in Dubai can be very costly given the scarcity of water and expense of irrigation. In fact, the Montgomerie course uses more than 1 million gallons of water a day, at a cost of approximately $1.5 million annually, which, when added to the other maintenance costs, is exorbitant. Sultan and I were in agreement that, much as in Arizona and other arid parts of the United States, a different canon should be developed. Thus, the Eco-Signature aspects of the courses had as much to do with conservation, recycling water, and use of indigenous plants and materials in out-of-play areas as it did with providing a habitat for native flora and fauna. By creating habitats that enhance the local flora and fauna, we bring life to areas that were unable to sustain such life previously. The result will be two environmentally friendly golf courses that truly leave the land in better condition than when we started. I would like to think that we will set a new standard for the design and development of sustainable and environmentally friendly courses for the region.

As part of my pledge to Sultan Ahmed bin Sulayem, I wanted to create more of a business-to-business relationship, and to be more strategic and less tactical. In short, I wanted to bring Medallist Developments into Dubai to work with Nakheel to develop a Norman Estates within JGE, thereby making a direct investment in the project—something that no other designer or consultant had previously done in Dubai. To this end, I held one of our Medallist board meetings in Dubai, so that the board could see firsthand the opportunities that were available in the market and so that Nakheel could have greater insight into Medallist and my partners in Macquarie Bank. To me, the Norman Estates product was a perfect fit for both parties. For Medallist, it enabled us to come into a new market, essentially riding the coattails of a $300 million development and creating a successful product that would be a calling card for our doing more work throughout the region. For Nakheel, it would validate their ability to sell other precincts within the overall project to qualified foreign investors.

When we looked at the overall picture of the new market, we recognized that there was potential for just about everything that GWSE offered in our business portfolio, as well as creating new opportunities that were unique to the UAE. In short, we could use all the arrows in our quiver. Immediately, we were able to expand our initial toehold for Greg Norman Collection into a more expanded strategy, one that included not only Nakheel's megaprojects but a dedicated retail plan with concept stores in major shopping centers. GNC would be quickly ramped up and positioned as an upscale lifestyle brand, eclipsing our U.S. rivals, Ashworth and Cutter & Buck, and positioning us against such lifestyle stalwarts as Polo and Nautica.

We took a different tack with Greg Norman Estates, however. In Dubai, wine and spirits are sold only through hotels and resorts. Thus, the UAE is never going to hold great promise for Greg Norman Estates. However, we recognized a different opportunity, one that would be unique to Dubai. African & Eastern, the UAE's largest distributor of wine and spirits, is owned in part by Foster's, so unlike in the U.S., where Foster's does not have its own distributorship, in Dubai we had the opportunity to better control the distribution of our products. At the same time, we recognized that Foster's owned one of Australia's premier springwater plants, Wattle Springs in Ballarat, Victoria. So we developed a plan to create an Australian-branded springwater that we would label Australis for distribution in the UAE.

As they say, imitation is the sincerest form of flattery. Our model was very much built on the success of Fiji water. We worked on the premise that the consumer generally has a positive view of Australia as a clean, green environment. In this instance, my brand was not the driver for the product. Rather, my involvement served as validation of the authenticity of an Australian product. For Foster's, the business was complementary to what they were doing with African & Eastern and Wattle Springs. If successful, this could lead to our expansion into other markets, including the United States.

With our existing businesses able to enter the Dubai market, we thought further about new opportunities. What is unique and dynamic about this market? What additional opportunities are there for us to capture?

One of the first things we elected to do was introduce Outback Steakhouse to Retail Corp, a sister corporation to Nakheel. As the developer of major shopping malls and residential communities, Nakheel had a need to provide restaurant concepts for their developments. As such, an opportunity to partner with Outback or Darden held great promise. Equally, Retail Corp was looking to find Western retail and franchise concepts for rollout in the UAE, for which Outback was well suited. At the same time, we were in loose discussions about incorporating our restaurant business, Greg Norman's Australian Grille, into the Outback portfolio of restaurants (which includes Carrabba's Italian Grill, Fleming's Prime Steakhouse and Wine Bar, Roy's, and Bonefish Grill). Outback CEO Chris Sullivan felt that there was room in his portfolio to position our restaurant between the Outback and Fleming's brands. This project, if successful, will serve as a pilot for our strategy in the United States.

As an interesting aside, I formed a brand joint venture with Australia's oldest corporation, Australian Agricultural Company (AACO), in 2005 to export premium-quality Australian beef to the

U.S. under the brand Greg Norman Australian Prime. Given the un-
tried nature of branding a beef product, it is our intention to market it to the trade, particularly the white-tablecloth restaurant
business. Not surprisingly, we wanted to sell our product to Outback and their portfolio of restaurants. After all, wouldn't it make
sense for Outback to serve an Australian beef product? As good a
relationship as I had with Chris Sullivan, we needed to earn our
own stripes, so to speak, and we found it particularly challenging to
make inroads into the relationship that exists between Outback and
their current beef provider, Cargill. Knowing that Cargill does not
have great penetration in the Middle East, it is also our hope to
have Greg Norman Australian Prime provide our products to the
Outback portfolio in the UAE. In doing so, we may be able to lever-
age Greg Norman Australian Prime into a stronger position with
Outback in the U.S.

Because Dubai is a financial center, it was part of our agenda to
build relationships in not only the UAE but other GCC states to
raise capital for a number of our ventures, Medallist Developments
in particular. We also wanted to present investment opportunities
to our new partners. One such opportunity revolved around GPS
Industries, a Vancouver, Canada, technology company that I have
had an involvement with since 2004. GPSI is one of three major
providers of GPS distance measuring to the golf industry. These
systems are typically cart-mounted, showing distances to the pin
and providing advertising, scoring, and course management opportunities. What attracted me to GPSI wasn't just their product and
the patent portfolio they controlled, but their recognition that by
providing a golf course community with differential GPS they could
effectively create the backbone for Wi-Fi enabling an entire community. That, in turn, would generate reoccurring income as a service provider offering Wi-Fi, voice-over IP, and wireless broadband.
Understanding that Nakheel would probably benefit from having a
wireless solution for its island communities and marinas, we cultivated the idea of having Nakheel's parent group, Istithmar (which
is Arabic for "investment"), make a direct investment in GPSI. At
the same time, the company could implement systems that would

both enhance the value of GPSI and differentiate Nakheel from their competition by providing their residents with e-communities.

The business opportunities in Dubai seemed endless. Obviously Nakheel had a fairly substantial marketing budget, because with the development of their new golf properties, they asked us to assist them in securing the host-venue rights to the World Cup (a U.S. PGA Tour–sanctioned event). While we had some reservations regarding the value proposition of the event due to the weakness of its field in recent years, Nakheel felt there was great connectivity between the title, World Cup, and their project, The World. Because GWSE runs a U.S. PGA Tour–sanctioned event, the Shark Shootout, they asked us to assist them in trying to broker a deal with the U.S. PGA Tour. So in January 2005, at the PGA Merchandise Show in Orlando, Florida, we arranged a meeting with PGA Tour representatives to explore the opportunity. Out of respect for our relationship with Nakheel, we did not want to earn a commission for making the introduction. Instead, we postured ourselves in such a way that our events-management group, Greg Norman Production Company, might enter into an agreement to manage the event.

Two months later, one of Nakheel's executives placed a telephone call to Bart Collins. "I don't know how to say this," he said. "I sense that you don't know anything about it. So we thought we should be up front with you."

"What is it?" asked Bart.

"Well, Ed Moorhouse and three senior members of the PGA Tour were just in Dubai pitching us on a completely different golfing event called the Road to Dubai, which would be held here and televised internationally."

An incensed Bart Collins immediately called me. "We tried to extend an olive branch and mend fences by saying that our client might be interested in running a PGA Tour event. Then they fly to Dubai and attempt to cut us out of the whole thing."

I was standing in my hotel room when I took Bart's call, and, I must admit, for a split second I felt like throwing the phone against the wall—just as I had done nearly two decades earlier when James Marshall made his insensitive remark when I told him I was going to be a father. Now a lot older and a little wiser, I simply shook my head. "A leopard never changes its spots," I said. "Let it pass."

With the sheer magnitude of our offerings in Dubai, losing out on a single deal was not going to harm us. What goes around comes around.

We now had a proven model with which to enter emerging markets. We were already being asked to invest in Oman, Abu Dhabi, Bahrain, and Qatar.

Great White Shark Enterprises was embarking on something of a World Business Tour. And unlike with the World Golf Tour, this time we weren't going to be derailed.

PART SEVEN

THE BACK 9 OF LIFE

CHAPTER THIRTY-ONE

As I APPROACH the latter stages of my life, I sometimes look back on all that has happened to me, as though I were at the turn in a full 18-hole round of golf. On the first 9, I went out strong, enthusiastic, even brash. At the same time, I was a little unsure—testing my swing, careful on my approaches, and trying to understand people.

I also think of life as being somewhat compartmentalized—especially my life. From birth to the age of eighteen, you're just a kid, absorbing life and learning as much as you can. From eighteen to twenty-one, you begin developing an idea of what you want to do and how to go about it. For the next ten years, you're trying to establish yourself. From thirty to forty, you solidify what you have. You get married, have children, become more patient, and slow down a little bit. Sometime after you hit forty, you start thinking about where you're going to be and what you're going to be doing when you're fifty-plus. And by the time you reach the turn, at age fifty, you're wondering if you have all your ducks in a row.

With the baby boomer generation now solidly in the throes of middle age, I would think that many people are looking at life in a fairly similar light. They're wondering, just as I am: "How did I do on the front 9 of life? And what's in store for me on the back 9?"

For me, personally, I feel like I shot a respectable score for my first fifty years—maybe 3 or 4 under par. As I head into the back 9, I've calmed down and settled into a bit of a rhythm. I have a better feel for the clubs now, the tools of life. And even though I'm more patient and wise, I still have a fire deep in my belly. I really want to finish strong—just the way I started.

Up to this point, for the most part, I've focused on family, friends, and golf. But now the majority of my time will revolve around my business interests. I also intend to spend as much time as possible with my kids, whose needs have changed with time. They will soon be going through that next stage of life where they try to establish themselves, and I want to help them get where they're going. The change will be good.

There is, of course, one thing I don't particularly relish as I get older. Physically, I just can't do what I used to be able to do as a professional golfer. Unfortunately, having hit more than four million golf balls over the last thirty years, my body has shown signs of wear and tear. As we all know, the golf swing is a very unnatural movement. Early in my career, people promoted what was called the "reverse C" in swing mechanics. But that only exacerbated lower back trauma. Fortunately, I took a very proactive stance in physical fitness and conditioning by advocating a balanced approach. I've always looked at myself as an athlete, and as such I have always had a mixed physical fitness regime involving cardiovascular work, weight training, and stretching; I am mindful, as well, of proper nutrition. My fitness regime will always be a big part of my life. It has played a major part in enhancing my performance, extending the longevity of my career as a professional golfer, and serving as a great stress reliever.

Notwithstanding these efforts, I've suffered a number of material physical issues that I've had to contend with over the years. In the late 1980s they were a bit more manageable and involved some arthroscopic work on my knees, a number of cortisone injections, et cetera. Back then I still had a feeling of invincibility, and I often think back to the time when my good friend Dr. Norton Baker would give me fairly painful cortisone injections just prior to teeing off in a tournament. I don't know if I would be quite so cavalier about that today.

The first major setback involved my shoulder. Like most injuries, it was manageable at first, but when I cold-topped my drive on the 18th tee at the 1995 Masters as a result of my ongoing problems, I knew I needed help. This time, however, I would undertake considerable due diligence in identifying the right doctor and procedure. After numerous meetings and consultations, in April 1998 I underwent shoulder surgery at the Steadman-Hawkins Clinic, performed by Dr. Richard J. Hawkins. It was a groundbreaking operation because the procedure used a heat probe to tighten a joint that is vital to the golf swing.

The surgical procedure required a six-month layoff that I put to good use by accelerating my seven-year plan. When I was given the green light to begin the process of rehabilitation, I committed myself to it as much as I would preparing for the British Open, because I knew that's what it would take for me to be competitive again on tour. Depending on the procedure, rehabilitation can truly test a person's conviction for a full recovery, and I was thankful for my trainer and great friend, Pete Draovitch, who worked with me through the entire process.

Soon after that procedure, I accepted a seat on the board of directors of the Steadman-Hawkins Research Foundation. That got me involved with fund-raising and developing the Steadman-Hawkins biomechanics programs, which are specifically targeted to the golf swing. Because of my work with the Steadman-Hawkins Research Foundation and my ongoing relationship with Dr. Hawkins, in 2000 I was recruited to play an advisory role for the University of Pittsburgh Medical Center (UPMC) and their new $42 million sports medicine unit. This facility was truly world class, but it had not gained the recognition of other top physicians and similar sports medicine units, such as Steadman-Hawkins, the Andrews Clinic, the Job Clinic, and others. UPMC wanted to broaden their awareness, develop golf-specific programs, and explore the potential for a warm-weather campus in Florida.

At about the same time, I began having difficulties with my right hip and came across Dr. Marc Philippon and his patented arthroscope. At the time he worked out of Holy Cross in Fort Lauderdale. In 2001, I underwent a revolutionary surgery that saved people from total hip replacements. Until my work with Philippon, the procedure was not used for golf-specific injuries. Now, however, it is a common practice, and in addition to Peter Jacobsen and Jesper Parnevik, other athletes such as Mario Lemieux, Tara Lipinski, and Priest Holmes have had their careers prolonged by Dr. Philippon's arthroscopic procedure. I immediately introduced UPMC to Philippon, and the hospital brought him on board as its surgical resident—along with Draovitch, who also made the transition to Pittsburgh.

My work with Steadman-Hawkins and UPMC was pioneering in many ways. Both facilities established a strong biomechanics program for golf, with the objective to develop swing mechanics for the next generation of golfers. We wanted to help prolong their careers and their quality of life, as well as educate the coaches about the minor nuances of changing a young person's swing and what the consequences may be twenty years down the line. I've thoroughly enjoyed the process of immersing myself in the science of sports medicine, and I distinctly remember taking pride in seeing the response of Dr. Scott Lephart of UPMC, when he realized I had read his book on proprioception and was somewhat well versed in the terminology and findings.

Aside from sports medicine, I have also been a proponent of the PGA Tour being proactive in having a set policy for performance-enhancing drugs. While it's true that golf is very much a clean sport and not one whose players would benefit from anabolic steroids, it has often been rumored that certain players take beta-blockers or performance-enhancing drugs. I made reference to this issue back in the late 1980s without much success. More recently, at the 2003 British Open, the subject of beta-blockers was again topical, and I remember commenting to both the media and the Royal & Ancient Golf Club of St. Andrews that I would be more than happy to lead the players in accepting drug testing as a means of gaining some momentum toward the creation of set policies. Today, however, I'm aware of nothing in the PGA Tour bylaws or rules that prohibits players from taking performance-enhancing drugs. So if there is no rule or regulation, you cannot blame players for trying to find that extra edge, given the magnitude of what they're playing for.

I wanted to maintain a competitive schedule of approximately a dozen professional events each year, but I just haven't been able to. I just will not step out on the golf course without being 100 percent. As a result, I've taken as much time as necessary to work myself back into condition. I have five or six different routines that include gym work, lifting weights, and various cardiovascular exercises. My favorite routine is to take long bike rides, where I frequently pedal thirty to forty miles a trip. When I'm back in shape and find I can perform, I'll be back out there. But I won't hang around taking up space. I've got to be able to compete at the highest level.

In most professional sports, athletes eventually retire. But golfers carry on, either competitively or simply playing exhibition matches or corporate outings. I don't believe there will ever come a day when I put my clubs in the closet and never touch them again. I'll probably phase out my professional career gradually, maybe playing a mix of regular tour, senior tour, and international events. While I may not be a fixture as part of the Sunday telecast each weekend, I continue to promote the game around the world, playing in overseas events and exhibitions, conducting golf course design and development work, and furthering my other business interests. Annually, I fly more than 300,000 miles, which is equivalent to circumnavigating the globe more than a dozen times. All the while I try to represent the sport of golf, all my business interests around the world, and the ideals of my native Australia.

In recognition of my career as a professional golfer and because of my contribution to the game, I was inducted into the World Golf Hall of Fame in November 2001. I was honored to have been inducted along with Payne Stewart, Karsten Solheim, Judy Bell, Donna Caponi, and Allan Robertson. Personally, I was very gratified to have been voted in by PGA Tour ballot.

Overall, it was a fantastic evening with wonderful energy, camaraderie, and, I must say, great support from my family, friends, and cohorts. In advance of my acceptance speech, both Steve Elkington and Commissioner Tim Finchem made introductory remarks, which were well received by everyone in attendance and on the live broadcast by The Golf Channel. Interestingly, though, Finchem credited me with giving vision to the international golf movement and the World Golf Championships. For a moment, I felt as though Finchem, who had previously cut my legs out from under me, was now offering me a pair of shoes. But it was a wonderful evening, and I was not about to let Finchem's comments dampen my spirits.

Every inductee is given a ceremonial locker and asked to place in it some career items. For mine, I chose, among many other items, the laminated driver I crafted by hand as an apprentice back in 1975. It still has my initials in the face inset. I also chose the King Cobra irons I used to win the 1993 British Open at Royal St. George's, the yardage book I used at the 1981 Masters, one of my trademark wide-brimmed hats, and the flight helmet I wore when I spent two days with the U.S. Navy aboard the aircraft carrier USS *Carl Vinson.* My locker is a menagerie of stuff.

The World Golf Hall of Fame is a very special place. It not only celebrates golf, it also keeps alive the memory of the game's great players. Sometimes I think it's easy to forget them. Everybody grows up in their own time bubble. It's easy, in our modern day, to think only about the current generation of great golfers, like Tiger Woods, Vijay Singh, Phil Mickelson, Ratief Goosen, and Ernie Els. People in the generation before me remember Arnold Palmer, Jack Nicklaus, Gary Player, Tom Watson, Raymond Floyd, and Lee Trevino. But there are too few of us who reach even further back. There's just not enough recognition or respect given to the past champions of golf. In the old days, touring pros were second-class citizens who had to change their shoes out in the parking lot in the pouring rain. And they certainly didn't have the opportunity to go out and compete for $5 million purses. The entire atmosphere is different in modern golf. And yet, if it weren't for guys like Willie Park, Bobby Jones, Byron Nelson, Gene Sarazen, Sam Snead, and countless others, I would not have been able to enjoy all the success I experienced as a professional golfer.

In addition to my induction into the Hall of Fame, there was one other event that I hold near and dear to my heart: my participation in the 2000 Summer Olympics in Sydney. In reality, it seemed more like the "Australian Olympics," as the entire country rallied behind the organizing committee's efforts to showcase Australia to the world. I was absolutely delighted when I was asked to carry the Olympic torch across the Sydney Harbour Bridge on its path to the stadium. Because the opening ceremonies needed to take place in the evening (so that they could be broadcast in the morning in the U.S.), I carried the torch across the bridge at approximately 6:30 A.M. Sydney time. I remember thinking, "Who the hell is going to be out there watching me at that ungodly hour?" But I was surprised and humbled to experience more than 10,000 spectators who brought traffic to a complete halt for more than an hour on what is Sydney's major thoroughfare between its two central business districts. I was also asked to participate in the closing ceremonies, in which I hit golf balls off a floating shark and later sang "Waltzing Matilda" with a host of Australian icons. I enjoyed each of those moments. But more than once, I thought back to the words of wisdom imparted to me by Charlie Earp. "Greg, everywhere you go, you're carrying the Australian flag with you," he said. "You're representing your country. Don't ever forget that." And I never have.

In the aftermath of the Olympics and Hall of Fame ceremonies, I started receiving more calls than usual to participate in golf tournaments. Tournament directors and sponsors asked me to play in their events. "We need you, Greg," they'd say. "You'll put people in the seats and increase television ratings." Over the following few years, I did help some friends out and play in a few tournaments. And in 2005, when I hit fifty, I played in a couple of senior majors. But in all honesty, I have little desire to go out there and play week in and week out for twenty weekends a year. I also have little interest in helping the PGA Tour. Although I've made these feelings known, I'm still asked to play a lot more golf.

Why do the fans still connect with me after all these years? I think people liked watching me play golf. I wasn't afraid to enjoy myself on the course, and I wasn't afraid to show my frustration. People might have liked me, in part, because I always wore my heart on my sleeve. I think that over the years, the fans have grown to appreciate how I handled myself in the aftermath of several highly publicized defeats.

The Masters has been a cruel temptress for me. Even though I suffered a number of heartbreaking defeats there, I was also close enough to taste victory several times. Still, I love the tournament. I don't think there is an event anywhere that has brought me more enjoyment or shaped my development more profoundly as a player or as a person. Losing at the Masters actually made me more resilient. And now, no matter what happens to me, I know I have the ability to put it behind me, or even turn it into a positive experience.

I love the game of golf. No sports psychologist can ever understand what it is actually like to execute a pressure shot, when your heart is pounding and your adrenaline is surging. There is no better feeling when you're successful—and no more humbling feeling when you fail. If I stop playing golf tomorrow, I'll have achieved nearly everything I wanted—more than most, a little less than others. I've felt agony and ecstasy. I've experienced things that very few people ever will. One thing I'm very proud of is that I was consistently up near the top of the leaderboard. Sometimes I ran through the finish line, sometimes I stumbled across it, and sometimes I fell flat before I got there. Some people said I choked.

I have always wondered about this notion of choking. Few people in life, let alone sport, could ever comprehend the feelings of the moment. People in life choke. Making poor decisions is part of the overall big picture that we all live in, whether we play sports or not. When I watch the Olympics, I watch with respect and awe, because these athletes have one shot in four years and that might be the only chance in their sporting career to achieve excellence. But I note that if the gold medal is not sitting around their necks at the end of the day, they are still revered for finishing second (silver) or third (bronze), or if they do not win a medal, they receive recognition for achieving a personal best. It's interesting to see how success and failure are perceived differently in different fields.

In those moments of reflection on what might have been, I think back to when I was nineteen or twenty years old, making twenty-eight dollars a week as an assistant pro under Charlie Earp at Royal Queensland and wondering whether I would ever get a chance to play in a four-round tournament. It's *then* that I know I was lucky to be playing in the Masters, or the U.S. Open, or the British Open, or the PGA Championship.

I'm glad I got caught in that uncontrollable dumper when I was eighteen. It led me toward golf. And that has made all the difference in my life.

CHAPTER THIRTY-TWO

Conduct yourself with integrity.

Discipline and patience.

Due diligence.

DIN and DIP.

These are just some of the things I learned on the golf course. In truth, I firmly believe that my playing career was a stepping-stone to something else. So many of the things I did then, I do now—only now I do them in running a successful business.

My standards were always high in golf. Keeping them high in business turned out to be a major factor in structuring my partnerships and attracting new clients.

In golf, I played my own game. I knew my limitations, so I started slow, planned for the future, and got better. When ready, I jumped from Australia to the Japanese and European Tours to the U.S. PGA Tour. And that's exactly how I played it in business. I started slow, with endorsement deals, and then, when ready, I created my own brand and formed my own company.

I always played golf more for the enjoyment of the great golf courses I was able to experience than for the amount of prize money. So when I started my golf course design business, I was already leaning toward designing classic, timeless golf courses. And when I began to lead a team, I learned that if you provide the right direction, people will feed off your enthusiasm and find their work more gratifying.

On the golf course, I learned from Bruce Crampton that I needed to keep my playing partners honest. So I challenged Mark McCumber or Jumbo Ozaki or anybody else who needed to be challenged. In our golf equipment distribution business, I challenged the OEM (original equipment manufacturer). And in the wine business, I challenged our partners with respect to our cost of goods, margins, et cetera.

In my pro golfing career, all those losses by miracle shots strengthened me. I learned to always expect the unexpected. Nothing could be as reverberatingly bad as when Larry Mize sank that pitch shot on the 11th hole at the 1987 Masters. And nothing ever has been—at least not in business. Even when we reached for the brass ring in our expansion of Greg Norman Collection and failed, I was able to look at it calmly, figure out what to do, and build the business back up. Actually, all I did in that situation was get back to basics, which is exactly what I used to do when mired in a golf slump.

When I lost a golf tournament, I performed a postmortem in order to cut my risk of losing again. And now I constantly monitor the performance of my businesses so that I can learn from the mistakes made, and so I may reduce my risk in future business dealings.

All these lessons I learned in golf. But, as they say, Rome was not built in a day. I didn't learn everything all at once, and I certainly didn't build my businesses all at once. Rather, I began thinking about life outside golf during my heyday as the number one golfer in the world. I'd seen too many athletes wind down their careers and then have nowhere to go. Many gravitated toward television or some other stopgap. But I never wanted that for myself. I wanted to put myself in a position where I had enough going on around me so I would have avenues to pursue when I stopped playing golf full-time.

The plan I put into place in 1993 was a major turning point in my business development. Only thirty-eight years old at the time, I set several goals to reach by the new millennium. But only three years later, I decided to accelerate that plan as much as possible. After Acushnet bought out Cobra, and in the wake of what happened to me with the World Tour, I no longer wanted to wait the full seven years. In fact, the year 2000 quickly became obsolete, almost an afterthought. During the six months of rehabilitation from shoulder surgery, I simply started working as hard and as fast as I could to develop my businesses to a point where I no longer had to rely on golf for my livelihood. And what were the results? Well, I don't want to say I achieved 100 percent of my goals. But I can say that I met my expectations. Things are vastly different today than they were in 1993. In 2006, I was nominated to the H. J. Heinz Company board of directors. Also, rather than writing columns for golf magazines, I'm now regularly asked to write columns for business magazines. And instead of reporters asking me for interviews for their sports sections, I'm now frequently interviewed for such forums as *BusinessWeek*, the *Australian Financial Review*, and Bloomberg.

In the minds of most businesspeople, I've developed a multi-faceted, entrepreneurial organization. But that is not necessarily true for the vast majority of the general public, who still view me primarily as a professional golfer. Overall, though, I believe I have successfully leveraged my career in golf to something greater in business.

In my journey, there turned out to be a natural progression with both people and organizations. I started with an agent who took advantage of my naïveté in the world of business and finance, which taught me to take control of my own destiny. Then I spent thirteen years with IMG, a management company that I eventually outgrew. And finally, I formed my own company, Great White Shark Enterprises. Along the way, there was another progression of sorts, one that went from a modest business enterprise to something that was extensive, diverse, and uncommon.

It all started simply enough. As with most pro golfers, I began by picking up fees for endorsing various products or organizations. From Chevrolet to Land Rover, from Cobra to MacGregor, I viewed them all as partners. Some came and went, and some stayed. And as I began to expand my business beyond endorsement-only contracts, I did so by being an entrepreneur, by partnering with the right people, and by providing a value proposition. I formed my own golf course design business, which today has opened more than fifty courses worldwide and has just as many under contract. And I'm proud to say that this part of my business turned out to be everything I wanted it to be.

From golf course design, I moved into all the elements of creating and building up a brand, including the design and marketing of my own shark logo. The fact that I was still playing a lot of professional golf clearly helped me promote my own brand, not to mention its related products. During my playing days, I also became involved in a number of ventures that went beyond licensing and branding. I learned when to build equity in my own brand and when to add value to other brands.

Along the way, I also learned to identify and exploit a specific niche. In golf course design, we pioneered emerging markets in Asia. With Cobra, we created senior and women's golf clubs. In wine, we marketed Australian wine in America *and* launched a new series of California varietals, which is something that had never been done before. All along the way, too, I was provided with an outlet for my curiosity and creativity. At Cobra, I was heavily involved in research and product development. With Greg Norman Collection, I helped design and then field-test a variety of clothing. And with Greg Norman Estates, I became involved in most aspects of the wine business: tasting, bottling, marketing, label presentation, and distribution.

With each new enterprise, I also learned how to take advantage of adjacent space opportunities. Golf course design led to the turf business and the development business. My joint venture with Cobra led to the formation of the leading golf equipment distribution business in Australia. And Greg Norman Estates, as part of the food and beverage industry, eventually led to Greg Norman's Australian Grille and our premium beef business, Greg Norman Australian Prime.

Basically, over the years, one thing has led to another. I'm particularly proud of the brand joint venture model. It's something we created, and as far as I know, it is unique to GWSE. We license the Greg Norman name, but at the same time, we have a controlling interest in the venture and as such direct how the product or service is developed, marketed, and distributed. At the same time, we are always gauging the balance of our various businesses (the fulcrum, so to speak) and designing our exit strategy, where all our efforts, all our plans, and our blood, sweat, and tears are turned into cash.

From the moment I set that seven-year plan in place, I have always tried to be *proactive* in building my business assets. Dubai is a perfect example. If we hadn't been the tip of the spear in pioneering that emerging market, GWSE would not have been able to capitalize on and create opportunities for our businesses there. And for me, personally, it is extraordinarily exciting to be involved in the birth of a city-state. I may never have another opportunity like this again. Looking out thirty years and knowing where Dubai is heading, it will be an amazing story to tell my grandchildren.

Through the years, as my knowledge of business grew, I developed something of a commonsense business model, based on my experience, values, and principles. It was relatively easy to put this model together because business principles are not that difficult to articulate. However, what I consider to be the more difficult part of running a business is much more complicated and indefinable. Human resources has the potential all by itself to make or break a business. While some of my businesses are built around consumer products, many are service-oriented, and in each case, our most valuable assets go out the front door at the end of the day. After it's all said and done, it won't matter how smart a businessperson you are, how great a salesperson you are, or how innovative your product is. If you don't understand human nature and get a grip on how to handle it, it could be the potential ruination of your business.

I've discussed this issue with many corporate executives over the years, and all agree that employee mind-set is a key component of success. While I hire people who are smarter than I am and let them use their talents and express their opinions without fear or favor, there is no room for ego in my office. If I see it or sense it, I remove it immediately.

With leadership, you can inspire people, empower them, and unlock their full potential to take action. In so doing, they become leaders in their own right. Along with that, however, I hold *everybody* accountable for their actions, including myself. Without accountability, results can become a matter of hit or miss.

Another thing I pride myself on is openly admitting when I am wrong and then correcting my mistakes. In so doing, I'm able to build trust with my staff and friends, because they know that there will be no retribution or undue punishment if they make mistakes. All I ask is that they admit their mistakes, be willing to learn by them, and make sure the same problem does not come up again. Trust is a key component in forging a cohesive work environment, as well as a strong friendship.

At the same time, corporate executives must also acknowledge that interpersonal relationships, politics, rumors, and disinformation exist in any organization. Effective communication, then, becomes vital in ensuring that these human tendencies do not become a cancer quietly destroying from within. You don't want the tail to wag the dog. One such example surfaced in early 2006, when my staff learned that Laura and I had separated and that a divorce was imminent. Clearly, there were serious concerns over my ongoing commitment to GWSE and what the impact of our financial settlement might be on the company. As soon as I heard of people's concerns, I sat down with my entire staff and explained to them exactly what the situation was: that Laura and I were getting a divorce but that it would not have a material effect on the business.

While I normally attempt to keep my personal and business lives separate, these people had committed themselves to me, and I felt that transparency was essential for treating them with the respect they'd earned. I also mentioned to them that a divorce is between the two people involved—and no one else. With that, I was essentially asking them to respect my privacy. Overall, the staff respected my open dialogue and moved forward in a productive manner.

Like everybody, I have bad days outside the office. But whenever I walk in the front door, I want everybody to feel like I'm up and in a good mood. If I'm drained and tired, and people see it, then they're going to ask, "What's wrong with Greg?" And that may filter all the way through the organization. So I don't ever let that happen. People will follow the leader whether the leader is up or down, exuberant or depressed, tranquil or troubled. So it's always better to be up, exuberant, and tranquil rather than down, depressed, and troubled.

Human resources will always be a challenge. So as I move forward, there are two major policies I'll employ in order to keep human resources problems to a minimum. First of all, I intend to run a tight ship and have as few employees as possible. Second, when I do expand, the people I hire will be top of the line in regard to both their technical merits and their ability to work in a team environment. I know that sounds funny coming from a professional golfer. Even though golf is not a team sport, business definitely functions better when people perform as a team. Individuals who cannot meld into the group and work with others often disrupt the process and inhibit productivity.

Not long after the turn of the millennium, when I achieved many of my goals and GWSE really started to expand, I decided to bring on a chief financial officer to look after the company's finances and put in a strong system of checks and balances. Unlike my previous appointment of senior executives, I did not have an individual in mind, so I engaged an executive search firm to assist us. Given the importance of identifying the right person, I had our president and in-house counsel narrow thirty candidates down to four. After that, I personally conducted the final round of interviews, and ended up selecting Jack Schneider of Ernst & Young. Jack was not only a CPA, he also had a law degree, which allowed him to provide advice on both financial and legal matters. It's not often that one finds an attorney or CFO who has a good commercial mind and can contribute in a variety of ways.

I was excited to have Jack on our executive team, in part because I thought I could learn something from him. And sure enough, not long after he arrived, he pointed out to me that one thirty-second decision on my part could sometimes result in more than forty hours of work for a senior executive, which may or may not turn out to yield results. After he gave me a couple of examples of how he and Bart Collins had spent a week or more each on a couple of my quick decisions, I realized that I had to be more cognizant of the impact such requests might have on them. When you run a lean organization with action-oriented people, extra assignments may divert their time from other more important projects.

Even though I've been quite successful with the people I've brought into my company, I've still made some mistakes in business. But that's to be expected, because just like golf, business has its inevitable ups and downs. You can drive poorly, you can three-putt, and once in a while somebody else can chip in to beat you. The big difference for me, personally, is that, in business, every move I make is not being scrutinized by the media. When I was out on the golf course, I was in my domain and I was happy. But off the course, the other aspects of professional golf did not come naturally to me, and as a result, I didn't particularly like them. Actually, that is one reason I practiced so much. Practice kept me on the golf course. I made a lot of mistakes early on in my career because I really didn't have a clue to what I was doing. I had no guide to advise me on how to handle being scrutinized for everything I did, for every word I said, and for every bad shot I hit. No matter how many victories I achieved, it never seemed to be enough for the media. That's one reason I was always a reluctant celebrity.

I feel a lot more comfortable in the business world because I'm not under the microscope. I haven't always made the right decisions, but rarely does anyone outside GWSE know that. I like my business world because it's private—and I intend to keep it that way.

People are always asking me what my net worth is, but they never get anything out of me. Nor will they ever get anything out of my employees. That's because none of them actually knows what I'm worth, with the exception of Jack, who is the only one who has looked up my skirt. I've always been a big believer in separating my business enterprise from my wealth management. This really goes back not only to the lessons I learned from James Marshall and

IMG, but also to my loose-tight management practices. I've always maintained that I will utilize my time, effort, name, and likeness as currency for building up my businesses, rather than putting my own capital at risk. Therefore, I have maintained a separation of church and state in these two elements of my business. It's no disrespect to anybody in my company. It's just important for me to keep everything separated. It's worked well for me, and I intend to keep it that way.

Over the years, the successes have accumulated. In fact, Bart recently brought to my attention some consumer research on wine that stated that the three most recognizable Australian brands are Foster's, Qantas, and Greg Norman. When I think back to 1976, when I knew that I wanted to be aligned with an iconic Australian brand, I didn't think the day would ever come when my brand would stand shoulder to shoulder with these great Australian companies.

Ever since that day, as I walk up to my airplane or open a bottle of Greg Norman wine, I sometimes pause for a moment to appreciate what I've achieved. I don't do it so much to make myself feel good, though. I do it as a reality check. It actually renews and re-energizes me. Why? Because it reminds me of how hard I worked to get where I am and that I have to work just as hard to maintain it all and keep the businesses expanding.

I struggled for years to move beyond my persona as a professional golfer. Even though I'm proud of my past, and even though I intentionally leveraged my pro career to get to where I am today, I really wanted to move beyond golf. I wanted to be known as a businessman in my own right. Well, not long ago, something happened that gave me an indication that I might be on the way to achieving that goal.

I was on my boat out in the Caribbean near the Turks and Caicos, a small group of islands about ninety miles northeast of Cuba. A few friends and I had left to go fishing at four o'clock in the morning so we could get the morning marlin and tuna bite. Most of my friends were catching some shut-eye while I captained the boat to a well-known fishing location that I have frequented over the years. I was doing about thirty knots when I noticed a blip on my radar screen rapidly approaching our position. "Wow, this thing is moving fast," I thought to myself. It turned out to be a Coast Guard cutter, and within a few minutes, I was talking to them on the radio. They asked me a series of questions, including who the captain was, what our objectives were, our identification, our serial registration, and so on. After a few minutes, they asked me to stop so they could continue their inquiry. I believe they thought I might have been running illegal drugs. In that case, I knew it was probably part of standard procedure for them to obtain a visual sighting.

When the Coast Guard cutter finally pulled up near my boat, the sun was just peeking over the horizon. As we chatted back and forth for a few minutes, the commander of the vessel suddenly recognized my name. "Hey, are you Greg Norman, the wine guy?" she asked.

"Yes!" I responded excitedly, with my hands over my head. "Yes! I'm Greg Norman, the wine guy."

That young Coast Guard officer knew me not for golf but for Greg Norman Estates. It was wine that finally got me over the hump.

CHAPTER THIRTY-THREE

BACK IN THE MID-1990S, a prospective client asked me to evaluate possibly building a golf course on some property he owned along the banks of the White River near Meeker, Colorado. After I got up there and looked around for a day or so, I gave him my professional assessment. "You would be absolutely crazy to ruin one of the most magnificent valleys in America," I said. "I wouldn't build a golf course here if I were you. I'm saving you ten million dollars. Don't do it."

My prospective client decided not to build a golf course on his property, and after expressing some disappointment, he flew back home to Kansas. But I stayed. I had immediately fallen in love with this entire area: the mountains, the river, the wilderness. It just seemed like an unbelievable, untouched piece of paradise to me. So after exploring the area, I decided to buy an 8,300-acre ranch named Dry Creek. None of the land bordered the river, but there were rock canyons, dense forests, and dark timber throughout.

For years, I spent time hunting the Dry Creek property. In 2004, I purchased the 3,300-acre Pollard Ranch, which included one and a half miles of the White River. As I was making plans to build a vacation home on the property, I received word from Henry Kravis (of Kohlberg Kravis Roberts) that he was looking to sell Seven Lakes Lodge, his custom-built 300-acre hunting lodge in the White River National Park. The acquisition of Dry Creek, Pollard Ranch, and Seven Lakes Lodge allowed me to put together approximately 12,000 contiguous acres of pristine ranch and river property where

I'm now able to enjoy the recreational hobbies of hunting, fishing, and ranch life that I had grown to love since my early days of being on the cattle station in Australia.

One of the first things I did after finalizing the deal was to bring in a private company, Colorado Fisheries, to give me advice on how to restore my river. Essentially, I adopted my principle of inviting the environmentalists to work with me on the project, giving them a sense of ownership and having them understand my commitment not only to preservation, but also to the local community. One of the things they pointed out to me was that cattle and sheep owned by a previous owner of Pollard Ranch had significantly eroded vegetation in many areas of the riverbank. As a result, the fish population was adversely impacted. Well, I wanted to bring back the normal amounts of cutthroat, rainbow, and brown trout. So I obtained permission from the Colorado Department of Wildlife and the Environmental Protection Agency to undertake a major river reclamation project. And over the next year, we returned the river to its pristine natural state, which nicely complemented the elk, bears, mule deer, mountain lions, and all the other wildlife that migrate to the area.

I try to spend as much time as possible up at my ranch in Colorado. In the summers, I'll jump on my John Deere 670D motor grader and cut some access roads through the property. I'll pack a lunch, operate the equipment by myself, and work for eight to ten hours a day for maybe two or three days in a row. For me, it's a way to unwind. I've never been one to sit around during my free time.

I'm an outdoorsman at heart, but through the years I have seen quite a bit of neglect and devastation. I get concerned, for instance, when I go scuba diving and see an entire reef being bleached out by locals chasing fish, or when I observe the desecration of wildlife, forestry, and fishing in rare and supposedly protected wilderness areas. Every person on this planet has to take care of the environment and try to leave it in better condition for the next generation. In a bid to contribute, I have invested my time and money in two organizations that are specific to the environment: the Environmental Institute for Golf (EIFG) and Living Oceans.

In 2004, I agreed to serve on the board of the EIFG and chair its advisory council. The EIFG was established by the Golf Course Superintendents Association of America (GCSAA), whose members, in my opinion, are the unsung heroes of our sport. Steve Mona, CEO of the GCSAA, approached me about getting involved because he thought, given my involvement with golf course design, residential development, and turf grass, I was well positioned to connect with golfers, the corporate world, and environmentalists. I agreed to serve, knowing that the EIFG would utilize me as a resource rather than just a figurehead. I see this as an opportunity to demonstrate that from recreational, economic, and environmental aspects, golf courses are, in fact, community assets. The EIFG is committed to strengthening the compatibility of the game of golf with our natural environment, and with time we have rallied the support of golf's administrative bodies, including the USGA and the PGA of America, to form a united front. In the first five years of operation, our efforts have been focused on five specific areas: water management; integrated plant management; wildlife and habitat management; energy and waste management; and golf course location, design, and construction. We have also developed EDGE, a Web-based tool that serves as a central clearinghouse for environmental information relating to golf courses. By uniting golf course architects, superintendents, governing bodies, and environmental organizations, we believe that a collaborative effort will lead to programs and services that benefit everyone who comes in contact with the game of golf.

The second organization I'm involved with, Living Oceans, was established by Prince Khaled bin Sultan of Saudi Arabia to preserve and protect our world's oceans. This particular relationship was a natural for me, because from the first time I explored the underwater beauty of the coral reefs off Australia's Magnetic Island, I was hooked. I have enjoyed many magical underwater experiences over the years, but, most important, the water has long been an escape for me. It has provided countless opportunities to experience some quality time away from golf, business, and everything else that is on my plate.

Living Oceans has formed partnerships with scientists and environmentalists around the world in an effort to educate people about our oceans. As a first step, the organization's work includes mapping many of the world's coral reefs, essentially taking an audit of the ecosystem, gauging the health of the fish and living coral, and assessing any dangers. This effort is critically important, and it will provide a basis from which to gauge progress or degeneration over a period of time. While various governmental institutions have undertaken similar projects, they have never been applied with consistency on a macro level. Thus far, Living Oceans has initiated studies in the U.S. Virgin Islands, the Seychelles, and the Red Sea, and I am pleased that the Great Barrier Reef will be a focal point for Living Oceans in the near future.

Another thing I care deeply about is the fight against cancer in children. This particular interest was brought home to me by Laura's brother, Dr. Richard Andrassy, who is one of America's leading pediatric cancer surgeons. I watched him perform surgery on babies so small that you could hold them in the palm of your hand. And I'd often accompany him on his rounds where we'd visit with children suffering from all stages of cancer. Some were living in sterile chambers so they could remain isolated from infection. And almost all were happy to see us, even though they had no idea who we were. These were children who, like my young friend Jamie Hutton, had never experienced the ocean, or hiked through the woods, or taken a whack at a golf ball. So I decided to do something to help. I began, as most people do, by donating money. But knowing I could do more, I expanded my efforts. I made CureSearch National Childhood Cancer Foundation one of the beneficiaries of the Shark Shootout, in order to raise awareness and additional funds for the organization.

Overall, I put in time and donate to many worthy causes that remain off the radar screen to the general public. One that made it into the public eye occurred in November 2001, when I participated in the Skins Game with Tiger Woods, Colin Montgomerie, and Jesper Parnevik. I was fortunate enough to win all eighteen skins and donated a significant portion of my $1 million to Fiduciary Trust, a division of Franklin Templeton Investments. That donation was specifically earmarked for family members who lost loved ones in the tragic events of September 11, 2001.

Back in 1987, when I was searching for a way to give something back to the game in Australia, my father suggested that we set up a golf foundation for young people in Queensland. As a result, over the past twenty years, we have built a foundation that not only caters to the development of aspiring professionals but makes the game accessible to everyone who is interested.

I believe I understand what access, encouragement, and a positive role model can mean to a young golfer. And I also know that the game of golf requires self-discipline, determination, and passion, which are qualities that help to develop character and personal strength in young people. I remember many years ago when I invited two of the foundation's participants to travel to Florida and spend some time with me. We picked the best performers, both academically and on the golf course. I wanted them to experience America and understand what a person had to do to become successful. The only condition I put on the two participants was that they had to do everything I did.

Well, one of those kids was Karrie Webb (who coincidentally happens to be from my father's hometown of Ayr, Queensland). She was only sixteen or seventeen at the time, but I could tell that there was something special about her. When I got up at five o'clock in the morning, so did she. If I hit 500 balls in practice, she did too. If I went to my office, she went with me. Karrie has a thirst for learning and success. I never once heard her complain, nor did she ask for anything. When I put her on the plane to go home, I remember predicting that this girl was going to be a success in life. "I don't know if it'll be on the golf course or in some other field," I said, "but she has everything a person needs to make it in this world." When Karrie Webb was inducted into the World Golf Hall of Fame in 2005, I couldn't have been more proud. And I was extremely disappointed when, due to a previous commitment, I was unable to accept her invitation for me to introduce her at the ceremony.

Whether it was junior golfers from my foundation in Queensland or other Australians spending time in the States, I always tried to host Australians at my home. I often think back to 1976, when I first came to the United States and played in the World Cup with Bob Shearer. It was a daunting experience, but I was fortunate that friends such as George Kelley gave me a bit of a road map. So I tried to pass it on when others came to the United States.

My visitors have included Australian cricketers Dean Jones and Allen Border, and young Australian golfers such as Robert Allenby, Aaron Baddeley, and Adam Scott during the Florida Swing on Tour. I've also had the good fortune to host the likes of former prime minister Bob Hawke, tennis players Lleyton Hewitt and Pat Rafter, and television personality Pat Welch. I'd like to think that, in some small way, I've helped them with their orientation to the States, whether their visits were personal or business. I also like to have an open-door policy to give my friends a respite, access to the Medalist Golf Club, and a few cold beers. I might add that, personally, I enjoy their company and feel it helps me stay connected to Australia.

One of the prouder moments I've had as an Australian and as a businessman came in November 2004, when I was honored by the American Australian Association, the largest nonprofit organization in the United States devoted to relations among the U.S., Australia, and New Zealand. First established by Rupert Murdoch, Sr., in 1946, its goal is to encourage stronger ties among the three nations, particularly in the private sector. I was honored for my contributions to American-Australian relations and my success in business. While I had received a number of accolades through the years, mainly for my golfing achievements, that particular recognition was extremely special to me because it was about being an entrepreneur, and because of all the distinguished Australians who were nominated before me. These included Rupert Murdoch; Geoffrey Bible, CEO of Philip Morris; Peter Lowy, managing director of the Westfield Group; Douglas Daft, chairman and CEO of the Coca-Cola Company; Andrew N. Liveris, president and CEO of the Dow Chemical Company; and Charlie Bell, former president and CEO of McDonald's Corporation. The AAA opened my eyes to something I am most proud of: that for a small country, Australia produces not just world-class athletes but world-class businessmen. You might be surprised at just how many Australians hold key positions in corporate America and around the world.

Immediately after the American Australian Association dinner I flew to Pittsburgh for a benefit with my good friends Henry and

Elsie Hillman. Nearly a thousand people gathered at a hangar in-side the Greater Pittsburgh Airport to raise more than $4 million for the University of Pittsburgh Medical Center's Hillman Cancer Center.

In 2005, after an Indian Ocean tsunami claimed 230,000 lives, I recruited former presidents George H. W. Bush and Bill Clinton for a benefit golf tournament at the Medalist Golf Club. Actually, Laura deserves credit for that idea. When it was announced that the two ex-presidents were joining forces to raise much-needed funds for tsunami relief, she turned to me and said, "Why don't you get the two of them to play golf and raise some money?"

I found that both men, who were already engaged in tsunami fund-raising efforts, were happy to oblige. So once we all agreed on a date, I got on the phone and started making calls. I made more than 100 calls and assembled 72 golfers to show up for our one-day event. Many others who didn't play golf sent in money. It rained the entire day, but both presidents played every hole and had a great time. Most important, with Bush representing the Red Cross and Clinton representing UNICEF, we were able to raise some $2.1 million for tsunami relief.

It was later brought to my attention that in a six-month span from October 2004 through March 2005, my regular charitable activities and a number of high-profile events helped raise nearly $10 million. Personally, I derive a lot of self-satisfaction from know-ing that, because I believe very much in the old scripture saying: *To whom much is given, much is expected.*

One of the great things about being fifty-one years old is that younger players sometimes seek me out to ask my advice on a vari-ety of subjects. And I am always happy to respond, mainly because I like to help. One young pro recently called me and related that he was having a problem concentrating for the entire round of golf. So many negative thoughts were in his head that he couldn't keep his mind on the putt he had in front of him. "I know it happens to every golfer," he said. "What kinds of things did you do to stay fo-cused? What should I do?"

"Flush the toilet," I said.

"Flush the toilet?"

"Yeah, I used to flush the toilet. You need a trigger mechanism to stay in the moment. Sometimes I'd have a conversation with myself. Sometimes I'd mentally write down all my negative thoughts on an invisible piece of paper, crumple it up, put a match to it, and throw it up in the air. 'Poof!' All the negative thoughts were gone and I was back in the moment. But most of the time, especially when I was lining up a putt, I'd flush the toilet."

"Tell me about that," said the young man.

"Well, you know how you squat down to line up a putt? If I had negative thoughts in my head, that is the time I would get rid of them. With my wide-brimmed hat, it was easy, because nobody was able to see my eyes. I'd look down at the ground and mentally pull together all of my negative thoughts. Then I'd hold my putter up to the left and bring it down as if I were pulling the chain of an old-time toilet. And that would flush all the waste away."

"You're kidding."

"No, I'm not kidding. Every pro has to have their own mechanism for staying in the moment. That one worked for me. Now, it might not work for you. But you've got the idea now. So all you have to do is come up with your own method."

In recent years, I've noticed that some younger players on tour break eye contact with me in the locker room or on the practice tee. I'm told that sometimes I appear to be unapproachable or hard-edged, or even that I have an intimidating stare. None of that gives me any joy, because I genuinely believe I am very approachable, and of course, I'm always pleased to engage with any of the younger players on tour.

When I'm asked to provide some general advice, I advise young golfers to go out and speak with experienced professionals. Listen to them, hear what they have to say, and learn from them.

If I'm asked about handling money, the first thing I say is that it's hard to make money but it's easy to lose it all. You might read in books how other athletes have been taken advantage of by people they've trusted. Well, I've been there, guys. It happens in life, and it happened to me. So seek the advice of financial experts, understand what they say to you, and keep control of your own finances.

When a young professional expresses some concern about the

PGA Tour and then asks my advice on what to do, I am direct and honest. The only way you are going to feel comfortable within yourself is to try to understand the internal workings of the Tour. But that is difficult to do. If you want to fight the PGA Tour on some issue, it will cost you money. Are you willing to fight them for three, four, or five years? Because that's what it will take. Actually, it may take longer, because the Tour will wait you out. Whether you're a member for ten years, fifteen years, or twenty-five years, you as an individual golfer are nothing more than a pass-through entity. But also keep this in mind: You don't want to do anything that will drag down our Tour. Overall, it has been very, very good for everybody who plays the game. The players are pretty much recession-proof. I believe Commissioner Finchem and the Tour, in general, have done a great job in making that a reality. Always remember, however, that the PGA Tour is *your* tour. It is a membership organization. The administrators work for you, not the other way around. It's up to the players to monitor the direction of their Tour, to understand its problems, if any, and to help shape its future. I sense, however, that many players are happy with their security blanket and are not that keen to question what is taking place behind closed doors. In my opinion, there is absolutely no problem in asking tough questions. Just as in my overall business philosophy, accountability is a crucial element.

And finally, if I'm asked about proper conduct when playing golf, my opinion never wavers. We must police ourselves while playing professional golf. We don't want referees on the golf course (like they have in soccer, rugby, or football) telling us what we did wrong or what we did right.

One of the fundamental principles in golf is that, while on the course, each individual must live up to the highest standards, morals, and ethics that he or she can possibly muster. We must look out for each other. We must care for each other. And we must stand up for each other. We all owe that to the game of golf.

Come to think of it, we owe that to the game of life as well.

CHAPTER THIRTY-FOUR

A COUPLE OF YEARS AGO, while playing in a PGA event, I was paired with a young man who had been on tour for only a short time, and I saw him do something wrong. We were playing under wet conditions, and we were allowed to lift, clean, and place on the fairways. But the young man had driven his ball in the left-side rough (not in the fairway), and it looked like it had plugged. I just happened to be glancing over there when I noticed him pick up his ball, clean it, and put it back down.

"Did you see what he just did?" I asked my caddie, Tony Navarro.

"Sure did," Tony replied.

I thought for a minute about going over to him immediately, but then I realized that this young man was a rookie and, as such, was probably nervous and prone to making mistakes. We had only a few holes left to play, so I told Tony I'd handle it after the round. "I don't want to disrupt his play at this point," I said.

On the 16th hole, I called an official over, explained the situation, and told him that I didn't want to make a public song and dance about it. "I'll deal with it quietly," I said. And he agreed to let me handle it.

Once we had signed our scorecards and were leaving the scorer's tent, I pulled my young playing partner aside. "Hey, bud, can I talk to you for a second?" I asked.

"Sure, Greg," he replied.

"Come on over here behind the tent for a minute, will you. I don't want anybody to hear us."

So we went behind the tent by ourselves. And then I put my hand on the young man's shoulder. "Look, what you did back there on the 15th hole broke the rules," I said softly. "You did two things wrong, for which you normally would have been penalized. Here's what you should have done. Because your ball was not in the fairway, you should have informed me, as your playing partner, that you had casual water and that your ball was plugged. Then it would have been up to me to determine whether or not you could lift, clean, and place. You cannot predetermine that on your own. Second, you can never touch your golf ball unless you've said something to me or an official."

As I was explaining all this, my partner was looking me straight in the eye, listening intently, and nodding his head positively.

"Now, I'm just giving you a warning shot across the bow," I concluded. "I've given you the benefit of the doubt because you're new out here. But don't expect this again. Because the rules of the game of golf are there to protect you."

The young man really seemed to appreciate what I had to say to him. And I firmly believe that by speaking to him privately about his mistake, I prevented him from taking a penalty in a later tournament.

I'm pretty sure that, had this situation happened twenty years ago, I wouldn't have reacted so tactfully. I've definitely mellowed over the years, and I'm a calmer person. And I think more before I act. It's a natural progression in life, I believe. The best of us grow, not only physically but also in how we deal with people. We think more about the responses that people have to an "in your face" confrontation.

As a kid, I reacted emotionally when I thought somebody had done something wrong—like the time I chased a guy on the rugby field for raking my face with his cleats. In that particular instance, I never did catch the guy *and* I got thrown out of the game. Later, as a young man, I made the impulsive comment that many golfers on the European Tour did not have the guts needed to win when victory was in sight. I had incorrectly perceived that some of these players were weak because they didn't practice as hard as I did. Today I regret making that statement, not because of all the negative press I received but because it was a public indictment of my peer group and not very professional.

These days, if someone does something I perceive to be wrong, rather than get in their face, I'll try to handle it a little more diplomatically, just like I did with my young playing partner. Don't get me wrong, though. I'll still say something. I'll never just let it go or walk away. But I do think it's wise to consider how your message comes across and whether there will be negative consequences to your actions. I've learned that you can still make the same point without causing a lot of consternation among people. Experience is a wonderful thing.

In my younger years, I was a perfectionist, driven to see what I could pull out of myself. Did I push myself too hard? I think I did. But would I be where I am today if I hadn't done that twenty-five years ago? Probably not.

When you're young, your dreams are your blueprint of reality. You think that with success comes happiness. But that's not necessarily true. True success, I believe, lies in being able to take something from every situation—every lucky bounce, every heartbreaking defeat—learn from it, and move forward. Normally, when you win at something, you move on without thinking. But when you fail, you analyze what went wrong and as a result often take more away from the experience.

Life, however, is a circle. History repeats itself. If you learn from your failures—whether in golf, business, or life—then you can do better the next time. You don't learn anything in life without failure. Believe me, I know. And it's how you turn those failures into something positive that separates the men from the boys. Some of my acquaintances think that the two worst things that ever happened to me were the James Marshall episode and the 1996 Masters. But in my view, those were actually two of the *best* things that ever happened to me.

Even though I lost a lot of money because of Marshall, it made me more aware of what I had to do in the future. In the 1996 Masters, when I blew that 6-shot lead on the final day, I was heartbroken at first. But the aftermath of that entire episode moved me so deeply that I came to realize that there was much more to life than winning golf tournaments. Both of those negative experiences changed my life. They made me a better man.

Because of the competitor I am, I certainly would have liked to have won more majors. But I can say unequivocally that winning the green jacket would not have improved my quality of life one bit. What matters most is the commitment you make to yourself and the effort you put in each and every time you go out there. And that's true whether you're playing golf, engaged in business, or just trying to get through life. The days you cry your eyes out and the days you celebrate with your friends—to me, that's what it's all about.

I don't wake up every morning feeling sorry for myself. Actually, it's quite the opposite. I wake up feeling completely fulfilled by what golf has given me and by what I have extracted from the game. I also wake up with a view toward getting something done each and every day. One thing that hasn't changed for me over the years is my energy. I still have a lot of energy, and when I rise early in the morning, I don't want to fail at whatever I'm going to do that day. There's that fear of failure I think I was born with. It'll never go away.

My daughter, Morgan, is very much a mirror image of me. She'll get up very early in the morning and get her work done. Her passion for life is incredible. She's just go, go, go. Often, we'll talk about how we both feel that there is so much to do. "I'll get all the sleep I need when I'm dead," I say to her.

I think engaging in a lot of physical activity is just part of who I am. I like doing things. I like getting my fingernails dirty. I've always been a workaholic, but even in my time off, I would rather be doing things than just sitting around on the beach. To me, an education in life is firing up all your senses at one time. Whether it's playing tournament golf, hunting, spearfishing, or skydiving, when everything is electrified, when every nerve, every neuron in your brain is firing—that's learning and living life to the fullest. And when I'm doing those things, I'm living in the moment. Morgan has observed that when I'm swimming off the Great Barrier Reef, I seem to merge into the environment and become like another fish. And Morgan should know. As she and her brother, Gregory, were growing up, they both (together and individually) accompanied me to many of the places I was exposed to when I grew up, including some of the wild and weird spots in the Australian outback.

I always thought I spent a great deal of time with my children until something happened when Gregory was about eleven or twelve. On one of my breaks from playing on the Tour, I asked my son if he wanted to practice some chipping and putting in the backyard. "No, thanks, Dad," he said. "But I'll gladly watch and help you."

After that practice session was over, I sat down with my son and asked him why he didn't want to practice with me. "Dad," he responded, "I've seen what this game has done to you, and the sacrifice of time away from the family for you to achieve all you did. So I don't want to be a professional golfer, I just want to enjoy the game."

Well, that turned out to be a real gut check for me. Afterward, I really tried to take both Gregory and Morgan with me as much as their schoolwork would allow. As a result, both of them have seen the world and experienced a great deal of the outdoors. And now that they're adults, we've continued to experience new adventures together. Both of them, for instance, wanted to go skydiving on their eighteenth birthdays. Well, I wasn't going to let an opportunity like that go by, so I joined them.

I still remember the time Morgan and I were looking out the door of that plane at 15,000 feet. It was the first time for both of us, and I remember thinking to myself, "What the heck am I doing up here?" With the rage of the engine and the wind noise, our hearts were racing a mile a minute. Then, when we finally jumped, and the parachutes opened, everything was perfectly silent. We were floating down through the air at the same speed. A couple of birds flew by. And I will never forget how, even though Morgan was several hundred feet away, I could talk to her like she was right next to me. It was a feeling of adrenaline-charged excitement combined with one of peace and serenity. I've never experienced anything quite like it.

All of the individual outings I had with my kids when they were growing up provided perfect opportunities for me to pass along some of the lessons I learned along the way. During trips to Wild Man River, Seven Spirit Bay (where an aboriginal elder took the kids to a 15,000-year-old burial ground), Bullo Station in the outback, and Truk Lagoon (Micronesia), I taught them about such things as DIN and DIP, about the 30/30/30/10 money rule, and urged them to apply themselves in school. "I wish I had paid more attention," I remember saying. "Because the two subjects I enjoyed most are now prevalent in my golf course design business. As a result, I've had to relearn many of the aspects of engineering and geography that help me understand topographic maps, drainage issues, construction, and other key elements of my work."

Those trips helped us build strong bonds. And now that my daughter and son are grown, our relationships are stronger than you can imagine. Both are pursuing degrees in higher education, and in the long run, they may choose to join me in business. If they do, I know it would be a great partnership in which we would learn a lot from each other. I could teach them the street smarts of running a business, and they could teach me the educational smarts I missed out on by not attending college.

I'm also blessed with a lot of very close friends because, in part, I work very hard at cultivating those relationships. I've stayed in touch with many of the people who went out of their way to help me in business: Tom Crow, Paul Fireman, Pete Dye, Bill Moss, Richard Sheppard, and Kerry Packer (who has since passed away), for example. Nelson Peltz, in particular, is one of my dearest friends to date, and he has been there for me through thick and thin, happiness and sadness. And I particularly try to stay close to people like Charlie Earp and others like him who went out of their way to coach and guide a young man with a dream. I feel so beholden to Charlie that when I was given the Francis Ouimet Award in 2005 for lifelong contributions to golf, I designated Charlie Earp's name in which to set up a scholarship.

I've always been a firm believer that a person finds out who his true friends are when he's down and out, when things look bleakest. Because I believe that, I'm always keeping an eye on the people I care about. My loyalty is strong. And when they're not doing well, I will reach out to them. After Bill Clinton had open-heart surgery in 2004, for instance, I flew up to see him in New York. I spent a couple of hours chatting with him, trying to cheer him up and reassuring him that everything was going to be okay. I remember being there when a phone call came in from John Kerry to inform the former president that he was going to concede the 2004 presidential election to George W. Bush. It was the day after Election Day, and Ohio was still in dispute at the time.

And when my friend Steve Elkington finished second in the 2005 PGA Championship by only one stroke, I called him up. "I'm very proud of you, Elky," I said. "Your swing was beautiful during the entire tournament. And that putt you hit on 18 was absolutely perfect. Why it didn't go in the hole, who knows? Did you know that you qualified for the NEC Championship because of your high finish? Keep up the good play. Go out there and win the NEC!"

I knew Steve was down, so I tried to get his mind off the disappointment. I didn't want him to dwell on the negative but to think about the positive. I also wanted to give him something to look forward to. "Hey, mate," I said. "Why don't you come out to Colorado with me. Bring your son. We'll go fishing, hunting."

I believe I've been successful in golf, business, and life because I make the time to work on my relationships with friends and family. And one of the ways I *make* that time is by not getting involved in a lot of meaningless drivel. I don't worry so much about the minutiae of life. Everybody has to understand that it is kind of like the Chinese water torture treatment. The drip, drip, drip slowly builds up to create problems. So the quicker you can eliminate the drip, the quicker you eliminate the torture.

I also try not to carry around a lot of excess baggage. I've mentioned before that whenever I have something on my mind, whether it's a minor problem in business or a major problem in golf, I make my decision, stand by it, and get on with my life. I remember DIN and DIP: Do It Now, and Do It Proper. If I'm troubled by something, the constant emotional toll holds me back from achieving new goals, and that, in turn, keeps me from enjoying life.

Unfortunately, it's not always that simple. My separation from Laura was clearly a defining moment in my life. I've joined the ranks of the nearly 50 percent of married Americans who divorce, and I now understand how difficult it is to separate from someone whose life has been interwoven with yours for more than twenty-five years. While I endeavored to take the high road, the anxiety and emotional turmoil that we went through were extraordinary. For me, it was like rolling my past fifty-one years up into a ball and having all the experiences, good and bad, not even come close to what the previous twelve months have been like.

Along the way, I had a strong support group of people who helped me deal with it. My daughter, Morgan, and my son, Gregory, were mature beyond their years. But, most important, I felt, they loved and respected both of us for who we were: their father and their mother.

The most surprising person who emerged in this entire ordeal, however, was my father. He was sympathetic, encouraging, insightful, and a source of great comfort and advice to me. After a conversation with Morgan and Gregory, I suddenly grasped something that I had never before really accepted. Through the eyes of my children, I realized that, for thirty years, my father had always been there for me. He was like a rock, ready to support me in all my times of need. I came to understand that, over the years, it was I who turned away from him, not the other way around. So, as devastating as it was to go through a divorce, in some strange way, it brought me closer to my father.

I've also realized that the people closest to me respect and honor me more for *who* I am than *what* I am. So now, more than ever before, I make a conscious effort to show respect for my mother and father, my children, and my close friends. And as always, I make sure they know I honor their decisions, their opinions, and their feelings.

I don't know if anyone ever fully recovers from the effects of a divorce. But I know that with the right attitude, and by adhering to my values and principles, I will get through this difficult period in my life. I'll remember the many good things and hold them close. I won't dwell on past negatives but will, instead, look forward to a brighter future. I'll learn, apply, and become stronger so that the next chapter in the back 9 of my life will be better. In the end, I believe I'll come out a stronger and better person because of it.

CHAPTER THIRTY-FIVE

IT HAS ALWAYS BEEN in my nature to go for it. Look the dragon right in the eye and take him on. Live by the sword, die by the sword. It was always that way in golf. And when I entered the business world, nothing changed. I stayed aggressive, kept attacking, and carved out my own future.

Golf used to be my vehicle for life. Now it's business. And the wins for my company have been every bit as fulfilling as those I experienced on the golf course. But I sometimes miss the day-to-day life of being a full-time professional golfer, largely because I experienced such a wide range of emotions. At times I was in the toughest, loneliest place in the world, which is leading a golf tournament. No one talks to you, and you don't talk to anyone. And then there were times when the camaraderie and the friendships I made were as good as a person can experience in life.

When I look back on my career now, I don't think as much about the tournaments won or lost as I do about the people I was able to spend time with and get to know. All too often, I took certain things for granted back then. I regularly became consumed with the negative things that people said without taking the time to fully appreciate their small acts of kindness. Now, however, it's a different story. I'm always on the lookout for signs of goodness in people. Sometimes, however, they're tough to find. Many individuals have a stoic, stonelike exterior that is difficult to penetrate. But if you take the time to really get to know people, then it becomes apparent that there is a lot of goodness inside.

Recently, I sat back and began to think about all the small acts of kindness that had been done for me over the years. They piled up pretty fast, and I realized just how fortunate I was to have had so many good people come into my life. There were Cyril King and Charlie Earp in my formative years. There was Sommie Mackay, the head of Precision Golf Forgings, who allowed me to work special hours so I could practice golf. There was John Klatt, who taught me the fundamentals of golf through his junior golf clinics at Virginia Golf Club. There was my buddy Bryan Smith, who was waiting on the 18th green with a bottle of champagne when I won my first golf tournament in Adelaide. There were also my traveling buddies in the early years: Bill Longmuir, Stuart Ginn, and Brian Jones. A bond developed among the four of us as we shared rooms in Japan, Europe, and other parts of the world.

And then there was the incomparable Jack Nicklaus—my childhood hero, a man who was already a legend in the world of golf. Jack sat down with me in the locker room at my first Australian Open and encouraged me. When I was anxious at my first Masters, he put his arm around me and mentioned that he was nervous too. When I was leading the 1986 British Open going into the final day, he pulled up a chair at dinner the night before and offered me some advice. The next day, when I won, he went out of his way to congratulate me. And I'll never forget standing together in his driveway in the rain talking about golf.

Back in the early 1990s, there was my personal trainer, Pete Draovitch, steering me on the path of physical fitness and nutritional understanding. To this day, he is still one of my dearest friends. In the 1996 Masters, there was Fred Couples, who, after hearing that I was having back problems, quickly sent over his back therapist to help me. On the Sunday of that tournament, there was Nick Faldo, who, rather than celebrate his victory, came up to me on the 18th green, hugged me, and told me: "Don't let the bastards get you down." In the days after that loss, there were thousands of good wishes I received from people all over the world. One from ten-year-old David Tiffenberg well represented all those messages. "Be happy and know that there are a million kids like me who love and respect you," he wrote.

Then I thought about Jamie Hutton, whose courage in the face of a devastating disease inspired me to win my first golf tournament in two seasons. I thought about Pete Dye going out of his way to teach me the ins and outs of golf course design, of Steve Elkington willing to take a punch for me, and of my steadfast caddies, Steve Williams, Bruce Edwards, and especially Tony Navarro. Words can never express what we went through over the years and the thousands of miles we traveled together. And now, of late, Chris Evert has been there as a friend, as have my colleagues at work, who have become good friends outside of office hours.

Of course, I also thought about my family. My four-year-old daughter, Morgan, slipping her hand in mine after the 1987 Masters loss and saying, "Daddy, I know you didn't win today, but we can still have a party." My seven-year-old son, Gregory, after my 1993 loss in the PGA Championship, breaking through the crowd and saying, "I'm proud of you, Dad." My mother taking me out on the golf course for the first time. My father instilling in me life's most important values.

A lot of people say I'm unlucky. They've seen me on the golf course swallowing some tough losses. But they haven't seen all the good things I've experienced. Life is a journey. All of our experiences get spread out over a long period of time, and things have a tendency to balance out. The truth is, I'm the luckiest guy in the world. But it has taken me a long time to realize it.

When I was younger, I was wrapped too tight around the axle. I was sometimes unbending, unforgiving, and hard. Being somewhat introverted, I had a tough exterior. But deep down, there was a good guy waiting to show himself—and, from those depths, a drive and a desire to improve that just needed to be pulled out. Over the years, I learned that life is not so much about having what you want as wanting what you have, and that, in the long run, you have to make peace with yourself before you can be comfortable with everybody else. I've learned to open my heart to all my friends and family. This I've learned only in recent times.

So I challenged myself to be the best person I could possibly be. I reached deep down inside and tried to pull out the goodness that I knew was there—that I know all people have. For me, personally, it's been a work in progress for fifty years. Some friends say that I'm softer now, more mellow. But I don't know that I've softened up so much as I have just worked hard to become a better person. And I suppose I'll use the time I have left to smooth out the rough edges.

In golf, you can always shoot a lower score. In business, you can always make another buck. And in life, you can always become a better person.

The next minute is the most important minute of your life.

You are limited only by your own imagination.

Your dreams are the blueprints of reality.

PRINCIPLES AND VALUES:
50 KEY LEARNINGS THAT DEFINE GREG NORMAN

- Dreams are the blueprints of reality.
- Find a better way, but don't take shortcuts.
- Always tell the truth.
- Separate yourself from the crowd.
- Control your emotions.
- Get anger out of your system as quickly as possible.
- Set high standards. They will drive you to achieve.
- DIN and DIP.
- You are judged by the company you keep.
- Learn the value of preparation.
- Be willing to change in order to succeed.
- Work to your weaknesses rather than focusing on your strengths.
- Face failure, learn from it, and move on.
- Seek the advice of others.
- Forge strategic and long-term relationships.
- Identify a niche and fill it.
- Study others. Apply what works. Discard what doesn't.
- Focus on delivering substance over style.
- Play your own game.
- Expect the unexpected.
- When looking for partners, search for companies with like-minded values.
- Don't stand by idly when the rights of others are threatened.
- Material change comes from those willing to challenge the status quo.
- Stay in good physical condition. It will make a significant difference in your mental outlook.
- Resolve conflict through personal interaction.
- Turn inertia into action.
- When presented with the right opportunity, go for it.
- Trust your instincts.

- Think of yourself as an entrepreneur.
- Learn to compartmentalize; give total focus to the task at hand.
- The nature of a true competitor is becoming more determined with every defeat.
- Victory is sweet, but how you handle yourself in defeat is often more telling.
- It takes time to establish something of value.
- Separate your personal life from your professional life.
- Treat your client's money as though it's your own.
- Don't change the people; *change* the people.
- Evaluate each business opportunity on its individual merit.
- Develop a detailed plan for each business and continually refine it.
- Find your adjacent-space opportunities.
- Know when to develop wholly owned businesses and when to partner with others.
- Be a good partner; respect and defer to others' talents.
- Know when to build equity in your own brand and when to add value to others.
- Always overdeliver on the value proposition.
- Every deal is different. Be flexible.
- Develop your businesses in emerging markets.
- Involve independent-minded people at the highest level of your organization.
- Empower your employees in a way that unleashes their talent and energy.
- Meet regularly with members of your team to explain your vision for the business.
- Begin with the end in mind.
- Attack life.

INDEX